Frommer's®

MW00963165

Provence & the Côte d'Azur

with your *family*

Louise Simpson &
Robin Gauldie

WILEY

A John Wiley and Sons, Ltd, Publication

UK Publisher: Sally Smith
Production Manager: Daniel Mersey
Commissioning Editor: Fiona Quinn
Development Editor: Donald Strachan
Project Editor: Hannah Clement
Cartographer: SY Cartography
Photo Research: Jill Emeny

Wiley also publishes its books in a variety of electronic formats. Some content that appears in print may not be available in electronic books.

British Library Cataloguing in Publication Data

A catalogue record for this book is available from the British Library

ISBN: 978-0-470-68336-1 (pbk), ISBN: 978-0-470-97695-1 (ebk)

Typeset by Wiley Indianapolis Composition Services

Printed and bound in China by RR Donnelley

5 4 3 2 1

Contents

About the Author vi
An Additional Note vii

1 Family Highlights of Provence & the Côte d'Azur 1

Best Things To Do 2
Best Dining Options 11
Best Accommodation 13

2 Planning a Family Trip to Provence & the Côte d'Azur 15

Visitor Information 18
Essentials 29
Accommodation & Eating Out 40
The 21st-Century Traveller 47
Fast Facts: Provence 49

3 Monaco & the French Riviera 55

Visitor Information 57
What To See & Do 59
Family-Friendly Dining 79
Family-Friendly Accommodation 84

4 Grasse & the Arrière-Pays 89

Visitor Information 91
What To See & Do 92
Family-Friendly Dining 107
Family-Friendly Accommodation 110

5 The Western Côte & Inland Var 115

Visitor Information 117
What To See & Do 118
Family-Friendly Dining 132
Family-Friendly Accommodation 137

6 Marseille & Aix-en-Provence 141

Visitor Information 143
What To See & Do 144
Family-Friendly Dining 160
Family-Friendly Accommodation 163

7 Nîmes & the
  Camargue 167

Visitor Information 169
What To See & Do 170
Family-Friendly Dining 186
Family-Friendly Accommodation 189

8 Avignon & the
  Vaucluse 193

Visitor Information 195
What To See & Do 197
Family-Friendly Dining 213
Family-Friendly Accommodation 217

9 Alpes de
  Haute-Provence 221

Visitor Information 223
What To See & Do 224
Family-Friendly Dining 235
Family-Friendly Accommodation 237

Index 239

List of Maps

Provence & the Côte d'Azur 16
Monaco & the French Riviera 56
Cannes 64
Monaco 66
Nice 67
Grasse & the Arrière-Pays 90
The Western Côte & Inland Var 116
St.-Tropez 122
Marseille & Aix-en-Provence 142

Aix-en-Provence 147
Marseille 149
Nîmes & the Camargue 168
Arles 174
Nîmes 175
Avignon & the Vaucluse 194
Avignon 199
Alpes de Haute-Provence 222

About the Author

Lead author **Louise Simpson** is a travel writer based in Southern France. Having studied French and Spanish at Cambridge University, she worked for a decade in London as a PR director for two leading travel PR agencies and as a writer for numerous UK newspapers and magazines including *The Independent on Sunday*, *Vogue*, *Timesonline* and *Financial Times*. She moved to Provence eight years ago, where she lives with her husband and two children. She has co-written this book with **Robin Gauldie**.

Robin first visited Southern France in 1972 and has returned almost every year since then, exploring every corner of the region. As a result, he could now drive most of Provence's winding mountain roads blindfold, but prefers not to. He spends part of each year in a ramshackle house in a tiny mountain village, from which he makes frequent forays in search of great places to eat and drink and things to do. A regular contributor to many British newspapers and magazines, Robin is the author of more than 20 guidebooks to destinations around the world, including France.

Acknowledgements

Special thanks are due to my husband, Jason, who shares my passion for food, travel and France. His patient support, as well as his food-tasting, pillow-testing and even proof-reading skills have proved invaluable to this book.

This book would never have happened without my dear friend, travel writer and editor par excellence, Anna Goldrein, or without the wise advice and understanding ear of Mark Henshall – our editor on this project.

Eternal gratitude is due to my parents for introducing me to Provence, to my parents-in-law for their ongoing support, to all my wonderful friends from the Mother-and-Baby group for sharing their advice and travel tips and to Fabrice at Chez Pascal in Beausoleil for keeping Jason, Alexandra, Charlie and me well-fed at all times.

Robin and I would like to give additional thanks to all those who have given their support over the course of this book including: Jill Emeny, Sally Smith and Karen Hamilton.

Dedication

To my lifelong travel companions – Jason, Alexandra and Charlie.

An Additional Note

Please be advised that travel information is subject to change at any time and this is especially true of prices. We therefore suggest that you write or call ahead for confirmation when making your travel plans. The authors, editors, and publisher cannot be held responsible for the experiences of readers while traveling. Your safety is important to us, however, so we encourage you to stay alert and be aware of your surroundings.

Star Ratings, Icons & Abbreviations

Every hotel, restaurant, and attraction listing in this guide has been ranked for quality, value, service, amenities, and special features using a star-rating system. Hotels, restaurants, attractions, shopping, and nightlife are rated on a scale of zero stars (recommended) to three stars (exceptional). In addition to the star rating system, we also use 5 feature icons that point you to the great deals, in-the-know advice, and unique experiences. Throughout the book, look for:

FIND	Special finds – those places only insiders know about
MOMENT	Special moments – those experiences that memories are made of
VALUE	Great values – where to get the best deals
OVERRATED	Places or experiences not worth your time or money
GREEN	Attractions employing responsible tourism policies

The following abbreviations are used for credit cards:

AE	American Express
DC	Diners Club
MC	MasterCard
V	Visa

And the amenities:

A/C	Airconditioning		Jacuzzi/Hot Tub/Whirlpool
	Baby Changing		Laundry Facilities
	Babysitting		Lockers
	Bar		Microwave
BF	Breastfeeding		Minibar
	Buggy rental		Picnic Area
	Café		Play Area
P	Car Park		Pool – Children's
FREE	Car Park – Free		Pool – Indoor
£	Car Park – Paid		Pool – Outdoor
	Children's Club		Restaurant
	Children's Menu		Reservations
	Cinema		Safe
	Cots Available		Shop
	Cycle Hire		Shower
	DVD		Shuttle Bus
	Fitness Centre		Snack Bar
	Fridge		Spa Facilities
	Full Kitchen		Sports
	Games		Tennis Courts
	Garden		TV
	Garden Centre		Washer/Dryer
	Golf		Watersports Rental
	High Chairs		Equipment
@	Internet Access		Wheelchair Access
	iPod Docking		Wheelchair Rental

A Note on Prices

In the Family-Friendly Accommodation section of this book we have used a price category system.

An Invitation to the Reader

In researching this book, we discovered many wonderful places – hotels, restaurants, shops, and more. We're sure you'll find others. Please tell us about them, so we can share the information with your fellow travelers in upcoming editions. If you were disappointed with a recommendation, we'd love to know that, too. Please email: frommers@wiley.co.uk or write to:

Frommer's Provence & the Côte d'Azur With Your Family, 2nd Edition
John Wiley & Sons, Ltd
The Atrium
Southern Gate
Chichester
West Sussex, PO19 8SQ

Photo Credits

1 Family Highlights of Provence & the Côte d'Azur

Everyone, from the Romans to Coco Chanel, has fallen for the sun-kissed charms of Provence and the Côte d'Azur. From the remote lavender fields of Haute Provence to the cheek-by-jowl golden beaches bordering the dazzling-blue Mediterranean, there's a corner of this southern French region to fit every family's agenda. Beachcombers can choose between watersports and posh nosh on the Côte d'Azur's sandy beaches, or the long, untamed coastline far from the crowds in the Camargue. Art lovers can admire works by the likes of Matisse, Picasso, Chagall, Cézanne and Renoir in galleries across the region. Activities for sporting families vary from tree-climbing to sailing, canyoning and white-water rafting; anyone with younger children can take advantage of the theme parks and adventure playgrounds. Local delicacies will keep gourmands happy: pancake-like *socca* in Nice; almond-flavoured *calissons* in Aix-en-Provence; and goats' cheese wrapped in chestnut leaves from Banon.

The new decade has brought renovation and innovation to southern France, in particular to its twin capitals, Nice and Marseille. The former is recapturing its Golden Age with the restoration of Belle Epoque landmarks and its high-tech tramway. Europe's largest-ever urban regeneration project is under way in Marseille with plans for a new rail terminal and port, with cutting-edge architectural designs dreamed up by Zaha Hadid and film director Luc Besson.

Contemporary architecture has been showcased in recent openings: Monaco's space age Ni Box entertainment complex complete with bowling alley and rooftop skating rink, Fréjus's neoteric Forum Théâtre modelled on the city's ancient Roman amphitheatre, and Marineland's 3.5€ million state-of-the-art polar bear home, complete with year-round snow, maternity den and seawater pool. Much-loved museums across the region, such as the International Perfume Museum in Grasse, Fondation Maeght in St.-Paul de Vence and Musée Picasso in Antibes, underwent top-to-toe renovations. The Oceanographic Museum in Monaco celebrated its 100th anniversary with the purchase of a 150-million-year-old reptile called Anna.

From new discoveries to long-running family favourites, my co-writer Robin and I offer you our tried-and-tested recommendations across Provence and the Côte d'Azur for this new edition.

BEST THINGS TO DO

Best Free Family Experiences
You don't have to raise your head from your beach towel to enjoy two of the region's best attractions for free: the sunshine and the bright-blue Mediterranean Sea.

But when you do look up, there are treats galore: from the striking white Calanques (p. 149) between Marseille and Cassis to the region's three national parks, Mercantour, Verdon and Luberon, where rare flora and fauna abound, as well as gorges offering watersports.

No trip would be complete without smelling freshly cut lavender at a market

Da Vinci Code addicts can explore the mystery of Mary Magdalene's remains at **La Basilique Ste.-Marie-Madeleine** (p. 127), while no museum in Provence is more child-friendly than Marseille's **Préau des Accoules** (p. 156), where tots to teens can learn about artists and even create their own masterpieces.

Fit in a free visit to a working glass-blowing factory where the sight of men in shorts and sandals blowing on molten glass down the end of long metal pipes is entertainment for all ages. **Cristallerie des Papes** (p. 208) in Fontaine-de-Vaucluse and **Verrerie de Biot** (p. 103) turn red-hot molten blobs into glassware of surprising beauty and complexity.

A must for all kids who've read Roald Dahl's *Charlie and the Chocolate Factory*, traditional sweet factory **Confiserie Florian** (p. 101) in Tourrettes-sur-Loup lets you watch its workers hand-dipping fruit into orange-coloured chocolate.

No trip to Provence would be complete without rummaging for lemons and smelling lavender in a market (p. 79, 106, 133, 160, 185, 212, and 236). Most towns have their own produce market,

be it a flower, fruit and vegetable market or a full-on affair with live chickens and fluffy bunnies. They can be a revelation to British children used to being trailed around boring supermarkets.

Best Attractions for Teens

Keep active teenagers busy with every imaginable watersport along the French Riviera coastline and the **Giens Peninsula**—famous for its windsurfing champions. Further inland, Haute Provence and the Alpes-Maritimes are home to the **Gorges du Verdon** (p. 228), the **Gorges de Saorge** (p. 101) near Breuil-sur-Roya, and the **Gorges de Daluis** (p. 101) in the Vallée de la Tinée. With their waterfalls and jaw-dropping descents, these gorges are perfect for rafting, canyoning, aquatic hiking, canoeing, tubing, hot dog, kayaking or swimming in rapids.

The best place for biking, karting and all things related (p. 211) is the Vaucluse. Vroom around the vineyards near Bedoin with **Découverte du Terroir en Buggy**, hire bikes in Avignon with **Holiday Bikes** or race down the piste in a soapbox-style cart with **Devalkart**. Meanwhile, the

Camargue offers some of the world's best riding, on the backs of its famous white horses. Our favourite is **Ranch La Brouzetière** (p. 183), with 30-minute pony rides for little ones.

After a busy day on the Riviera, teenagers will love watching a Hollywood blockbuster (in English) splashed up against Monaco Ville's rock at the **Open Air Cinema** (p. 61).

Best Attractions for Toddlers

A sure-fire winner for young kids is a trip to a farm: **Graine & Ficelle** (p. 97) near Vence, **Beaugensiers Farm** (p. 140) near Toulon and **Oiselet Farm** (p. 216) in the Vaucluse are perfect places to coo at rabbits and baby chicks. Meanwhile, turtles are the order of the day at the Var's **Village des Tortues** (p. 125)—a refuge for sick or abandoned turtles. My toddler son loves watching them nesting, incubating and bathing in pools.

Another perfect place for toddlers is **Jarditrain** (p. 201) near Carpentras, where 25 miniature trains putter through a garden of scale-model landscapes complete with stations, roads and villages. Motorised **Little Tourist Trains** (p. 77, 132, 157, 182, and 209) all over the region are also an easy way to explore cities with toddlers.

Best Indoor Activities for Rainy Days

Bowling alleys (p. 72) in Nice, Antibes, Cannes and Monaco on the French Riviera and Laser Games (p. 150) in Marseille are easy indoor winners for older kids.

Another way to pass a rainy day is with a kids' cookery class: try chocolate desserts at **L'Atelier de la Cuisine des Fleurs** (p. 102) near Vence or traditional Provençal cuisine at **Marc Heracle's Cooking School** (p. 156) near Aix-en-Provence.

The **Grottes de St.-Cézaire** caves (p. 96) are most beautiful when it rains, making them the

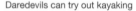

Daredevils can try out kayaking

Roman Arles

perfect wet-weather destination. At nearby **Parfumerie Molinard** (p. 102), kids (aged 4 and up) who have dreamed of designing their own perfume can take 30-minute workshops culminating in the presentation of a diploma and a bottle of their personally designed perfume.

Best Child-friendly Events

Whatever time of year you're planning to visit, local events can add colour to your trip: *www.discoversouthoffrance.com* has event listings covering the whole region. Some of Europe's most popular festivals take place in Southern France: flower parades at the **Nice Carnaval** (p. 61); lemon floats at Menton's **Fête du Citron** (p. 62); the **Festival d'Avignon** (p. 198), with its classical music; and the Riviera's jazz festivals (p. 62) in Nice and Juan-les-Pins.

Grasse is famous for its flower festivals—its May **Expo Rose** (p. 93) and August **Jasmine Festival**—while winter-flowering mimosa (p. 119) is celebrated in towns along the Var coastline between January and March. Families spending Christmas in the Var can see puppet shows and dancing displays at the **Children's Festival** in Hyères (p. 93).

Street festivals in Sisteron will keep children entertained with dancing, singing and theatrical performances; in Mornas, time-travel is the order of the day with summer historical reconstructions at the 13th-century Mornas Castle (p. 197), during which older children can take part in demonstrations of swordplay and quarterstaff combat.

Best Cities, Towns & Resorts

Vibrant **Marseille** (p. 148) and **Nice** (p. 64) are filled with world-class museums, art galleries and restaurants. Glitzy **St.-Tropez** (p. 120) and **Monaco** (p. 63) host A-list celebrities, Ferraris and yachts complete with helipads. Beach resorts such as **Fréjus** (p. 121), **Antibes** (p. 62) and **Ste.-Maxime** (p. 120) offer Blue

Gordes

Flag golden-sand beaches and bags of family-focused activities. Inland highlights include arty **Aix-en-Provence** (p. 146), Roman **Arles** (p. 173) and beautiful **Avignon** (p. 199).

Best Hilltop Villages Picturesque hilltop villages with jaw-dropping views are what Provence is all about. You'll find your own favourites; among ours are **Cabris** (p. 96), **Colmars** (p. 226), **Gordes** (p. 203), **Mons** (p. 123), **Tourtour** (p. 120); **Mougins** (p. 94) and **Roussillon** (p. 203).

Best Beaches If you long to be far from the crowds, I'd recommend the beautiful, wind-swept coastline of the **Camargue** and the tiny secluded beaches (accessible only by boat) along **Les Calanques** (p. 149).

Those who like the convenience of children's play areas, restaurants and striped recliners should head to beaches along the Côte d'Azur. Our favourites are the Blue Flag beaches in **Antibes**, **Juan-les-Pins** and **Fréjus**.

Best Natural Attractions Families wanting to get away from it all on the French Riviera should take a day trip to the beautiful **Îles des Lérins** off the Cannes coastline: the **Île Ste. Marguerite** (p. 68) houses the prison cell of the Man in the Iron Mask (subject of a 1998 film starring Leonardo DiCaprio), while the **Île St.-Honorat** (p. 68) is home to the Lérins monks, who produce fine wines and potent liqueurs for parental delectation.

If you're staying inland, you can enjoy the undisturbed beauty of Provence's nature reserves; the Alpes-Maritimes's mountainous **Mercantour National Park** (p. 98) is a haven for endangered flora and fauna, while the woodlands and cedar-cloaked valleys of the Vaucluse's **Luberon Regional Natural Park** (p. 204) are home to rare birds, butterflies and mountain flowers. One of France's newest nature reserves, the **Verdon Regional Natural Park** (p. 229), boasts the terrifying but impressive

Verdon Gorges (p. 228) and the shimmering Lac de Ste.-Croix.

Children also love learning about wolves at **Scénoparc** (p. 104) in St.-Martin Vésubie or taking the themed **Train des Merveilles** (p. 98) on a day trip to see the prehistoric rock engravings in the **Vallée des Merveilles** (p. 103).

Best Animal Attractions
Provence is rich in creepy-crawlies: my favourite place to learn about them is the home of the Vaucluse's insect man, **Jean-Henri Fabre** (p. 204). There are also hundreds of wriggling caterpillars and butterflies to explore at the **Jardin des Papillons** (p. 228) in Haute Provence.

In the Camargue, there's the **Parc Ornithologique du Pont de Gau** (p. 176)—a 'bird hotel' that looks after thousands of flamingos, egrets and other migrating birds, as well as taking in injured specimens. More unusual is the **Ferme aux Crocodiles** (p. 203) near Avignon, where more than 400 rare crocodiles keep company with giant tortoises and tropical birds in a huge greenhouse.

Aquariums worth a detour include the Camargue's **Seaquarium** (p. 177) in Le Grau-du-Roi, where highlights include a shark tunnel and basking sea lions, and the subterranean aquarium at Monaco's **Oceanographic Museum** (p. 73), where my toddler son loves the knobbly seahorses.

Best Gardens Menton is famed for its gardens (p. 71), while neighbouring Monaco has immaculately tended public spaces such as the **Roseraie Princesse Grace** (p. 71).

You and the kids can learn about Mediterranean flora and fauna at the **Forest Eco-museum** (p. 152) near Aix-en-Provence; English-language booklets are available to guide you around the forest trails.

Yellow submarine outside the Oceanographic Museum, Monaco

Palais des Pâpes

Best Castles & Historic Sites

Everyone loves a fairytale castle, and Provence's best example is the **Château d'Uzès** (p. 179), which is owned and lived in by the oldest dukedom in France. In nearby Avignon, there's little to beat the 14th-century **Palais des Pâpes** (p. 206) for over-the-top grandeur: it's the largest Gothic palace in the world.

With splendid gardens and even more splendid views, the pink *palazzo* of **Villa Ephrussi de Rothschild** (p. 74) in St.-Jean–Cap-Ferrat is one of the Riviera's finest Belle Epoque palaces; children love the English-language treasure hunt around its themed gardens.

If you want to see where hobbits might holiday, visit the **Village des Bories** (p. 207) in Gordes, where you'll find tiny, beehive-like stone houses that used to be built all over the Vaucluse as tool sheds and shelters.

Best Museums & Art Galleries

If you plan to visit just one art museum during your trip, make it St.-Paul de Vence's **Fondation Maeght** (p. 99), where you can introduce your kids to 20th-century greats such as Chagall and Matisse, and where its art-filled garden may well inspire your children to create their own masterpieces.

Other world-class museums for kids to see 20th-century art include St.-Tropez's airy **Annonciade Museum** (p. 129), boasting Braque, Signac and Matisse; and Marseille's **Musée Cantini** (p. 154), which has a collection spanning 1900 to 1960 including work by Dufy, Signac, Rothko, Kandinsky, Picasso and Hopper.

The don't-miss museum in Haute Provence is the **Musée de Préhistoire des Gorges du Verdon** (p. 230), designed by British architect Lord (Norman) Foster, which offers a themed trail to the Baume Bonne grotto by boat and to an archaeological village where kids can try their hand at living Stone Age style.

Best Theme Park/Water Park

On the French Riviera, Europe's largest marine park, **Marineland** (p. 70) in Antibes, is an obvious choice for a family day out: as well as a large aquarium and dolphin shows, you can visit two polar bears in their newly opened 3.5€ million refrigerated home. At the neighbouring adventure farm, **La Petite Ferme du Far West** (p. 70), toddlers will love gazing at the rabbits and having their faces painted.

Best Outdoor Activities Families who want to play at being Tarzan and Jane will love the **Indian Forest Sud** (p. 158) near Martigues, **Parc Arbres et Aventures** (p. 233) near Comars or the **Passerelle des Cîmes** (p. 210) in Isle-sur-la-Sorgue, with rope bridges connecting trails of varying height and difficulty.

Lovers of heights should try **Via Ferrata** (p. 106)—a form of rock climbing along iron-rung ladders that allows beginners to scale dramatic rock faces usually only attempted by experts—in the Alpes-Maritimes hinterland. Going underground, there's a subterranean form of Via Ferrata near Caille, where you scale cave ceilings to explore stalactites.

If you can face waking up at dawn, the best way to admire the lavender fields and olive groves of Haute Provence is from a **hot-air balloon** (p. 233)—they were invented by the French, after all. For an eco-friendly way to explore Marseille's coastline, contact **Naturoscope** (p. 158), who introduce families to the local environment through guided walks and snorkelling.

Best Confectioners Scoffing sweet treats is one of the indulgences of being on holiday, and Provence is one of Europe's best spots for confectioners. Among our favourites are **Les Caprices de Marine** (p. 185) in Arles, **La Maison de la Tarte** (p. 132) in Fréjus, **Patrick Mesiano** (p. 78) in Nice and Beaulieu-sur-Mer, and **Léonard Parli** (p. 159), where you can taste Aix-en-Provence's famous *calisson*.

In addition, make sure you follow locals to **La Cure Gourmande** (p. 184), a celebrated traditional biscuit- and chocolate-maker with shops across Provence.

Best Shopping You won't go far in western Provence without coming across *santons* (clay figurines); a good place to both see them being made and buy them is **Santons Fouque** (p. 159) in Aix-en-Provence. Another must in western Provence is Les **Indiennes de Nîmes** in Nîmes (p. 185), Arles and Avignon, that specialises in colourful

Artichokes on a market stall, Aix-en-Provence

Langue d'Oc—The Language of Poetry

When I was studying French and Spanish, Occitan was my least-favoured subject, but I consoled myself with the thought that I was unlikely ever to come across this ancient southern-French language again. More than a decade later, my husband and I bought a house in the Provençal countryside, and introducing ourselves to our elderly neighbours wondered why we were having such difficulty understanding them. It wasn't just our rusty French: we later realised that our 80-year-old neighbours laced their French phrases with Provençal, a regional dialect based on Occitan. Five years and many glasses of *vin d'orange* later, we finally understand what they are talking about, or we think we do.

Occitan, or *Oc*, was spoken all over *Occitania* (an area covering Monaco and southern France as far as the Dordogne, northern Italy and Spain). Having evolved from Vulgar Latin, the language became established through the success of 12th-century poets—the troubadours. Masters in the art of courtly love, these knights wooed virtuous women with songs written in Occitan that spoke of their patient devotion. Famous troubadours in Provence included Folquet de Marseille, Raimbaut d'Orange, Comtesse de Die and Raimbaut de Vaqueiras. After the 1539 Edict of Villers-Cotterêts ruled that Parisian French should be the language of all France, Occitan waned. However, it was kept alive through the centuries by writers and poets such as the Grassoise poet Louis Bellaud, and Frédéric Mistral, who wrote the 19th-century French/Occitan dictionary *Lou Tresor dóu Felibrige*.

Provençal fabrics and clothes for kids from 2 up.

You'll find more pretty clothes for tots to teens along the smart **Rue d'Antibes** (p. 79) in Cannes, home to all the chic French children's labels from **Tartine et Chocolat to Petit Bateau.**

In the perfume capital, Grasse, don't miss **Fragonard** (p. 106), for duck soaps and children's fragrances, and nearby **Fragonard Maison** for embroidered toy bags and cuddly toys. Other havens of sweet smells include the newly opened **Nature et Senteurs— Savonnerie du Duché Chantois**

(p. 186) in Uzès, with its organic range and name-inscribed soaps, and **Magie du Parfum** (p. 235) in Sisteron, full of aromatic perfumes and cosmetics.

Small is beautiful when it comes to toy shops, and our favourites are all diminutive treasure troves of traditional wooden toys: **En sortant de l'école** (p. 78) in Cannes, **Le Chat Botté** (p. 212) in Isle-sur-la-Sorgue, **Chez Tom et Léa** (p. 77) in Nice's Old Town and **Au Bois de Mon Coeur** (p. 184) in Uzès.

Since 2005, interest in this long-forgotten language has been revived through demonstrations against the illegal status of Occitan within France in Carcassonne, Montpellier and Béziers, as well as the annual *Estivada* festival in Rodez, celebrating Occitan language and culture.

You're most likely to see Provençal on restaurant signs: look out for *Lou* (the) before the restaurant name. See if you can spot any of the following on your travels: *Lou Pèbre d'Aï* (savoury), *Lou Fassum* (a cabbage-based recipe), *Lou Pitchoun* ('little one') or *Lou Pistou* (a garlic, basil and tomato-based sauce). You may even come across *Lou Cigalon*—an ironic reference to the 1935 film by Marcel Pagnol about a restaurant owner who is an excellent chef but refuses to serve his customers until his former employee opens another restaurant nearby.

Some Occitan words are very similar to their English counterparts or easily recognisable to Anglophones:

Animal	*Animal*
Apology	*Excusa*
Castle	*Castèl*
Colour	*Color*
Intelligent	*Intelligent*
Gift	*Present*
Question	*Question*
Rare	*Rare*
Village	*Vilatge*
Waterfall	*Cascade*

If you've run out of holiday reading, English-language **Book in Bar** (p. 159) in Aix-en-Provence and **English Book Centre** (p. 106) in Valbonne should bridge the gap. You can introduce children to Astérix at **The Comic Strips Café** (p. 77) in Antibes, which sells comic books galore.

BEST DINING OPTIONS

Best Fine Dining Although family dining and gastronomic cuisine don't naturally go hand-in-hand, there are a few places worth trying if your youngsters are fairly adventurous. At Michelin-starred **Les Terraillers** (p. 108) in Biot, kids (up to 10) can design their own three-course menu for 25€.

Best Fish Restaurant The harbourside **La Poissonnerie Laurent** (p. 161) in Cassis has been run by the same fishing family for 150 years; children are well catered for with an 8.60€ menu featuring fresh fish and vegetables.

Best Vegetarian Food Italian owner (and chef) Marco

Choosing a flavour of ice cream is always a difficult decision

decorated **Zucca Magica** (p. 81) in Nice with a Hallowe'en theme of wall-to-wall pumpkins. Children 10 and under eat free, and there are set menus of three courses at lunchtime and four in the evening (to which Marco always seems to add a couple extra).

Best Beach Restaurant Les Pêcheurs (p. 82) in Juan-les-Pins, overlooking the Cap d'Antibes, offers a stylish menu of grilled meat, fish and salads served beneath a canopy of pine trees. There are comfy recliners, beach huts to change into your swimming togs and even a car valet service.

Best Alfresco Dining The Auberge du Point Sublime (p. 235) near the Verdon Gorges and **La Taverne Provençale** (p. 108) in Gourdon are worth a trip for their views alone, while **Le Bananier** (p. 187) in Uzès, **Café**

des Arcades (p. 107) in Valbonne and **Le Café** (p. 85) in St.-Tropez are set on traffic-free squares where children can run around after the market has finished. For idyllic terrace dining on garden-fresh produce, our tips are **La Chassagnette** (p. 188) in Arles and **Restaurant à Deux Pas du Potager** (p. 214) in Avignon.

Best Ethnic Restaurant Don't go to Iberian-influenced Nîmes without tasting tapas, preferably at **La Bodeguita** (p. 186), a popular hangout for the bullfighting glitterati, who love to listen to the flamenco singers.

A good place to introduce your children to Moroccan cuisine is Valbonne's **Le Pigeot** (p. 108), with its hand-painted furniture and suitably low chairs.

Best Crêperie Transport yourself to Brittany, minus the rain, with a visit to a crêperie: worth a detour are **La Crêperie du Vieux Port**

(p. 133) in St.-Raphaël, with more than 20 pancake fillings, **La Crêpe au Carré** (p. 161) in Marseille, for excellent *galettes* (savoury pancakes) and ice creams, and **Les 2 Suds** (p. 188) in Arles, with its flower-filled garden.

Best Ice cream Stops The competition for Provence's best ice cream is stiff, but our top choices are the sundaes and unusual flavours such as fig and plum at Arles's **Soleileis** (p. 189), **Brasserie Beau Rivage** (p. 162) in Marseille, with yummy (if not very French) Snickers flavour, and the white chocolate ice cream at **Barbarac** (p. 136) in St.-Tropez. Old-timer **Fenocchio** (p. 85) in Nice offers a mind-boggling range of flavours, and **Glacier Gelato-show** (p. 215) in Orange sells *granita* in more colours than there are in the rainbow.

Best Scenic Picnic Spots Pretty castle gardens with

not-to-be-missed views include **Parc du Pharo** (p. 163) near Marseille's Vieux Port, looking towards the Château d'If and the Îles du Frioul, and the **Parc du Château** (p. 82) in Nice, with its man-made waterfall, play areas and rope web. In Orange, the **St.-Eutrope** hill (p. 217) is a shady picnic spot with views for miles from the ancient Roman theatre towards the Dentelles de Montmirail mountain range.

BEST ACCOMMODATION

Best Luxury Accommodation
The most family-friendly luxury hotel along the Riviera is the **Royal Riviera** (p. 85) in St.-Jean–Cap-Ferrat. As well as children's menus, interconnecting rooms, a cordoned swimming pool and a private beach, it offers younger guests

Orion Bed & Breakfast

complimentary gifts, table tennis and water-skiing.

The gorgeous **Auberge Cavalière** (p. 191) is ideal for families seeking an authentic Camargue experience yet desiring the luxuries of a four-star hotel: as well as its riding stables, there's a swimming pool and a well-regarded restaurant.

Best-kept Accommodation Secrets To enjoy Cannes without breaking the bank, check in at the **Villa d'Estelle** (p. 86), an apartment hotel minutes from the beachfront La Croisette, with tastefully decorated self-catering studios with up to three bedrooms.

In the back-country's St.-Paul de Vence, **Le Hameau** (p. 113) attracts families-in-the-know with its 17 air-conditioned rooms and apartments set in whitewashed 18th-century stables around a swimming pool and terrace.

For families wanting to head back to nature, it doesn't get much better than the **Hotel au Naturel Moulin du Château** (p. 237) in Haute Provence, a former olive-oil mill surrounded by olive groves—it's the only hotel within the Verdon Regional Natural Park.

Best B&B Our favourite B&Bs in the region are old farmhouses loaded with Provençal style and set within flower gardens, such as the **Mas de la Pierre du Coq** (p. 219) and **La Sommellerie** (p. 218) in the Vaucluse and **Clos des Cypres** (p. 111) on the outskirts of Grasse.

Best Campsite The best all-singing, all-dancing campsite on the French Riviera is **Camping du Pylone** (p. 87) in Antibes, next to Marineland theme park. Anyone looking to get away from the crowds should head inland to **Parc des Monges** (p. 111) in Auribeau-sur-Siagne.

In the heart of the Camargue, **Camping Crin Blanc** (p. 192) offers mobile homes and chalets, plus plenty to keep youngsters amused, including tennis courts, volleyball, a games room, a children's pool, table tennis, a playground and a summertime miniclub.

On a 5-hectare site near Apt, the friendly **Camping Le Luberon** (p. 220) is perfectly located for exploring the Luberon Regional Natural Park; choose between self-catering stone houses and wooden chalets.

Haute Provence has excellent campsites, notably the convivial **Camping L'International** (p. 238), where you can have fun with families from across Europe, and **Camping Les Collines de Castellane** (p. 238), with children's entertainment from face-painting to treasure hunts.

Best Eco-friendly Accommodation With treehouses scattered around a forested garden and an outdoor pool filtered through stones and aquatic plants, **Orion Bed & Breakfast** (p. 113) in St.-Paul de Vence is an eco-friendly paradise.

2 Planning a Family Trip to Provence & the Côte d'Azur

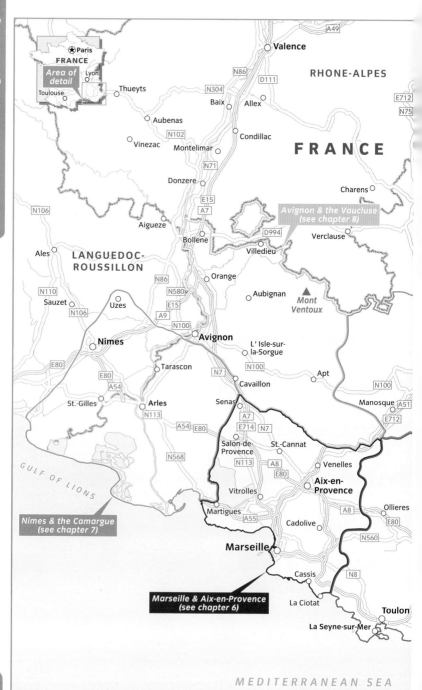

Planning any family trip, long or short, is a fine art: over-plan and your holiday can resemble a military expedition; under-plan and you miss out on some wonderful experiences because you're too often forced to make last-minute decisions without having the full information at hand. This is especially true if you're planning to stay anywhere along the Côte d'Azur, from St.-Tropez to the Italian border, during peak season, for which you'll need to plan well in advance. The best and most reasonably priced accommodation and the cheapest flights are snapped up early—organising on the hoof will leave you disappointed or out of pocket. It's a family trip, so make sure you get the children involved in the forthcoming adventure. Talk about what you'd like to see and do, prompted by some of the suggestions in this guide, and maybe draw up a rough timetable. However, make sure you leave some unplanned time in your schedule. It's often the unexpected events and encounters that leave the most magical holiday memories.

This guide takes in six administrative *départements*—the Alpes-Maritimes, Alpes de Haute-Provence (aka Haute-Provence), Bouches-du-Rhône, Gard, Var and Vaucluse. The sightseeing chapters are loosely based on each of these, although the Alpes-Maritimes is spread across two chapters, and the Nîmes and Camargue chapter includes Gard and part of Bouches-du-Rhône.

VISITOR INFORMATION

The advent of the **Internet** has made researching and planning holidays child's play, or almost. France's **official tourist board website**, *www.franceguide.com*, clicks through to separate sites for more than 30 countries, including *http://uk.franceguide. com* for the UK, *http:// us.franceguide.com* for the US and *http://ie.franceguide.com* for Ireland. Their online services include brochure-ordering and a travel shop with booking for accommodation and sports activities. The tourist board also has offices, aka **Maisons de France**, in 29 countries, offering the same services. In the UK there's one at Lincoln House, 300 High Holborn, London WC1V 7JH (📞 *09968 244 123*); in France, at 20 Avenue de l'Opéra, Paris (📞 *01 42 96 70 00*); in the US you can contact them at 825 Third Avenue, New York (📞 *514 288 1904*).

The official tourist board websites let you pick the region you're heading for—including Provence and Riviera Côte d'Azur—which generates a page with the full contact details, including relevant links for the regional tourist board (Comité Régionale de Tourisme or CRT), departmental tourist offices (Comités Départementales de Tourisme or CDTs) and the tourist offices (offices de tourisme) of major towns and cities. Note that you can't visit CRTs and CDTs in person.

The English-language **CRT** website for this region, known as Provence Alpes Côte d'Azur (PACA), is **www.discover-south offrance.com**, which covers everywhere from Arles to Nice. CDT websites (including **www. gard-tourisme.com** for Nîmes, Uzès and Aigues Mortes (which aren't in the PACA region but are part of Languedoc-Roussillon) are listed under 'Visitor Information' in the sightseeing chapters. Most of the CDT websites are translated into English and have some information on family holidays or children's activities. They all list every tourist office, *syndicat d'initiative* (small tourist office) or *mairie* (town hall) in the department. It's useful to print out and take with you the list of tourist offices in the department you want to visit.

For route planning ahead of a trip, or just general interest, **http://maps.google.com** has zoomable maps of just about anywhere, turn-by-turn directions to and from places and even detailed satellite images and StreetView—look at Marseille's Vieux Port, for instance, or even the hotel you're going to stay in. If you have the time to be really organised in advance, the excellent **www.viamichelin.com** can also give you detailed directions (plus maps) from your home town to your destination in France, including the location of speed cameras.

Child-specific Websites

A useful resource is **www.france 4families.com**, which has lots of general information about France from a family perspective plus guides to all regions, including Provence and the Côte d'Azur. Another good site is **www.totstofrance.co.uk**, which, as well as detailing family-friendly properties to rent, provides information on travelling in France with children, including tips on what to pack.

More general family-oriented sites are **www.takethefamily.com**, with tips, destination guides (including lots on camping in France) and a discussion board; **www.babygoes2.com**, with general tips and location reports; **www.travellingwithchildren.co.uk**, a comprehensive site with lots of tips; and **www.deabirkett.com**, a handy family travel forum for exchanging tips and views, run by the former *Guardian* journalist and children's travel specialist.

Entry Requirements & Customs

Passports & Visas

Citizens of European Union (EU) countries need an identity card to enter France. For the time being, this means a passport for UK nationals. Non-EU citizens also need a passport, and a few nationalities, including South Africans, require a visa. However, stays of more than 3 months by non-EU citizens also require a visa. For French embassies/consulates around the world see *www.diplomatie.gouv.fr/venir/visas/index.html*.

Taking Pets

Under the **Pet Travel Scheme** (PETS), UK-resident dogs and cats can travel to many other EU countries and return to the UK without being quarantined. Dogs and cats are issued with a **passport** (by a vet) after being fitted with a microchip and vaccinated against rabies at least 21 days prior to travel. On re-entry to the UK, you need to get your pet treated for ticks and tapeworm (by an EU vet 24 to 28 hours before being checked in with an approved transport company). For full details see *www.defra.gov.uk/animalh/quarantine/index.htm*.

Most French **hotels** and some self-catering properties permit animals, often for an additional small fee. The commercial website *www.visitfrance.co.uk* is a good source of pet-friendly, self-catering options.

Customs

Visitors to France from other **EU countries** can bring home any amount of goods for personal use except new vehicles, mail-order purchases or more than 800 cigarettes, 10 litres of spirits, 90 litres of wine or 110 litres of beer. Travellers from **outside the EU** must declare all transported goods and pay duty or tax on those worth more than 175€. All visitors leaving with more than 7,600€ must declare

the amount to Customs. The French Customs website, *www.douane.gouv.fr*, is translated into English.

Travelling with the Disabled & Elderly

For Grandparents

Older people planning to stay in *gîtes* (p. 43), small guesthouses or pensions may want to check up on access to bedrooms—many smaller hotels have steep, narrow stairs and no lift, while some *gîtes* have steep, loft-ladder-style stairs to loft bedrooms (see 'For Families With Special Needs', in the following section). If you take your grandchildren on outings, remember that over-60s generally get **discounts** on travel tickets, museum and zoo entry. Bring photo ID.

For Families with Special Needs

Older hotels, *gîtes* and some smaller museums and historic buildings have limited or non-existent **wheelchair access**. Many newer hotels, however, are well equipped with wheelchair-accessible ground-floor rooms and lifts. Most larger spa and 'thalassotherapy' resort complexes also offer good wheelchair access throughout, including access to pools. Beaches obviously present a challenge for wheelchair users, but some commercial beaches in resorts such as Cannes have wheelchair ramps and boardwalks. For visitors with limited sight or hearing, many major historic attractions (such as Avignon's Palais des Papes) have multilingual **audio-guides** for rent and **induction loops** for hearing aid users. Holiday Care (℡ *0845 124 9971*, *www.holidaycare.org.uk*) offers general advice for people with disabilities travelling abroad and links to other organisers, including specialist tour company **Canbe-done** (℡ *020 8907 2400*, *www.canbedone.co.uk*) which offers package holidays in several accessible hotels in Nice.

Drivers who have the new blue disabled driver card are entitled to the same parking concessions as French residents.

Eurotunnel has better wheelchair access than most ferries, and **Eurostar** (p. 32) offers first-class travel for second-class fares for people with disabilities.

Money

Currency

France, in common with 15 other countries at the time of writing, has the **euro** (€) as its currency. There are 100 **cents** in a euro, with notes for 5€ to 500€ and coins for 1 [ce] to 2€. For current rates and a currency converter, see *www.xe.com*. Note that in practice 500€ notes are not commonly accepted.

Credit & Debit Cards

Most French shops, restaurants and hotels take credit or debit cards, at least **Visa** and **MasterCard** (American Express and Diner's Club are only really accepted in expensive establishments). There is often a minimum spend of 7€ to 15€.

The only **places unlikely to accept cards** today are small businesses, B&Bs, small campsites and inexpensive rural inns. However, it's always wise to check in advance as there are exceptions to the rule. As always, watch out for **charges** when you use your credit or debit card abroad. At the time of writing, Nationwide and the Post Office offer credit cards that don't charge for each transaction made outside the UK (only charging for withdrawing money from an ATM), reducing your holiday bill considerably. This is a safer option than carrying around wads of cash. For further information about the best credit cards to use abroad, see *www.moneysupermarket.com*.

You now use your **PIN** when making a purchase with your card as well as using it at an ATM, except at some automated pumps at petrol stations out of hours (most petrol stations now have payment machines that do accept foreign cards).

The **prepaid debit card** is another excellent option for families. This is a 'virtual wallet' that you load with as much cash as you like before leaving home. You can then use it to withdraw cash from any ATM using a PIN. Older children can each be given their own, loaded with their spending money—a useful way of putting a cap on holiday budgets.

Credit card companies have become super-vigilant about approving cash withdrawals or purchases away from home, and may use computerised procedures to block any 'unusual' transaction that doesn't fit your everyday spending profile. This is meant to protect you (and the card company) against fraudulent use of your card, but it can be embarrassing if you're trying to pay for a tank of fuel or settle a hotel bill. Tell your credit card provider (preferably in writing) that you will be travelling abroad, and where and when you will be going. To be on the safe side, it's a good idea to keep a stash of emergency cash (enough for a tank of fuel and a night in a hotel) at all times.

For **lost or stolen cards** see p. 52.

Cash & Travellers' Cheques

There are 24-hour cashpoint machines (or ATMs) outside all French banks and in many supermarket lobbies—even relatively small ones in out-of-the-way towns; withdrawing cash is rarely a problem unless you've gone over your limit. You usually get a better rate at a cashpoint than an exchange booth (which may also take a commission). However, your bank will probably charge a fee for using a foreign ATM, so avoid drawing small sums every day.

It's also a good idea to bring some cash into France as a back-up, and to have two or more

cards in case of a hiccup. Remember, you can also make cash withdrawals from ATMs using a credit card as well as your debit card (though it's likely to cost you even more in interest payments).

Travellers' cheques are becoming a thing of the past, now cities and most towns have ATMs. However, if you do choose to take some as back-up, you can get them at banks, building societies, travel agents and the Post Office. Keep a record of their serial numbers in case of loss or theft and carry them separately from money and cards. You'll need to show ID when you cash one.

When to Go & What to Pack

The weather is generally mild in this region, with temperate winters and hot, dry summers: that is, a typical **Mediterranean climate**. Coastal towns along the Côte d'Azur boast 300 days of sunshine per year and rarely see any frost, whereas inland regions can experience temperatures as low as -10°C in winter. **Beach-lovers** are all but guaranteed sunny weather between June and October. Spring and autumn can see short but heavy bursts of rainfall, particularly in November, and the irritating *mistral* wind often blows between March and May.

To be on the safe side, it's best to **pack** winter clothes if you're visiting the region between November and April. However, it's useful to also take some T-shirts just in case. Whatever the time of year, you'll need comfortable **walking shoes** for all your sightseeing expeditions, and also **sunglasses**. And if you plan to eat in fancier restaurants during your stay, pack some smart clothes, including shirts and trousers for the boys.

A helpful tool for planning what to take and what to do is *www.meteofrance.com*; even with only basic French (you need to know the days of the week) you get a general idea of what to expect in your area from the clickable maps. Or call ☎ *08 92 68 02 XX* (XX is the number of the département: 04 for Alpes de Haute-Provence, 06 for Alpes-Maritimes, 13 for Bouches-du-Rhône, 30 for Gard, 83 for Var and 84 for Vaucluse). A good English-language site is *http:// weather.msn.com*.

Since the region is most popular among visitors—at least French ones—for its beaches and coastal resorts, it's at its busiest and most expensive at Easter, during the French May Bank Holiday (1st to 8th), and in July and August. The French holiday en masse in August, which means congested roads and resorts—particularly in the Alpes-Maritimes and Var, from Menton to Hyères. Family attractions also get very crowded at this time, so it's often best to arrive first thing in the morning to avoid the crowds and find parking spaces. On the other hand, this is when most festivals, events and activities, including children's beach clubs, take place. You'll find details of these on tourist office websites.

Public & School Holidays

French **national holidays** are called *jours fériés*. Banks and small shops close. However, larger supermarkets and department stores increasingly open in the morning. Most museums close but many other visitor sites stay open, as do the majority of restaurants. If there's a public holiday on a Thursday or Tuesday, many people take the Friday or Monday off as well—this is called *faire le pont* (to make a bridge).

The main public holidays are **New Year's Day** (1st January), **Easter Monday** (March or April), **Labour Day** (*Fête du Travail*; 1st May), **VE Day** (8th May), **Whit Monday** (late May), **Ascension Thursday** (late May, 40 days after Easter), **Bastille Day** (14th July), **Assumption of the Blessed Virgin** (15th August), **All Saints' Day** (1st November), **Armistice Day** (11th November) and **Christmas Day** (25th December).

Average Daily Temperatures												
	Jan	Feb	Mar	Apr	May	June	July	Aug	Sept	Oct	Nov	Dec
Temp. (°C)	12.2	11.9	14.2	18.5	20.8	26.6	28.1	28.4	25.2	22.1	16.8	14.1

Shopping in Provence

We've listed our pick of the region's best small shops and markets in the regional chapters. For one-stop shopping for family essentials (from food and drink to socks, nappies, baby foods, underwear, toys, barbecue kit, tents and camping accessories, and medicines) it's often quickest and easiest to head for a supermarket, usually located on the ring-roads of larger towns. If you're self-catering or staying in a *gîte* or campsite out of town, these can be a godsend, with easy off-street parking, air-conditioning and a user-friendly layout. Many even have a few shelves devoted to 'foreign' foodstuffs such as Marmite, baked beans and HP Sauce—usually racked in the 'exotic' section along with sauces and spices from India, China and Mexico. The Géant, Leclerc and Intermarché chains are our favourites; all larger branches have an in-store pharmacy as well as other satellite shops.

In larger towns, you'll find also find smaller Monoprix supermarkets on a main shopping street, which can cater to all your everyday needs, selling food and drink, clothes, accessories and baby items. For English-language books, magazines and newspapers, it's often best to head for the TGV station or airport, although you'll find a limited choice at some newsagents in towns.

There are five **school holidays** a year in France: two weeks in February, two weeks at Easter, all of July and August, one week at the end of October and two weeks at Christmas. Holidays are staggered around the country: Zone A includes Nîmes, Uzès and Aigues Mortes, Zone B covers the rest of the region, and Zone C is Paris. Most tourist sites take into account both the holiday period in their own area and Parisian holidays. For further details see *www.frenchentree.com*, then click on 'Living in France' followed by 'Education' then 'School Calendar'.

Tourist sites and roads are busier during these periods and hotels are often more expensive. However, remember that many of the museums, galleries and other venues host **extra children's activities** in the holidays and resorts have children's beach clubs plus special events and entertainment. If you do visit during busy periods, bear in mind that the French tend to go out after lunch so mornings are a good time to visit popular attractions.

Special Events

For our pick of the best family-friendly happenings throughout the year, from scary monster celebrations in Tarascon to sardine-eating festivals around Marseille, see the 'Child-friendly Events & Entertainment' sections of each sightseeing chapter.

Children's Kit

The following items can make travelling with babies or young children easier or more relaxing:

Bébétel Baby Monitor: Unlike battery-powered listening devices, this is not limited by range and suffers no interference, so you can use it in all hotel restaurants. You plug it into a standard phone line (there are foreign adapter sets) and programme in your mobile number (you may have to add the international code). If your child gets up or cries, the monitor calls you. It costs a hefty £150 or so from *www.bebetel.co.uk*, so check that your hotel doesn't already have one.

Littlelife Baby Carriers: These 'backpacks-with-children-in' are a great idea if you're doing a lot of walking or hiking and don't want to be encumbered with a buggy. 'Voyager' has a zip-off bag for drinks, snacks and wipes, for about £170; lighter models start at half that. You can get hold of them at *www.littletrekkers.co.uk* and outdoor pursuits shops. The same firm's compact, super-absorbent travel towels are also handy for travelling.

Portable Highchairs: Many French restaurants provide at least one highchair. However, if they don't, or it's taken, or it's a weird old-style one without a front bar, you may be left trying to eat with one hand and hold a squirming baby or toddler with the other. Lightweight options you can carry around include the supremely compact 'Handbag Highchair' (a loop of fabric that secures your baby to the chair), the foldable Handysitt toddler seat and the Early Years inflatable booster seat. All are sold at *www.bloomingmarvellous.co.uk*, with prices from £15 to £75.

Boardbug Baby & Toddler Monitor: Great for the beach or for shopping, this award-winning wristwatch-style monitor alerts you to whenever your little one (or ones—the parent one can be paired with up to three child units) strays from you, with adjustable distances from 2m to 150m. It costs about £55 from *www.safetots.co.uk.*

Baby Equipment Rental: Try Les Petits Nomades (☎ *08 20 82 13 37/04 91 37 66 91, www.petitsnomades.fr*).

Health, Insurance & Safety

Medical

Travellers to France from other EU countries now need to carry their European Health Insurance Card (EHIC) as proof of entitlement to free/reduced-cost medical treatment abroad. The quickest way to apply for one is online (*www.ehic.org.uk*), or call ☎ *0845 606 2030* or get a form from the Post Office. You still pay upfront for treatment and related expenses; the doctor will give you a form to reclaim most of the money (about 70% of doctor's fees and 35% to 65% of medicines/prescription charges), which you should send off while still in France (see the EHIC website for details).

Travel Insurance

The EHIC (see 'Health, Insurance & Safety', p. 25) only covers 'necessary medical treatment' and doesn't cover repatriation costs, lost money, baggage or cancellation, so it is not a replacement for **travel insurance**. Before you buy the latter, check whether your existing insurance policies and credit cards cover you for lost luggage, cancelled tickets or medical expenses. If they don't, an example of cover for a family of four travelling to France for 2 weeks, without any adventure sports, with a reputable online insurer such as *www.travelinsuranceweb.com*, is £20.49; an annual multi-trip policy costs £41.49, well worth it if you make more than two trips a year. Make sure your package includes **trip-cancellation insurance** to help you get your money back if you have to back out or go home early (more likely if you're travelling with children), or if your travel supplier goes bust. Allowed reasons for cancellation can range from sickness to natural disasters or a destination being declared unsafe for travel.

Non-EU nationals—with the exception of Canadians, who have the same rights as EU citizens to medical treatment in France—need comprehensive travel insurance that covers medical treatment overseas. Even then, you pay bills upfront and apply for a refund.

Staying Healthy

There are no real health risks when travelling in France and you don't need vaccinations. For general advice on travelling with children, consult your GP. For **emergency treatment, doctors** and **chemists,** see p. 52.

Bring along copies of **prescriptions** in case you or anyone in your family loses their medication or runs out. Carry the generic name of prescription medicines in case a local pharmacist is unfamiliar with the brand name. You should also bring along an extra pair of contact lenses or prescription glasses.

When flying, pack any **prescription medicines** you'll need while in the air in your hand luggage in their original containers, with chemist's labels. All gels, lotions, liquids, creams and ointments must be carried in containers no bigger than 100ml and presented for inspection before boarding. Larger quantities must go as checked luggage. For details, see your departure airport and/or airline website.

If you or your child have an illness that may make it impossible to explain what's happening to you/them, and that needs swift and accurate treatment, such as epilepsy, diabetes, asthma or a food allergy, the charity **Medic Alert** (*www.medicalert.org.uk*)

provides body-worn bracelets or necklets engraved with the wearer's medical condition(s)/vital details, ID number and 24-hour emergency telephone number that accepts reverse charge calls, so their details can be accessed from anywhere in more than 100 languages.

Safety

France—especially outside Paris and other major cities—is generally a very safe country. A traveller's main worry is being targeted by **pickpockets or petty thieves**—travel with your car doors locked as a precaution. It's obvious, but don't leave **valuables** in a car. As a parent, be especially wary of French drivers; many pay no heed to the speed limit, exceed the alcohol limit and drive aggressively. Virtually no-one here stops at **pedestrian crossings**, so tell your child to wait until vehicles have stopped before proceeding.

As everywhere, **hold hands with young children** and don't let them out of your sight unless they are being supervised by someone you trust. Avoid situations where young children could get swept away in a crowd and, with older children, agree on a **place to meet** should you get parted, such as the information desk at a museum. Make sure they have your mobile number and accommodation address on them, with instructions to ask for a member of the police (*agent de police* or *gendarme*) should they not be able

to find you. Their name should never be visible on their bag/clothing and tell them the importance of **never divulging their name to a stranger**.

Beaches can be lethal: you lay back and close your eyes for what seems like a second, and when you open them, your child is nowhere to be seen. With the sea close by, the potential for disaster is clear. The rule is to take it in turns to flake out while one parent keeps watch. If you're alone, you have no option but to stay hyper-alert. Alternatively, you could book them into a supervised children's **beach club** (ask at the local tourist office for details).

For peace of mind, especially if you have more than one child to keep an eye on, invest in **Boardbug** wrist-worn monitors (p. 25) with adjustable distance alarms for children of varying ages. You could also try a set of reins if you have a toddler who likes to go walkabout.

Responsible Tourism

No holiday abroad can be truly 'green'. But in practical terms, there's plenty that you can do to limit the impact of your holiday on the local and global environment. After arriving, don't use your car more than you must. Anyway, it's more fun to **walk or cycle**. Bikes can be hired in many places in France, or you might want to look into taking folding bicycles—you'll find a selection to buy at *www.foldingbikes.co.uk* or *www.onyourbike.*

com, which also rents bikes from £35 per week.

Don't use **air-conditioning** if you can avoid it, and turn it off when you're not in the room. Switch the **TV** off rather than leaving it on standby and don't leave **mobile phones, cameras** or **laptops** on charge longer than necessary (the charger goes on drawing power even after the equipment is fully recharged). Don't waste water (take showers not baths) and look for places to stay that use renewable energy (such as solar water heating). Buying **locally sourced food** in markets instead of processed supermarket food supports local producers and cuts down on 'food miles'—and market shopping in Provence is easy and fun for kids. It's even educational.

Air travel emits CO2, but aviation globally is responsible for only 2% of global emissions, and short-haul holiday flights contribute only a fraction of that total. **Driving** is probably the least environmentally friendly way of getting to the South of France from the UK. **Coach** travel, surprisingly, may well be 'greener' than rail travel (it depends which experts you listen to). **Rail** is usually claimed to be greenest of all, but those with qualms about nuclear energy should reflect that French trains are, in effect, nuclear-powered, as more than 80% of France's electricity is generated by nuclear power stations.

You can salve your carbon conscience by contributing to charities such as **Climate Care** (*www.climatecare.org.uk*), which claims to offset your CO2 in a number of ways, including funding sustainable energy projects.

Responsible Travel (*www. responsibletravel.com*) espouses sustainable travel ideas and has a handful of places to stay in Provence (ranging from villas, *gîtes* and cottages to apartments and hotels, as well as walking and cycling holidays), and you'll find a number of other travel companies which at least pay lip service to greener holidays through the **Association of Independent Tour Operators** (*www.aito.co.uk*).

TIP ▶ ## Resources for Single Parents ◀

For a good holiday page with contact details of useful UK associations and operators, see *www.singleparents.org.uk*. The US-based **Single Parent Travel** (*www.singleparenttravel.net*) is also good for travel advice. **Gingerbread** (0808 802 0925; *www.gingerbread.org.uk*)) is a British charity offering information and advice for lone parents. Members of both get discounts with tour operator **Eurocamp** (p. 34), which has an 'Arrival Survival' service to help lone parents unpack and settle in. Other camping operators offer discounts, as do most **youth hostels** (p. 45). **Lone fathers** should check out *www.onlydads.org*.

ESSENTIALS

Getting There

By Air As a general rule, **under-2s fly free** if they sit on your knee. Some airlines occasionally offer reduced fares for children between 2 and 12 years old, so it may be worth shopping around. However, these fares are usually only available on long-haul flights; on routes from the UK and Ireland to France, children usually pay the full fare. Many airlines, including Ryanair, charge for checked-in baggage, so verify exactly what you are paying for before you book. Many airlines also require that you opt out of booking extras that you may not need—such as travel insurance—by un-checking the tick-box on the screen when booking online. If you don't do this, you will be automatically charged for various things that you don't want. You may also pay a hefty charge at the airport if you do not check in online, so if this is a condition make sure that you comply and carry a hard-copy confirmation.

To **compare cheap flights** try *www.skyscanner.net*—and always watch out for special offers.

From the UK & Ireland The advent of **low-cost airlines** has made the region more accessible to holidaymakers. The situation fluctuates, but at the time of writing you can fly from the **UK** to **Avignon** (Vaucluse), **Mar-seille** (Bouches-du-Rhône), **Nice** (Alpes-Maritimes), **Nîmes**

(Gard) and **Toulon-Hyères** (Var).

Ryanair (UK ☎ *0871 246 0000*/France ☎ *08 92 23 23 75*, *www.ryanair.com*) flies from UK airports to Marseille, Nîmes and Toulon.

Flybe (UK ☎ *0871 700 2000*/outside UK ☎ *00 44 13 92 26 85 13*, *www.flybe.com*) flies to Avignon from Southampton, Birmingham, Manchester and Exeter, and to Nice from Southampton.

Easyjet (*www.easyjet.com*) flies to Marseille from Bristol and London Gatwick, and to Nice from several UK airports.

Jet2 (*www.jet2.com*) flies from Leeds Bradford to Nice and Avignon (summer only), and from Manchester to Nice.

Bmibaby (UK ☎ *0905 828 28 28*/France ☎ *00 44 845 81 11 00*, *www.bmibaby.com*) flies to Nice from Birmingham and East Midlands.

You can also fly to Marseille or Nice from the UK and Ireland with **British Airways** (UK ☎ *0844 493 0787*/France ☎ *08 25 82 54 00*, *www.ba.com*), **Air France** (UK ☎ *0870 142 4343*/France ☎ *08 20 82 08 20*, *www.airfrance.com*) and **Aer Lingus** (UK ☎ *0871 718 5000*/Ireland ☎ *08 18 36 50 00*, *www.aerlingus.com*).

From the US & Canada **Delta Airlines** (US ☎ *1 800 241 4141*, *www.delta.com*) is, at time of writing, the only airline flying direct to the South of France from the US, with flights between New York JFK and Nice. Alternatively, fly to Paris and take a connecting flight or

Flying with Children

If possible, keep children with colds grounded, as ascent and descent can be especially painful—and even dangerous—when they have congested sinuses. If that's not an option, give them an oral child's decongestant an hour before ascent and descent, or administer a spray decongestant before and during take-off and landing.

When travelling with a baby, you might want to invest in a **Baby B'Air Flight Safety Vest**, which attaches to your seatbelt to protect lap-held little ones during turbulence, and allows you to sleep knowing your baby can't fall from your arms. It costs about £27 from *www.babybair.com*. Check first that your airline doesn't already have baby holders to lend to you.

---

train (p. 58) to Nice. Airlines that fly regularly between the US and Paris are **American Airlines** (📞 *1 800 433 7300, www.aa.com*), **British Airways** (📞 *1 800 AIR-WAYS, www.ba.com*) and **Continental Airlines** (📞 *1 800 525 0280, www.continental.com*). **Air France** flies to Paris from the US and Canada, and **Air Canada** (📞 *888 247 2262, www.air canada.com*) flies there from Toronto and Montreal.

From Elsewhere There are currently no direct flights from **Australia to Paris**; your best bet is a connecting flight or Euro-star/TGV via London. **South African Airways** (📞 *0861 359 722, www.flysaa.com*) flies to Paris from Johannesburg and **Cape Town.**

By Ferry & Car The shortest, cheapest and most popular crossings are from Dover to Boulogne, Calais and Dunkerque. **P&O Ferries** (UK 📞 *08716 645 645*/France 📞 *08 25 12 01 56, www.poferries.com*) sails from Dover to Calais in just over an hour. All vessels have children's

play areas and entertainment, including films and video games. **SeaFrance** (UK 📞 *0871 663 2546*/France 📞 *08 25 08 25 05, www.seafrance.com*) has similar onboard facilities, as does **Norfolkline** (UK 📞 *0844 499 0077 www.norfolkline.co.uk*), which sails from Dover to Dunkerque, just north of Calais.

Brittany Ferries (UK 📞 *0870 907 6103*/France 📞 *08 25 82 88 28, www.brittany-ferries.com*) sails from Poole to Cherbourg and from Portsmouth to Caen, Cherbourg and St-Malo. These are overnight crossings, with four-bed cabins available as well as onboard children's areas and entertainment, and are certainly worth considering for families from southwest England.

LD Ferries (UK 📞 *0906 75 33 451, www.ldline.co.uk*) sails from Dover to Boulogne, Newhaven to Dieppe (about 4 hours) and from Portsmouth to Le Havre (about 6 hours). LD Ferries also offers a seaborne option for families from Ireland, with an overnight crossing from Rosslare to Le Havre.

TIP ▶ What You Can Take on Your Flight ◀

You can usually take just one bag on board with you. Generally, maximum dimensions are 55cm x 40cm x 20cm. Maximum permitted weight varies between 10kg and 15kg, so check with your airline. Note that all carry-on items—including handbags, laptop computers and cameras—must go in one single bag. You can take your mobile phone on board, but it must be switched off before boarding. Liquids, gels, ointments, lotions and aerosols such as shaving foam and deodorant may be taken on board only in containers with a maximum capacity of 100ml, packed in one transparent, resealable plastic bag (use zip-up freezer bags). You can, however, get around this partly by buying liquid items like sun lotion, shampoo or conditioner in the departure lounge pharmacy *after* passing through security. If you need to carry liquid medicines in quantities greater than 100ml and don't want to put them in your checked luggage, you can usually arrange in advance to collect your prescription from departure-lounge branches of Boots at most UK airports.

Baby milk and some essential liquid medications may usually be taken on board in quantities larger than 100ml, but you must present them for inspection at security and must have a prescription and ideally a doctor's confirmation that medicines are essential during your journey.

It's a good idea to wear slip-on shoes when flying, as airport security sometimes demands that footwear should be removed from screening. Tying and untying several sets of laces just adds to the hassle of boarding.

Savvy parents can also stretch the limits of their checked luggage allowance by wearing garments with lots of pockets into which heavy items such as books and cameras can be stuffed, leaving more space in your bag. Multi-pocketed, sleeveless photographers' jerkins are good for this, and easy to take off at security. You can even get a small laptop into the largest pockets. You can also cheat the system by strapping a bum-bag round your middle instead of carrying a handbag, or by carrying bulky cameras on a belt pouch.

Remind small boys that even **toy guns** are seriously frowned upon—you'd be surprised how many people get a ticking-off over these!

For those travelling from Scotland or northern England, ferry options include **P&O Ferries**, sailing overnight between Hull to Zeebrugge in about 12 hours; **DFDS** (UK ☏ *0871 522 9955 www.dfdsseaways.co.uk*), sailing from Newcastle to IJmuiden (near Amsterdam) in the Netherlands overnight (in about 16 hours); and **Norfolkline**, sailing from Rosyth, just outside Edinburgh, to Zeebrugge on an overnight 18-hour crossing. Four-berth cabins are available on all these routes, and all vessels have children's facilities such as playrooms and films; DFDS also has its 'Jack the Pirate' club with supervised activities such as face-painting and treasure hunts for under-12s. Check with your ferry company on what is and isn't permitted (some don't accommodate travel cots, for instance).

Bear in mind that these options can be very much more expensive and time-consuming than simply driving south to Dover and taking a short sea crossing. Driving to Dover from Edinburgh, for example, should take around 9 hours each way; including fuel and ferry, this option costs as little as £200 return, less than half the cost of a return fare from Rosyth to Zeebrugge with Norfolkline.

Driving time from most of the French ports to Avignon is notionally around 9 hours, but that assumes pausing only for fuel and toilet stops. You also need to allow up to an hour for disembarkation. In practice, doing it in one go will take at least 12 hours, which is too much for most families; plan a stop on the way and make the journey part of the holiday. One place that's great for children who need to let off steam after long hours in the car is the **Walibi Rhône-Alpes** theme park (*www.walibi-rhone-alpes.fr*). A bit over midway between the Channel ports and Provence (48km east of Lyon and just off the motorway), Walibi has water rides and other activities, family-friendly restaurants and a choice of accommodation packages in hotels, campsites, *gîtes* and guesthouses.

By Train For families starting their trip from London or southeast England, going by Eurostar is beyond a doubt the best way to get to Provence in high season.

From mid-July to mid-September you can travel from London St. Pancras or Kent (Ashford/Ebbsfleet) to Avignon in just over 6 hours with **Eurostar** (UK ☎ 08716 645 645/France ☎ *08 25 12 01 56, www.eurostar.com*), leaving around 07:00 and arriving at 14:13. Children under 4 go free if you sit them on your lap all the way; return fares for a family of two adults and two (fare-paying) children start at around £800. The rest of the year, you can take the Eurostar to Lille Europe to connect with French high-speed trains (TGV) to Avignon. This only involves a change of platform; you can also connect with TGV trains to the South of France at Paris, but this involves a long, time-consuming slog by public transport across the city from Gare du Nord to Gare de Lyon so is not recommended for families with young children.

Rail Europe (UK ☎ 08448 484 064, *www.raileurope.co.uk*) is the most convenient place to book, but also check out *www.seat61.com* for timetables and other useful tips.

There are baby-changing facilities on all Eurostar trains and TGV trains. Note that Avignon's TGV station is several kilometres from the centre.

By Bus National Express (☎ 08717 818181, *www.nationalexpress.co.uk*), the UK partner in the Eurolines bus consortium, runs overnight services from London Victoria to Avignon twice a week, and to Nice once a week. However, with journey times of 19 hours and 22 hours, respectively, and fares that aren't that much lower than train fares, this isn't an attractive option for families; return prices for a family of two adults and two children in August are around £750.

Packages, Deals & Activity Holidays

Package deals let you buy your aeroplane, ferry or train ticket, accommodation and other elements of your trip (e.g. car hire or airport transfers) at the same time, often at a discount. However, they may include hidden charges that you would avoid by booking direct with a hotel or carrier. The obvious appeal for parents is that package deals save you time researching and booking.

Activity holidays are roughly the same, with the addition of some kind of sporting, creative or cultural activity, although sometimes you make your own travel arrangements.

Escorted tours, where you are taken around the various sites, can be anathema to family holidays, where you need to remain flexible in case the children get bored/tired/ill. Such holidays also take away the exhilaration of getting out there and discovering the destination for yourselves—one of the best lessons you can give children.

The following are a few of the best package holiday companies. You will find many more on the Internet and advertised in Sunday papers. Check that your travel

insurance (p. 26) covers you should your operator go bust.

Brittany Ferries ★ ★ ★

📞 *0870 556 1600, **www.brittany ferries.com**.*

This ferry company is also an award-winning tour operator, and can make parents' lives easier by booking hotels, apartments, *gîtes*, camping chalets, theme parks, cycling and boating holidays in conjunction with travel on its ferries. All properties are inspected and, handily for those anxious about the language, there's a 24-hour hotline with English-speaking staff to deal with plumbing problems or the like. The excellent online search facility lets you refine your *gîte* search by distance from a beach, availability of baby equipment and so on, and there's plenty of information provided on each property. You can also book mix-and-match holidays that allow you, for instance, to treat yourselves to a night or two in a posh hotel after spending a week in a chalet.

Keycamp

📞 *0844 406 0200, **www.keycamp. co.uk**.*

This company offers tents, mobile homes and chalets at campsites across Europe, including seven in the Var between Toulon and St.-Raphaël. All sites have children's clubs, a swimming pool or pools and a variety of play, sporting and practical amenities. You can see the attraction of this kind of holiday for those with young children—lots of ready-made playmates and a range of activities. Expect a 7-night stay in a two-bedroom mobile home without linen to cost about £1,000 (1,480€) in July and August. The price drops significantly out of high season. You get a discount for booking online and they can also arrange your travel and car hire.

Similar firms include **Eurocamp** (*www.eurocamp.co.uk*), offering six sites in the Var and one in Port Camargue; **Thomson Al Fresco** (*www.thomsonalfresco. co.uk*), with four sites in the Var, including the Résidence du Colombier in Fréjus (p. 121); and **Canvas Holidays** (*www. canvasholidays.com*), with eight sites in the Var. Companies use some of the same campsites.

VFB Holidays ★

📞 *01242 240 340, www.vfbholidays. co.uk.*

This award-winning, reputable firm is a good option for cottages, *gîtes* and villas in Provence and elsewhere; the online search facility invites you to click on 'family friendly' as one of the selection criteria for accommodation. A sample price for a villa sleeping four plus a baby in the Lubéron hills for a week in June is £1,000. You can get discounts on airport parking and hotels too.

Siblu ★ ★

📞 *0871 911 0022, www.siblu.com.*

Formerly known as Haven Europe, this company offers tents, mobile homes and chalets at three sites near Fréjus and St.-Raphaël. All sites have free supervised children's clubs, water parks with indoor and outdoor pools, a toddler's pool and slides, play areas and sporting and housekeeping amenities. You can rent 'baby packs', which include buggies, highchairs and baby baths and more, as well as beach and activity packs for older children. Single parents take note of the discount: a 7-night stay in La Baume near St.-Raphaël starts at £723 in July for one adult and two children; the price includes a £100 single-saver discount plus online booking and independent travel discounts (ferry crossings can be arranged).

Getting Around

By Car Although far from environmentally friendly (or cheap, given fuel prices), having a set of wheels allows you the necessary flexibility when it comes to exploring the South of France, especially rural areas such as the Camargue, Haute-Provence, the Vaucluse and inland parts of the Alpes-Maritimes and the Var.

If you're bringing your own car, you'll need to have your **driving licence**, the original of the **vehicle registration document**, a current **insurance certificate** and, if the vehicle isn't registered in your name, a letter of authorisation from the owner. Your British insurance will give you the minimum legal cover required in France but it's advisable to ask your insurer for a **green card** (international insurance certificate). These are no longer compulsory but provide evidence of minimum insurance cover. Get yourself some extra peace of mind by arranging **24-hour breakdown assistance** too (p. 36). Note that, if you break down on a motorway, you can only call the official breakdown service operating in that area; there are orange emergency telephones every 2km. They charge a fixed fee of 68.60€ for repairing or towing a vehicle, or 85.75€ at night (6pm to 8am), but make sure you get a receipt. You can call your own breakdown service after being towed off the motorway.

Those coming into France must display an international **sign plate or sticker** (e.g. GB) as near as possible to their rear registration plate. Carrying a **red warning triangle** is strongly advised, even if your car has hazard-warning lights, because breakdown may affect your electrics (they're compulsory for cars towing a caravan or trailer). You should also buy a complete **spare-bulb kit** before you go, because it's illegal to drive with faulty lights. You need to **adjust your beams** for right-hand drive, which means buying special stickers to affix on your headlights. All of this gear is available from shops at the Channel ports.

The **French road system** is generally excellent. **Motorways** are uncrowded compared with British ones, though on most you have to pay a **toll**—Calais to Nice costs about 90€. If you're not in a hurry, it's often preferable to take a *route nationale* (RN or N)—a main road, usually single-lane, that sometimes takes you through scenic towns. Motorways have parking/rest areas every 10 to 20km and 24-hour petrol stations with basic car maintenance services every 40km or so. Visa and MasterCard are accepted at tolls and petrol stations (except some automated out-of-hours pumps).

The website *www.autoroutes.fr* (with an English version) will give you information about routes, toll charges, service stations, rest areas, restaurants, petrol stations and hotels along the way. It even works out how much petrol you will use to get from one place to another. If you understand French, **Autoroute FM** (107.7 FM) broadcasts live traffic information on motorways.

Don't drink and drive at all. Apart from the safety of yourself and your children, there are frequent random breath tests and the alcohol limit is just 0.05%. The **speed limits** are 130 km/h (80 mph) on toll motorways, 110 km/h (68 mph) on dual carriageways and motorways without tolls, and 90 km/h (56 mph) on other roads except in towns, where it's 50 km/h (31 mph). On wet roads the limits are, respectively, 110 km/h (68 mph), 100 km/h (62 mph) and 80 km/h (50 mph); in fog with visibility of less than 50m it's 50 km/h (31 mph) even on toll motorways. For cars towing a caravan, if the weight of the trailer exceeds that of the car, the limit is 65 km/h (40 mph) if the excess is less than 30%, or 45 km/h (28 mph) if the excess is

Driving Rules & Advice

Traffic rules in France resemble those in force in Britain—the key difference is that in France you *drive on the right*. Don't forget this for a moment when you exit a petrol station or junction. In built-up areas, you must give way to anybody coming out of a side turning on the right (the infamous *priorité à droite*). This rule no longer applies at roundabouts, where you give way to cars that are already on the roundabout. Common signs you will see are *chaussée déformée* ('uneven road/temporary surface'), *deviation* ('diversion') and *rappel* ('continuation of restriction'). The official text of the French **highway code** is available in English at **www.legifrance.gouv.fr**. For **road signs**, see **www. permis-enligne.com**, or your road atlas will probably picture many of them. Note that you must be at least 18, not 17, to drive in France. For **child car seats**, see p. 37. Children under 10 may not sit in the front.

more than 30%. Speeding is always supposed to result in fines and a court appearance, but a cash fine often suffices for foreign drivers.

Car Rental The best way to hire a car in France is in advance via the **Internet** so that you have **proof of your booking** when you arrive. When collecting your car, as well as your reservation print-out you need a **driving licence** for each driver, additional **photo ID** (your national identity card or passport), your passport if you are a non-EU resident and a credit card in the main driver's name (sometimes two cards for expensive models). Different rental firms have different lower age limits for drivers; it's generally between 21 and 25 but it can depend on how expensive the model is, and you may have to pay a young driver's surcharge. For child-seat hire, see the 'Painless Travel by Car' section, p. 37.

Car hire in France has got much less expensive in the past

few years. However, prices seem to vary enormously, even between cars of similar size. Make sure you get a few quotations from different firms (you can compare prices at **www.carrentals.co.uk**), and check that they include unlimited mileage, full insurance, tax and 24-hour breakdown assistance. With some cheaper deals, you may need to buy a **damage excess liability waiver** so you're not liable for a considerable initial chunk of loss or damage to the car. This starts at about 15€ a day. Good deals are often available if you book via low-cost airline websites at the same time as buying your flight ticket. All of the major car companies operate across France; the following websites will tell you which operate where:

Avis **www.avis.co.uk**

Easycar **www.easycar.com**

Europcar **www.europcar.com**

Hertz **www.hertz.co.uk**

National/Citer **www.citer.com**

Painless Travel by Car

When travelling long distances by car, it may be worth timing your trip to coincide with a child's nap time, or even leaving after dinner and unloading them into bed at your pre-booked accommodation. Think about investing in an in-car satellite navigation system (**SatNav**). They are now relatively affordable, and many couples cite them as marriage-savers! They're particularly handy for parents who are trying to map-read and deal with the demands of children in the back. However, be vigilant about removing it from your car when you leave it parked on the street—or someone else will remove it for you. Other desirables and essentials are:

- A fully charged **mobile phone**
- **Breakdown cover/roadside assistance**. **Europ Assistance** (📞 *0844 338 55 33, www.europ-assistance.co.uk*) has fair prices and an excellent reputation. If you do break down, tell the operator you have children so they'll prioritise you. If you're somewhere other cars could run into the back of you, such as on the hard shoulder of the motorway, it's wise to get children out of the car. If you have a hire car, make sure the booking includes 24-hour roadside assistance.
- **Child seats**. Under-10s *must* be seated in the back in France, except babies in rear-facing safety seats, though the latter must not be used if the front passenger seat is fitted with an airbag. Laws that came into force in the UK in 2006 require children under 13 (or under 136cm in height) to use a specialist seat for their age, except in certain mitigating circumstances. There is no such law in France and the types of car seats provided by the car-hire companies vary. Easycar, for instance, provides infant seats for babies up to 9 months (or 9kg) and boosters for children up to 10; Europcar provides different seats for 0–12 months, 1–3 years and 4–7 years. You need to reserve them when you book your car; expect to pay about 17€ to 30€. If that seems expensive, it's relatively hassle-free to bring your own car seat or booster by plane—they just go in the hold with your luggage (although they may come out at a separate point in the baggage hall; ask a member of staff if yours doesn't materialise). A good source of information on car seats for both the UK and abroad is *www.childcarseats. org.uk*.
- A **first-aid kit**; **window shades**; **children's travel pillows**; a **portable highchair** (p. 25); a **cooler box** to replenish with drinks and snacks each time you set off; **wipes**, **nappies** and **plastic bags** (for nappies or motion sickness); **blankets**, **sweaters** and a **change of clothes**.
- **Audio CDs** of your children's favourite stories or songs, **sticker books**, **crayons and paper**, a **magic slate**, or a compact **travel book** with games and activities such as the *Amazing Book-a-ma-thing for the Backseat* (Klutz, £10.99, from *www.amazon.co.uk*).

If you bring a car rented in the UK into France, you must inform the rental firm that the car is being taken to France in order to ensure you're covered there. You might need to show the French police the rental agreement to prove you have this insurance.

Motorhomes These are subject to the same road rules as cars. You can stop for a few hours in a motorway service area, but note that toll tickets are only valid for a limited time. You're also not allowed to stop overnight at the roadside. To find out about the 1,700 places adapted for motorhomes (that provide waste disposal and water, for example) in France, including campsites, see the French-language *Camping-Car Magazine* (available at newspaper kiosks), or check sites for your destination at its website, *www.campingcar-magazine. fr*, ahead of your trip.

If you're not bringing your own motorhome, you can hire one in Marseille or Nice: try *www.motorhome-hirefrance.com* or *www.aviscaraway.com*. A four-person motorhome with unlimited mileage for one week in high season can cost 1,000€ to 1,500€, with special terms for long-term rental (2 months or longer). Damage excess liability waiver and 24-hour breakdown assistance are optional but highly advisable. You can also get child seats, bedding sets, bike racks and satellite navigation (the latter with a hefty deposit).

By Train France's national rail system, run by the **SNCF**, is efficient and inexpensive compared with the British network, and a very good way of getting between cities and larger towns. Its famously zippy **TGV** (*train à grande vitesse*, aka 'very fast train') network is ever-expanding—see *www.tgv.com* (available in English) for an excellent clickable route map that then takes you to *www. voyages-sncf.com* (also available in English) to book tickets. The South of France is pretty well served by the TGV: it stops at Aix-en-Provence, Antibes, Arles, Avignon, Cannes, Hyères, Marseille, Nice, Nîmes, St.-Raphaël and Toulon.

The **regional train service** (*www.ter-sncf.com*) covers smaller towns such as Aigues Mortes and villages along the Côte Bleue coast. It also runs a good seaside service between Menton and Cannes. However, to explore the region properly, particularly the Camargue, Haute-Provence, the Vaucluse and inland parts of the Alpes-Maritimes and the Var, you'll need a car.

Expect to pay about 30€ for a single ticket from Marseille to Nice (about 2½ hours), and 14€ for a child aged 4 to 11 (under-4s travel free on a parent's lap on all trains, unless you want to pay for an extra seat to ensure you have sufficient room). However, if you're travelling with at least one child under 12, ask about the *Decouverte Enfant* offer, which gives a discount for up to five members of the party. The very clear

What Things Cost in Provence	€
1 litre unleaded 95 petrol	1.27
Rental of medium-sized car (week)	200€–1,350€
City/town bus fare	1.20€
City/town bus fare, child aged over 5	same
Single train fare Nîmes to Avignon, adult (45km)	9€
Single train fare, Nîmes to Avignon, child 4–11	5€
Single TGV fare Marseille to Nice, adult (211km)	30€
Single TGV fare, Marseille to Nice, child 4–11	15€
Admission to zoo, adult	13€
Admission to zoo, child 4–12	7€
Admission to public museum	free
Cinema ticket, adult	8€
Cinema ticket, child	6€
British newspaper	2.50€
Local telephone call (per minute)	0.03€–0.09€
European telephone call (per minute)	0.22€
Fixed-priced menu at mid-price restaurant	14€–18€
Under-12s menu at mid-price restaurant	9€
1 litre of milk in supermarket	1€
1 litre bottle of water in supermarket	0.60€
6 Golden Delicious apples	3.50€
5 bananas	1.99€
Packet of 30 Pampers in supermarket	11.30€
900g tin of baby milk in supermarket	14€
Ham and cheese baguette from bakery	3.50€

online booking system will tell you if you need a seat reservation (compulsory on TGVs).

By Bus Getting around by bus is fairly easy, though be aware that they are infrequent and sometimes leave at unsociably early hours—this is because they normally do the school run. Some inter-town buses are less frequent during school holidays. Most regional bus companies have their own websites and are included in the 'Getting Around' section of the sightseeing chapters; you can also get a timetable from the local bus station (and

sometimes the tourist office) when you arrive, although if you're going to explore the region by public transport, it's good to do your research in advance to plan your itinerary.

Town and city centres in this part of the world are fairly compact and easy to get around, so you won't really need to use a bus except in sprawling Marseille (where you can also hop on a Métro or tram). Nice also opened a tramway in 2007.

By Taxi Taxi **fares** in this region vary enormously and you are advised to ask how much a journey will cost before you commit to taking one. For example, in sleepy Tarascon, a taxi over the bridge to Beaucaire (about 1km) would cost a minimum of 10€. Nice is also renowned for expensive taxis, whereas those in Nîmes and Marseille are very affordable. If you're arriving at an airport or train station, there's usually a fairly frequent bus or train alternative.

By Bike If you don't bring your own bikes, tourist offices can give you lists of hire outlets or you may find that your accommodation offers bike loan or hire. All hire shops have **helmets** and most can also provide child seats and sometimes child trailers. Avoid busy towns and roads and stick to quiet country lanes, though the nature of French driving means you must be vigilant at all times. Taking your bike on trains is a complex issue: you need to talk to the SNCF in each individual case. Tourist offices and their websites have details of cycle routes in their respective areas.

ACCOMMODATION & EATING OUT

Accommodation

If you're planning to holiday along the Côte d'Azur, you have to plan carefully to avoid overpriced and overrated accommodation. Room rates are often high, and a seemingly endless list of expensive extras will push

your bill up even higher. From St.-Tropez east to the Italian border, good-value hotels, B&Bs and campsites tend to be booked up well in advance.

Further west, you'll find plenty of long, empty beaches along the Camargue coastline, accompanied by low-key, better-priced resorts catering to French families, as well as well-serviced campsites and holiday villages. The verdant regions of the Vaucluse and Alpes de Haute Provence, as well as the mountainous hinterland of the Alpes-Maritimes and the Haut Var, offer hundreds of *gîtes*—some with pools, mountain bikes for loan or hire, and other kit for active families—as well as more campsites, small country hotels and farmhouse accommodation.

We have based the **price categories** used within the 'Accommodation' sections of the sightseeing chapters on the following ranges, based on lodgings per night for two adults and two children, without breakfast except in the case of B&Bs and some hotels (see individual hotel reviews for details).

Very expensive: More than 360€

Expensive: 280€–360€

Moderate: 160€–280€

Inexpensive: Less than 160€

The costliest options are mostly **châteaux-hotels** (in key inland tourist areas such as Avignon and Grasse), luxurious **resort hotels** or über-stylish **boutique properties** in glitzy beach destinations such as St.-Tropez, Cannes or Antibes, with private beach strips, gastronomic restaurants, swimming pools, health and beauty spas, tennis courts and super-attentive service. These can be fabulous places to splash out on for the odd night or two.

In the moderate to expensive categories you'll find good seaside hotels, often with pools, games for families, supervised watersports and services including child-minding and babysitting. In the moderate and budget categories, you'll find a range of off-the-peg, minimal-frills hotels and apartments run by chains that span France.

Almost all the hotels and *chambres d'hôte* chosen for this guide offer **family rooms** for up to four, or interconnecting rooms or suites with comfortable sofa-beds. In a hotel, an *appartement* isn't what we'd call an apartment (there are no self-catering facilities) but a one- or two-bedroom suite. Most hotels and *chambres d'hôte* will provide baby cots either free or for a nominal extra charge. Continental breakfast is often included in the room price. At the lower end of the price range, it generally comprises croissants, preserves, coffee and (often watered-down) juice, while at the top end the content is similar but the quality and quantity is superior. Either way, children (and adults) may find French hotel breakfasts monotonous after the first few days. If breakfast isn't included in the room rate, eating at a nearby café—and there are

usually plenty—is generally a better bet than paying extra in your hotel, as hotel breakfasts throughout Provence are exorbitantly overpriced.

Hotels

For family trips, it makes more sense to deal directly with individual hotels and other accommodation suppliers than book them through a website or booking agency. Doing it by e-mail (or, the old fashioned way, by fax) lets you explain your needs and make sure that the hotel provides the services and facilities you require, from bottle warmers and cot linen to games consoles, DVD players and mountain bikes. It also means you have the details in writing in case of queries or misunderstandings when you get there (in the worst-case scenario, you have proof if the hotel doesn't deliver what was promised). Hotels often offer special low-season deals or last-minute prices on their websites, though these are rarely available at peak family holiday times, and should always be treated with caution—the rooms being offered at rock-bottom prices are usually the worst and smallest in the hotel, with no view and a poor location, and are often long overdue for renovation.

Still, for late-booking deals, some of France's **centralised booking services** can turn up trumps—for smaller hotels in Provence and all over France, check out *www.guidesdecharme. com* and *www.logisdefrance.com*.

No-frills Hotels

Strategically located near airports, train stations and motorway junctions, France's no-frills hotels are not places to spend more than a night or two. However, they do offer great convenience and excellent value for money if, for example, you are arriving late at night, taking an early flight or train, or driving through France and in need of an overnight stop that doesn't involve straying too far off the *autoroute*. With one single bunk above a double bed, cabin-style bedrooms can be a bit spartan, though younger family members tend to find them rather fun.

These hotels can usually be booked online. The most basic, virtually unmanned module hotels simply issue you with a one-time PIN code when you book—punch in the code on a keypad to enter the hotel and access your room. Even the simplest of them offer a continental breakfast of coffee, juice, croissants and preserves for around 5€ per person.

Among the most ubiquitous chains are **Formule 1** (*www.hotelformule1.com*), which offers rooms for around 30€ per night, with washbasins but shared WCs and showers. **Etap** (*www.etaphotel.com*) has similar accommodation for around 40€ per room per night, with ensuite shower and WC.

Campanile (*www.campanile.com*) has properties all over France and a wide range of special offers for families, including interconnecting rooms for around 90€ (sleeping up to five people). In Provence you'll find Campaniles in Aix, Arles, Avignon, Marseille, Nice, Orange and Toulon. Its sister-chain, Kyriade, also has value-for-money hotels in Aix, Antibes, Arles, Avignon, Cannes, Fréjus, Marseille, Menton, Nice and elsewhere. We wouldn't recommend these hotels for a long family holiday, but for one night—or even a weekend—they are very well-priced, squeaky clean, user-friendly and above all easy to find.

More up-market, and better for longer stays, are the apartments of the **Citadines** chain (*www.citadines.com*), with a double bedroom plus a small sitting room with a comfortable sofa bed and a fully equipped kitchenette, cots by request, air-conditioning and Wi-Fi. Ideal for families visiting bigger cities, they can be found in Marseille (in the heart of the Prado district and close to the old harbour), in Nice (close to the Promenade des Anglais), in Aix and in Lyon—handy for a stopover between Provence and the Channel ferry ports.

Hotel-residences

Hotel-residences are common along the Côte d'Azur and offer the best of both worlds: these are apartment complexes attached to hotels, so you have the flexibility of self-catering along with the use of hotel facilities such as restaurants, bars, pools, a gym and health centre, a spa and often a children's club as well.

Holiday Villages

Provence has numerous 'holiday villages' both along the coast and inland, often in lakeside or riverside locations, and these are great for families on a budget, offering clean, simple accommodation in self-catering chalets, apartments or sometimes mobile homes with enough space outside for toddlers to romp safely. The big attraction is that, in addition, they offer the kind of facilities you would expect to find in a more expensive, full-service hotel, such as pools for children and adults, supervised children's clubs and activities for children of all ages, and facilities for sports such as tennis, volleyball and archery.

Vacanciel (*www.vacanciel. com*) has several holiday villages in the region, in a choice of seaside, lakeside and mountain locations. You can also try **Club Med** (*www.clubmed.com*) in Opio; **VVF Vacances** (*www. vvf-vacances.fr*) in Grasse, La Colle sur Loup and Toulon; and **Pierre et Vacances** (*www.pierre etvacances.com*) in 16 locations across the Alpes-Maritimes, Var and Bouches-du-Rhône.

Gîtes, Villas & Apartments

We have lumped all of these together because they come under the heading of self-catering options—though, of course, in the grandest of Riviera villas that catering may be undertaken by your resident cook or housekeeper, whereas in a rural *gîte* you might barbecue dinner in the garden, and in the simplest holiday apartment you may be reduced to heating up a tin of beans on a two-ring electric hotplate.

The Provençal coast is not the best place to look for a quaint old seaside cottage. However, you don't have to head very far inland to find lovely converted stone farmhouses, often with fairly extensive gardens and their own swimming pools. Built originally for large peasant families, these houses have more than enough space for most British families. I think they offer the best family accommodation in Provence, with very affordable prices compared with hotels, and usually excellent facilities. You can count on a fully equipped kitchen, usually with a dishwasher and a washing machine; secure parking; and in most cases satellite TV and/or a DVD player. However, check facilities carefully before committing yourselves. Sites with pools cost more, but that's money well spent. Location is important too: ideally, you want to be within walking distance of a village with a couple of shops and at least one café-bar. You can book *gîtes* directly on several good websites, including *www.gîtesdefrance. com*, *www.interhome.co.uk* and *www.frenchconnections.co.uk*, though for peace of mind I would strongly recommend booking through one of several specialist UK-based companies that offer high-quality *gîte* and villa accommodation in Provence, and also ease your way

Gîtes d'Enfants (Children's Gîtes)

This school-holiday programme allows children aged 4–16 to enjoy country life and outdoor activities with other children (often including the host's own family) at an establishment—usually a farm—inspected by the French department of health and social services. Activities might include butter making, rambling, making herb gardens, picking flowers, going on picnics, dance and foreign-language lessons, handicrafts, canoeing, riding and sailing. You're probably thinking you came on holiday to spend time *with* your children, not to fob them off on somebody else. However, if they're independent and enjoy discovering nature and wildlife, they might enjoy doing this for a week. If you stay in a hotel nearby, you can pop in and see them every day, while grabbing some 'adult time' and perhaps even a bit of pampering. It's generally a good idea, at least the first time, to send a child with a sibling, cousin or friend of a similar age. There are **Mini-Gîtes** for ages 4–10, generally accommodating just two to five children on a farm, **Junior-Gîtes** for six or more children aged 6–10, where the owner is helped by a trained assistant, and **Clubs Jeunes** for between 12 and 35 children aged 11–16, with more active sports. Expect to pay just under 300€ per week. Some places offer activities by the day.

For children's *gîtes* by *département*, see **www.gîtes-de-france.fr**. Some owners speak English, where indicated, but this is obviously a great way for children who speak some French to improve their language skills.

by booking flights and car hire. Such specialist *gîte* and villa companies are listed on **www. holidayfrance.org.uk**, the official website of the Association of British Tour Operators to France, and on **www.aito.co.uk**, the website of the Association of Independent Tour Operators.

Campsites

The French have camping down to a fine art, and many French families spend their summer *vacances* under canvas in huge tents with multiple compartments, canopies and fully quipped outdoor kitchens. To cater for them, campsites in Provence range from huge and bustling four- and five-star resorts on the Riviera and the Côte d'Azur—complete with pools, aqua-parks, private beaches, watersports and tennis courts, as well as children's clubs, childminding and babysitting—to small sites tucked away in quiet valleys or beside mountain lakes in the Haute-Provence and the Vaucluse. If you're looking for a spell at a beach campsite but don't fancy the hurly-burly of the Côte d'Azur, the place to head for is the

Camargue coast. Here, there are miles of empty sand even in high summer, and youngsters can walk straight from the tent to a beach with pedalos, canoes and watchful lifeguards.

If you're planning to tour the region by car (or if you're driving to Provence from the UK), camping can be a great option. You don't have to worry about finding a place to leave the car, unloading valuables or navigating your way through a baffling maze of narrow one-way streets to a hotel in one of the region's historic towns—you just roll up, park and pitch your tent. Most French campsites have at least a basic restaurant (in summer) serving child-friendly meals, drinks and snacks, usually until about 10pm, and most rural sites have pools for toddlers as well as for teenagers and adults. They'll also have communal showers, barbecue areas and usually a coin-operated launderette. Several British companies, including **Canvas Holidays** (p. 34), offer camping holidays in Provence. These companies save you the trouble of pitching your own tent by providing ready-made accommodation under canvas with separate 'rooms' for different members of the family.

If you'd like something a little more solid and luxurious but still with that campsite feel, many sites on the Provençal coast also offer accommodation in self-contained self-catering bungalows or mobile homes with two or more bedrooms, kitchen-diner, ensuite shower and WC. UK-based holiday company **Alan Rogers Travel** (☏ *01580 214 000, www.alan rogers.travel*) offers a hand-picked selection of excellent campsites throughout France. **Club Cantabrica** (☏ *01727 866 177, www.cantabrica.co.uk*) offers lodge-style accommodation in beachside campsites at Port Grimaud and Antibes, starting at only 75€ per person per week, with coach transport from the UK, free child travel and a range of family saver packages.

Youth Hostels

For families, youth hostels in Provence are generally a desperate last resort if there isn't anywhere else to stay. They are usually chock-full of young backpackers throughout the year, so turning up without a reservation isn't a good idea. If you are on a minimal budget and don't mind mucking in, however, they are undeniably cheap and fun, with family rooms sleeping four to six people in bunk beds, communal kitchens, launderettes and games rooms. Single-parent families (p. 28) sometimes get special rates.

The French hostelling association website, *www.fuaj.org*, translated (somewhat eccentrically) into English, has links to individual hostel websites (where they exist) but does not list privately run hostels or those run by other organisations.

Expect to pay around 12€ per person in a four-person room,

including breakfast, plus 23€ for annual family membership of FUAJ.

Dining

Some people come to France for the cuisine alone, in the belief that France is still a country in which you can walk into a modest small-town bistro and discover a meal worthy of the most demanding gourmet. Sadly, that isn't always the case in Provence. The region has more than its share of world-famous, Michelin-starred restaurants patronised by the rich and famous, but mass tourism and the Provençal fondness for quick money have also seen the arrival of venues where the food is mediocre, the service surly and indifferent, and the prices over-inflated.

That said, most restaurants and cafés (with the odd notoriously rude exception) are welcoming to children. The climate encourages alfresco eating, and the historic centres of many towns and villages are traffic-free, which means that you can let the children potter around the village square while you enjoy a post-prandial coffee.

Many restaurants in this region have **children's menus** (generally about 10€), although the standard choice is *steak haché* (a burger by any other name) and chips, pizza or pasta as a main course, followed by ice cream. A quick alternative for those bored of sitting down is eating on the street—you can get great pizza by the slice (about 0.50€ to 4€) from stalls and corner shops in most coastal towns and resorts.

Vegetarians will find the Côte d'Azur the best place to go, and other areas of Provence less user-friendly. Meat or seafood products in one form or another manage to find their way into even the most innocuous-seeming salads, and the really imaginative vegetarian fare generally appears on the *degustation* menus of the region's poshest and most expensive restaurants. However, there are some honourable exceptions, which are flagged up in the relevant regional chapters.

Restaurants and cafés generally have at least one **highchair**, but these are available on a first-come, first-served basis, so a portable highchair (one that can double as a child's car seat), a blow-up travelling booster seat or a foldable fabric one is almost a must (p. 25 for some recommendations).

Mealtimes on the Côte d'Azur in summer are less rigid than in much of France, although outside major coastal cities and resorts it can still be hard to find restaurants serving sit-down meals outside the standard lunch and dinner hours (generally noon to 3pm and 7 to 10pm). In smaller, hinterland towns and villages, don't expect to find anywhere serving lunch after 2pm. That said, *brasseries* are often open all day, providing parents with an opportunity to get family blood-sugar levels back up to normal with sweet or savoury pancakes or ever-useful standbys such as *sandwich jambon* or *sandwich fromage*. These bar-restaurants—and other French eating and drinking spots—became a bit more family-friendly from 2008, when the French government finally banned smoking in bars and restaurants entirely. However, smoking is still permissible at outdoor tables, so you and your family may still be exposed to fumes when dining alfresco.

INSIDER TIP >>

Always take a portable changing mat and wipes with you to restaurants as very few places in Provence have a nappy-changing area.

The 'Family-friendly Dining' sections of the sightseeing chapters in this book cover as wide a range of eating options as possible, from tasty, street-level pizzerias to dazzling gastronomic restaurants that welcome children but will also appeal if you fancy a rare night out without them. Bear in mind that virtually every restaurant offers set menus (*menu*) for lunch and dinner, which are a lot more budget-friendly than ordering a la carte. **Price categories** are based on two adults and two children eating two courses plus drinks:

Expensive: More than 120€

Moderate: 45€–120€

Inexpensive: less than 45€

THE 21ST-CENTURY TRAVELLER

Mobile Phones

Mobile phones are indispensable for travelling families, and most British mobiles automatically switch to a French network on arrival. Check before leaving that your phone is set up for international roaming and that you can access your voice mail while abroad.

Under pressure from the EU, mobile phone companies have abolished exorbitant roaming charges and have made big cuts in the cost of phoning and texting across most of Europe, including France. However, if you expect to make a lot of calls, you may be able to cut your costs still further by buying a French pay-as-you-go SIM card, available before you leave the UK from *www.0044.co.uk* (which sells pay-as-you-go packs from £39.99, with calls costing 20p per minute), or in the US from *www.gosim.com*.

Mobile phone coverage in southern France is generally good, but in mountainous areas or the deep valleys of Alpes de Haute-Provence it may be difficult to get a signal. Note that you can sometimes use text messaging even when the signal isn't good enough for voice.

If you're planning a longer stay or come to France regularly, you could buy a pay-as-you-go (*sans abonnement*) phone from one of the Orange, Bouygtel or SFR shops that can be found on

TIP **Provence's Best Child-friendly Chains**

The great food at **La Piazza Papa** (*www.piazzapapa.fr*), including the pasta, is made on the premises, and there's a choice of good-value menus, including a *menu bambino* with pizza or chicken with spaghetti, dessert and a 'goody bag' present. Branches are at: 33 cours Mirabeau (04 42 26 72 02) in Aix-en-Provence; 15 quai Rive Neuve (04 91 59 82 24) in Marseille's Vieux Port; 13 bis cours Saleya (04 93 85 61 91) in Nice; and 8 boulevard Amiral Courbet (04 66 76 01 21) in Nîmes.

A national chain specialising in steaks, **Hippopotamus** (*www.hippopotamus. fr*) keeps under-12s entertained with crayons, drawing books and balloons before they tuck into their two-course children's menu. There are Hippopotami at 33 quai des Belges (04 91 59 91 40) in Marseille's Vieux Port; 16 avenue Félix Faure (04 93 92 42 77) in Nice; and 802 Ancienne Route de Générac (04 66 04 80 60) in Nîmes.

the main streets of most French towns, or from a large supermarket such as Intermarche, Leclerc or Géant.

US Travellers

For those from further afield, such as the US, the situation is basically the same provided you have a world-capable multiband phone on the GSM system, with international roaming activated. Again, installing an international SIM card can save you money if you plan to make a lot of calls. The website *www.gosim.com* is worth checking before you leave.

How to Dial Within Country on a Mobile

To use a mobile within France, you will need to dial the country code (00 33) then the local phone number (dropping the initial zero from the 2-digit regional code). To call another UK mobile, even if both phones are in France, dial (00 44) then drop the initial zero.

For information about **area** and **international dialling codes** and public phones, see p. 53.

Internet & Wi-Fi

Large cities and most towns have a choice of Internet access points, whether in **cybercafés, public libraries** or the **tourist office**. Tourist offices will provide you with a list, and websites such as *www.cybercafe.com* and *www. cybercaptive.com* can be helpful. A good French site is *www.cyber cafe.fr*. You can also get (expensive) Internet access in some post offices, and some major cities have Internet kiosks in the street.

To **retrieve your e-mails**, ask your internet service provider (ISP) if it has a **Web-based interface** tied to your existing account. If it doesn't, set up a **free Web-based e-mail account** with *www.hotmail.com* or *www.yahoo.com*, for example.

You might want to start one up anyway as a back-up to your existing account.

Most **hotels** have a terminal in the reception area where you can access the Internet (for free or a small charge) or a means by which you can access it from your laptop. The latter could be either through a modem connection/dataport in your room (you'll pay for it as you would a phone call, and this can be expensive; you might also need an adaptor) or, increasingly, through **Wi-Fi**, for which you'll need to obtain a code from the receptionist (it's a good idea to check in advance if it's available in your room as well as in public areas and if there's a charge). Wi-Fi is also available in many **airports and cafés** (see *www. journaldunet.com/Wi-Fi*).

If you're a touch typist and need to do a lot of e-mailing, **French keyboards** don't work on the QWERTY principle and will slow you down. For example, the '@' sign (known as *arrobaz* in French) is normally above the number 2.

FAST FACTS: PROVENCE

Area codes See 'Telephone', p. 53.

Baby equipment Most hotels, B&Bs and *gîtes* can provide cots, often for a charge (around 8€ on average), and some offer other equipment such as bottle warmers and changing mats. Some places do not provide linen for their cots because of allergy risks. For equipment rental, see p. 25.

Supermarkets, especially larger ones such as the Carrefour, Géant or Auchan chains, are good for baby equipment, from nappies and jarred food to baths and car seats. Many out-of-town *centres commerciales* (shopping malls) have baby and toddler supermarkets such as **Bebe 9** (*www.bebe9.com*)—there are branches at Aix, Carpentras, Cavaillon, Fréjus, Gap, Marseille and elsewhere.

Babysitting Most expensive and some moderately priced hotels offer babysitting services, usually sub-contracted to local agencies and requiring at least 24 hours' notice. You usually pay the sitter directly and rates average 8€ to 13€ per hour. Some *gîte* owners also offer babysitting.

Banks Normally open from 9:30am to 4:30pm Monday to Friday except public holidays. Branches in smaller towns and suburbs often close from 12.30 to 2pm. Most have 24-hour **ATMs** (p. 22).

Breastfeeding Breastfeeding in public is much less common in France than in the UK, and you may get stared at, especially if you're feeding an older infant. It's odd, considering that naked breasts are a far from unusual sight along the Provençal coast in summer. You can brazen it out, since breastfeeding is your right, or you may prefer to find a secluded spot.

Lire & Learn

An excellent way of interesting children in Provence is through children's classics set within the region. Ste.-Maxime's Plage des Éléphants is immortalised in Jean de Brunhoff's *Voyage of Babar*, while older children might enjoy Agatha Christie's murder mystery classic, *The Mystery of the Blue Train*, set along the French Riviera. Other fun books to get your children in the mood include:

Children of Summer, by Margaret J. Anderson, which tells the tale of French entomologist Jean Henri Fabre, a Provençal farmer fascinated by the insects of his homeland, recounted through the eyes of his 10-year-old son Paul. This novel should stoke children's interest in Provence's vast summer menagerie of creepy-crawlies, from giant green grasshoppers to maternal scorpions, shrill cicadas and the cannibalistic praying mantis.

Rabbit Pirates, by Judy Cox and Emily Arnold McCully, is an illustrated picture book about two gastronomic rabbits (aptly named Monsieur Lapin and Monsieur Blanc) running a café in Provence.

The Truffle Hunter, by Inga Moore, is a picture book with excellent illustrations about a truffle-hunting pig—perfect for young children visiting the truffle-rich Vaucluse.

Camille and the Sunflowers, by Laurence Anholt, and *Visiting Vincent van Gogh,* by Caroline Breunesse, describe Vincent van Gogh and his home in Arles through illustrations. Both books are good for younger children visiting the Bouches-du-Rhône.

La Gloire de Mon Père and *Le Château de Ma Mère* (available in a one-volume translation as *My Father's Glory* and *My Mother's Castle*), by Marcel Pagnol, are humorous memoirs of a Provençal childhood set in the thyme- and rosemary-scented hills above Marseille, and good books to read aloud to your children.

Business Hours For those used to Britain's 24/7 shopping culture, France requires a change of pace and a lot more planning. You can't just nip out for a pint of milk at any time of the day or night. Shops outside large towns generally open at 9 or 10am (7 or 8am for bakeries) and close at 6 or 7pm, with a 2-hour lunch break from 12:30 to 2:30pm. In summer, many large **supermarkets** stay open all day until 9 or 10pm in the evening. Some shops (but few supermarkets) open on Sunday morning if there is a Sunday market nearby, but close on Monday. For out-of-hours shopping, a good tip is to look in the slightly scruffier parts of cities such as Marseille, Nice and Avignon, where shops for locals often stay open longer.

Restaurants generally open from noon to 2:30pm and 7 to 10pm; larger towns and resorts

Getting the Children Interested in Provence

As well as using this book to involve your children in planning their trip and picking the sights they want to see and the things they want to do, introduce them to publications such as *Bonjour France!* (Rebecca Welby, Beautiful Books), with games, maps, puzzles and activities for 7- to 12-year-olds. It also includes ideas for beach games and indoor games for rainy days. Most of the well-loved Madeline books by Ludwig Bemelmans, about the escapades of a French schoolgirl, are set in Paris, but *Madeline Says Merci: The Always Be Polite Book* (republished in 2006 and available from **www.amazon.co.uk** and **www. amazon.com**) is a good way of getting youngsters aged 4 to 10 interested in France and French ways and learning some essential French phrases.

Astérix, the cunning little Gaul, and his lumbering sidekick Obélix are also good comic-book companions for children travelling in France. Astérix's home is in Brittany, but he passes through Provence and its great seaport, Marseille, on at least one of his adventures in the ancient world. The Astérix books are available in English as well as French. The French take *bandes dessinées* (comic books) much more seriously than we do, and most bookshops have long shelves packed with graphic sketches for all ages (be aware that some of them are perhaps a little *too* graphic for younger readers). True fans should visit the **Comic Strips Café** bookshop (p. 77) in Antibes.

---

usually have some with *service continu*.

Public **museums** close on Monday or Tuesday and on public holidays, but most tourist sites open on public and school holidays. The Côte d'Azur is a less seasonal holiday region than many parts of France, but even so, many attractions and hotels close for part or all of the winter and many **restaurants** take a break of up to a month, usually after Christmas. In the mountainous hinterland, where winters are harsh but where winter sports do not really flourish, many *gîtes*, **campsites** and **rural hotels** close for the winter.

Car Rental See p. 36.

Climate See 'When to Go', p. 22.

Currency See 'Money', p. 21.

Customs & Duty-free See p. 19.

Doctors Some hotels have an expensive private doctor on call, and most accommodation providers will be happy to help you contact a doctor in a minor emergency. Local newspapers list doctors on call (*medecins de service*).

Driving Rules See p. 36.

Electricity Electricity runs on 220-volt, 50-cycle AC and is adequate for UK appliances, but you will need an adapter (available from French supermarkets) to use the two-pin sockets. Most hotels will lend you one.

Embassies & Consulates British Embassy, 35 rue du Faubourg St.-Honoré, Paris ☏ 01 44 51 31 00, *www.britishembassy. gov.uk*, open 9:30am–1pm and 2.30–6pm Mon–Fri.

British Consulate, 24 avenue du Prado, Marseille, ☏ 04 91 15 72 10, open 9am–noon and 2–4.30pm Mon–Fri.

Emergencies Hotel staff are trained to deal with emergencies, so call the front desk before you do anything else. Otherwise, for an ambulance call ☏ 15, for police ☏ 17, and for the fire service ☏ 18. You will be expected to pay for ambulance service and claim reimbursement from your insurer, so adequate travel insurance is essential. In minor emergencies, unless it is dangerous to move the injured person, it will probably be quicker to drive yourself to the nearest hospital than to wait for an ambulance. Note that hospitals are sometimes signposted *Hôtel de Dieu* rather than *Hôpital or Centre Hospitalier*.

Holidays See p. 23.

Hospitals See 'Emergencies', in the section above this.

Internet & Wi-Fi See p. 48.

Legal Aid Contact your embassy, consulate or insurance company.

Lost Property Go to the nearest police station. For lost passports, contact your embassy or consulate. For lost credit cards, see 'Money & Credit Cards', below. If you think your car may have been towed away for being illegally parked, ask at the local police station.

Mail City post offices are generally open Monday to Friday 8am to 7pm and Saturday 8am to noon. In smaller towns and villages, they are usually open Monday to Friday 9am to 12:30pm and 2 to 5pm and Saturday 9am to noon. Postcards or letters to the UK weighing less than 20g cost 0.55€ and take 1 to 5 days. Stamps are sold at tobacconists (*tabacs*) as well as post offices. If you need to receive mail while travelling, ask the sender to address it to your name c/o Poste Restante, Poste Centrale, in the relevant town. You will need to show proof of identity and pay a small fee to collect your mail.

Maps For online sources to plot your route, see p. 19 and 52. On the road, equip yourself with a good road atlas. The *Michelin Tourist & Motoring* atlases (available from *www.amazon.co.uk* and at petrol stations, port shops and aboard ferries) have the best detail.

Mobile Phones See p. 47.

Money & Credit Cards See also 'Money', p. 21. For lost/stolen cards, call the relevant company immediately—for **AmEx** ☏ 01 47 77 72 00, for **Visa**

📞 08 92 70 57 05, for **Diners** 📞 08 10 31 41 59 and for **MasterCard** 📞 01 45 67 84 84. In emergencies, you can have money wired to you online, by phone or from an agent's office through **Western Union** (📞 08 00 83 38 33, *www. westernunion.com*).

Newspapers & Magazines
British newspapers (often available on the day of publication) are sold at many newsagents and newsstands along the Riviera and the Côte d'Azur, in Marseille and in Avignon, but are less widely available in rural areas. *The Connexion*, published monthly at 2.40€, is an English-language newspaper aimed at British expatriates living in France.

Pets See p. 20.

Pharmacies Chemists are signposted by a prominent green cross; staff can provide **first aid** in minor emergencies and dispense a range of remedies (including some antibiotics) that would require a doctor's prescription in the UK. Rotas of pharmacies operating outside normal hours (9am to 1:30pm and 2:30 to 8pm Monday to Friday, and 9am to 1:30pm Saturday) are posted in every pharmacy window.

Police In emergencies call 📞 17. For thefts and insurance claims, file a report at the nearest police station.

Post Offices See 'Mail', above.

Safety See also p. 25. The usual common-sense tips apply as they would at home. Don't leave

money or valuables where they can be seen (theft from cars is common) and be wary of pickpockets and bag snatchers. Do not walk alone at night in unlit public spaces.

Shopping Hours See 'Business Hours', above.

Smoking See p. 47.

Taxes Value-added tax (TVA) of 19.6% is included in the price of most goods and hotel and restaurant services.

Taxis There are taxi ranks at all airports, in city centres and at main railway stations and bus terminals. Taxis can also be flagged down on the street, or called from the reception desk of hotels, restaurants and bars. Check that your taxi has a meter and that it is switched on, and ask the driver for an estimated fare before setting out.

Telephone All phone numbers are 10 digits, including a two-digit **area code** (📞 04 for Provence) that you must dial even when calling from within the area. Numbers starting with 📞 06 are mobile numbers and will cost more to call. 📞 08 00- and 📞 08 05-prefixed numbers are toll-free within France. Other numbers with the 📞 08 prefix have differing rates.

To call a French number from abroad (or when using a British mobile phone in France) drop the initial 0 of the area code after dialling the international code (📞 00 33 from the UK). To call the UK from France, dial 📞 00 44 then the

British number minus the initial 0. International mobile phone charges can be high, as can those from hotel phones. To save money, buy a phonecard (*télécarte*) from a post office, tobacconist or newsagent and use public phone boxes. *Télécartes* start at 7.40€ for 50 units. Phone-boxes with a blue bell sign can take incoming calls.

Time Zone France is 1 hour ahead of UK time and 6 hours ahead of EST in the US.

Tipping *Service compris* means a service charge has been added to your bill. However, an extra tip (10% to 15%) may be added if you wish.

Toilets & Baby-changing Public toilets can be found in most large towns in railway stations and bus terminals, but can be less than pristine. Toilets at

autoroute service areas can be even smellier. Bars, cafés and large supermarkets and department stores are a better bet. Few places except large family-oriented tourist attractions such as theme parks, aquariums and museums have baby-changing facilities (such facilities are also available at airports and on intercity TGV trains), so arrive armed with a portable folding mat.

Water French tap water is safe to drink. Many restaurants automatically serve you a carafe of chilled tap water (*eau de robinet*), though most waiters will enthusiastically try to persuade you to buy expensive *eau minerale* (bottled mineral water), either *sans gaz* (still), *gazeuse* (sparkling) or *pétillante* (mildly fizzy).

Weather See p. 22.

3 Monaco & the French Riviera

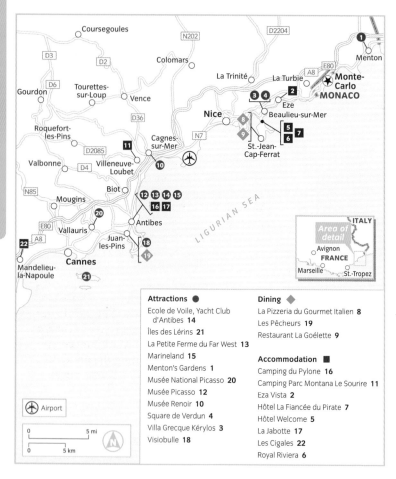

Attractions ●
Ecole de Voile, Yacht Club
    d'Antibes **14**
Îles des Lérins **21**
La Petite Ferme du Far West **13**
Marineland **15**
Menton's Gardens **1**
Musée National Picasso **20**
Musée Picasso **12**
Musée Renoir **10**
Square de Verdun **4**
Villa Grecque Kérylos **3**
Visiobulle **18**

Dining ◆
La Pizzeria du Gourmet Italien **8**
Les Pêcheurs **19**
Restaurant La Goélette **9**

Accommodation ■
Camping du Pylone **16**
Camping Parc Montana Le Sourire **11**
Eza Vista **2**
Hôtel La Fiancée du Pirate **7**
Hôtel Welcome **5**
La Jabotte **17**
Les Cigales **22**
Royal Riviera **6**

Airport

0 — 5 mi
0 — 5 km

Stretching from Menton near the Italian border to Mandelieu-La-Napoule near the Var, the French Riviera coastline is a golden playground for aristocrats, actors and well-heeled Europeans. Listen to jazz as you wander down its palm-fringed avenues and bathe in the bright-blue Mediterranean, beside sun-drenched shores that have lured so many admirers, from Coco Chanel to F. Scott Fitzgerald. With 3,000 hours of sunshine a year, this all-seasons destination has much to offer active families: citrus-filled gardens in Menton for mums pushing prams; bowling and skating at the new Ni Box in **Monaco;** and private beaches in Cannes with bouncy castles for toddlers, parasailing for teens and striped recliners for sleep-deprived parents.

Sandy seaside resorts such as Antibes, Juan-les-Pins and Cannes provide popular bases for families holidaying on the Riviera, but make sure you fit in a day trip to Nice: the region's capital greeted the new decade with freshly renovated Belle Epoque squares, high-tech trams and world-class museums where kids can learn about art through brightly coloured canvases by Chagall or Matisse.

Aquaria along the coastline also offer not-to-be-missed days out. The Oceanographic Museum in Monaco celebrated its 100th anniversary with a Damien Hirst exhibition and the purchase of a 150-million-year-old reptile called Anna. At the same time, Europe's largest marine park, Marineland in Antibes, showed off its latest arrivals: two polar bears whose 3.5€ million refrigerated home comes complete with year-round snow, 24-hour surveillance and a maternity den. By contrast, the sale of the much-loved Cap-Ferrat Zoo in Saint-Jean-Cap-Ferrat to a British hotel developer upset so many Rivera-based families that local newspaper *Nice Matin* joined forces with Villefranche-sur-Mer council in a campaign to buy it back.

The term 'French Riviera' is often used interchangeably with Côte d'Azur ('azure coast'), a phrase conjured up in the 19th century by would-be poet Stéphane Liégeard to sum up the bright-blue sea and cloudless skies of this golden coastline. However, these two names don't actually refer to the same precise area: the Côte d'Azur stretches from Menton in the Alpes-Maritimes to Hyères in the Var, while the French Riviera refers only to the Alpes-Maritimes coastline. Whatever you call it, be warned that separating the undervalued from the overpriced in this corner of Southern France needs careful planning, especially in peak season.

VISITOR INFORMATION

The French Riviera Regional Tourism Committee website, **www.cotedazur-tourisme.com**, has useful information on attractions and events, as well as a practical guide to help you prepare for your stay. The site also has listings for local tourist offices throughout the region. Other useful resources for parents staying on the Côte d'Azur include **http://kidookid.com** and **www. familyfirst.fr**, which both provide information in English on events, activities, shopping and childcare.

Getting There

By Air British Airways runs numerous direct flights between Nice and London airports, including Heathrow and London City; they take approximately 2 hours. **easyJet** runs flights between Nice and London airports Gatwick, Stansted and Luton, plus other UK destinations including Belfast, Bristol, East Midlands, Edinburgh,

Liverpool and Newcastle. **BMI** flies to Nice from Birmingham and East Midlands, while Flybe has flights from Southampton and Jersey. There are also flights with Aer Lingus to Nice from Cork, Dublin and London Gatwick.

Nice Airport is less than 10 minutes' drive from the Promenade des Anglais. You'll find cash machines, taxi ranks (Central Taxi Riviera Nice, ☎ 04 93 13 78 78) and stops for buses into the centre beside Arrivals at terminals 1 and 2. For more information, go to **www.nice.aeroport.fr** (with a version in English) or call ☎ 04 89 88 98 28. Car-hire companies at Nice Airport include **Avis** (☎ 08 20 05 05 05), **Budget** (☎ 08 25 00 35 64), **Europcar** (☎ 08 25 358 358), **Hertz** (☎ 08 25 342 343), **National Citer** (☎ 08 25 16 12 12) and **Sixt** (☎ 01 44 38 55 55).

By Train Eurostar (UK ☎ 0870 518 6186, **www.eurostar.com**) sells a combined Eurostar/TGV ticket to Antibes, Cannes and Nice; you change in Paris from the Gare du Nord to Gare de Lyon, or in Lille between platforms (a great time-saving option). The journey takes about 9 hours.

Regional TER trains can then take you along the coastline to most seaside resorts, including Golfe-Juan, Juan-les-Pins, Ville-neuve-Loubet-Plage, Cagnes-sur-Mer, Saint-Laurent-du-Var, Villefranche-sur-Mer, Beaulieu-sur-Mer, Eze, Cap d'Ail, Monaco, Roquebrune–Cap-Martin and Menton.

By Car See p. 37.

Orientation

The A8 runs along the coastline from the Italian border near Menton, past Nice and Cannes and into the Var. This *autoroute* artery serves all the Riviera's towns and resorts. It's usually the quickest way of travelling from A to B.

If you're in less of a hurry, you can enjoy the panoramas along the **Corniches** (p. 66)—three minor roads that wind from Menton to Nice. Major restaurants, hotels and attractions along the French Riviera are usually well signposted.

INSIDER TIP

An eco-friendly way of touring central Nice is by *Cyclopolitain* (☎ 04 93 81 76 15, **www.cyclopolitain.com**). From Tuesday to Saturday, you'll find these cycle-taxis at Cours Saleya, Place Magenta, Promenade des Anglais and the train station. My daughter loves the party-blower car horns. It's fun for toddlers to teens, but not so good if you have a buggy as there's nowhere to store it.

Getting Around

The French Riviera coastline is easily accessible by public transport. A regional TER train service runs along the coastline from Mandelieu-La-Napoule to Ventimiglia (across the Italian border), stopping at most seaside resorts, with several trains per hour to key destinations such as Cannes (takes 10 minutes from

Cannes

Mandelieu), Antibes and Nice; see ***www.ter-sncf.com*** (the site is in French, but it's fairly easy to find train timetables).

Bus services run from Nice Airport eastwards to Monaco (return journey for 28.50€ takes 45 minutes each way), Menton and Roquebrune–Cap-Martin and westwards to Saint-Laurent-du-Var, Cagnes-sur-Mer, Antibes, Juan-les-Pins, Golfe-Juan and Cannes (see ***www.nice. aeroport.fr***). Local tourist offices can provide details of other local bus services, taxis and bike-hire firms.

For those looking to rent a car, **Avis** (***www.avis.com***), **Budget** (***www.budget.fr***), **Europcar** (***www.europcar.fr***), **Hertz** (***www. hertz.com***) and **National Citer** (***www.citer.fr***) can be found beside the train station in Nice. Avis, Europcar and Hertz also have city-centre locations in Antibes, Cannes and Monaco. Sixt serves Cap D'Ail and Villeneuve-Loubet.

WHAT TO SEE & DO

Children's Top 10 Attractions

❶ **Smelling** the flowers in Nice's Cours Saleya (p. 64).

❷ **Learning** to sail at the Yacht Club d'Antibes (p. 76).

❸ **Getting** lost in the labyrinth at Villeneuve-Loubet (p. 63).

❹ **Listening** to jazz at festivals in Cimiez and Juan-les-Pins (p. 62).

❺ **Skating** on the rooftop at Monaco's Ni Box (p. 72).

Banks: In Monaco: familiar names such as Barclays, HSBC and Lloyds TSB appear in Monaco, but these are private banks and so not open to the general public. There are *bureaux de changes* in Parking des Pêcheurs near Monaco Ville and in Métropole shopping centre. In Nice, you'll find **HSBC** at 35 boulevard Gambetta and Barclays at 2 rue Alphonse Karr.

Hospitals: In Monaco: Princesse Grace hospital (☎ *377 97 98 97 69*, *www.chpg.mc*) runs a 24-hour emergency service, while CHU (☎ *04 92 03 33 33*) runs Nice's 24-hour emergency services for kids at Hôpital L'Archet, 151 route de Saint-Antoine de Ginestière, and for adults at Hôpital Saint-Roch, 5 rue Pierre Dévoluy.

Internet Cafés: Most hotels in Monaco have Wi-Fi hotspots. In Vieux Nice, Au Vieux Cyber (☎ *04 93 53 13 86*, *www.auvieuxcyber.fr*), 4 rue Rossetti, is open Monday to Friday 11am to 3pm and 4 to 8pm and Saturday afternoon from 4 to 8pm.

Pharmacies: Chemists are located all over central Monaco, with three along Boulevard des Moulins alone. After-hours pharmacies are on a rota basis: check at Princess Grace hospital. In Nice, there's a 24-hour pharmacy at 7 rue Masséna.

Post Offices: Post offices in Monaco are located at Palais de la Scala, 1 avenue Henri Dunant; Place de la Mairie in the Old Town; and 3 place du Campanin. In Nice, head to 2 rue Louis Gassin near Marché aux Fleurs.

Shopping: See p. 77 and, for markets, p. 79.

---

❻ **Pondering** over violin-playing goats at the Chagall Museum in Cimiez (p. 75).

❼ **Reading** about Astérix at the Comic Strips Café in Vieux Antibes (p. 77).

❽ **Discovering** knobbly seahorses at Monaco's Oceanographic Museum (p. 73).

❾ **Exploring** the Man in the Iron Mask's prison cell on the Île Ste. Marguerite (p. 69).

❿ **Watching** striped dolphins dive near Villefranche-sur-Mer (p. 75).

Child-friendly Events & Entertainment

Festival International du Cirque de Monte-Carlo ★★

Chapiteau de Fontvieille, 5 avenue des Ligures, Monaco, ☎ *377 92 05 23 45, www.montecarlofestival.mc*

From trapeze artists to clowns, this internationally acclaimed circus festival attracts big names in the business, and troupes of circus performers compete for the coveted *Clown d'Or* ('golden clown') in Fontvieille's permanent Big Top. My son Charlie was entranced by the black sea lions. The cheapest seats for families are the *gradins* (upper circle benches); half-price *fauteuils* (stalls) seats for children under 12 are available for shows during the second week. During the day, you can visit the animal pens.

*Jan. **Adm** from 25€, children under 12 10€. **Credit** AE, MC, V.*

Nice Carnival ★

*Nice, ☏ 08 92 70 74 07, **www.nice carnaval.com***

This 2-week extravaganza of flower parades, pop concerts and fireworks sees *Spitting Image*-style papier-mâché characters dancing through the crowds and a *Bataille des Fleurs* (Flower Battle) parading down the Promenade des Anglais. Dating back to the 13th century, the Nice Carnaval is a family-friendly celebration with the emphasis on fairytale creations rather than drunken debauchery. If you haven't booked in advance, you can buy tickets from temporary ticket booths (around place Masséna and promenade des Anglais) 2 hours before each event.

*Feb–Mar. **Adm** 10€–25€ (depending on day), children 6–12 5€–10€, children under 6 free on parent's knee. **Credit** MC, V.*

English-language Cinemas

If you have older children, go to see a Hollywood blockbuster in English at Monaco's **Open Air Cinema** (☏ 377 93 25 86 80, ***www.cinemasporting.com***), which runs from July to August. With the cinema screen splashed up against the rock, it's a memorable way to spend an evening on the Côte d'Azur. Films start at about 9:30pm (depending on when it gets dark).

For other English-language films, look for the 'VO' (*version originale*) symbol. For current listings for the following cinemas, go to ***www.angloinfo.com*** or see their websites.

Cinéma Cannet Toiles, 1 rue Victorien Sardou, Le Cannet ☏ *04 93 69 51 66*.

Cinéma Espace Centre, 5 avenue de Verdun, Cagnes-sur-Mer, ☏ *08 92 89 28 92*.

Cinéma Rialto, 4 rue de Rivoli, Nice, ☏ *04 93 88 08 41/08 92 68 00 41*.

Cinéma Sporting, Le Sporting, place du Casino, Monaco, ☏ *08 92 68 00 72, **www.cinemasporting.com***.

Cinémathèque de Nice, Acropolis, 3 esplanade Kennedy, Nice, ☏ *04 92 04 06 66, **www.cinematheque-nice.com**..*

Le Casino, 6 avenue du 24 Août, Antibes, ☏ *04 93 34 04 37/08 92 68 70 12*.

Les Arcades, 77 Avenue Félix Faure, Cannes, ☏ *04 93 39 00 98/04 93 39 10 00*.

Mercury, 16 place Garibaldi, Nice, ☏ *04 93 55 37 81/08 92 68 81 06*.

Fête du Citron ★

Jardin Biovès (opposite Menton tourist office), Menton, 📞 *04 92 41 76 76/04 92 41 76 95, www.fetedu citron.com*

Thousands of lemons and oranges are piled up around the Jardin Biovès in this 2-week citrus celebration, during which youngsters can explore the huge, zesty designs and watch the Sunday processions of edible floats through central Menton. Each year follows a different theme. The best time to visit is towards the beginning of the festival, when the fruit is still in peak condition.

*Feb and Mar. **Adm** 9€–17€, children 8–14 6.50€–13€, children under 8 free. **Credit** MC, V.*

Nice Jazz Festival ★★★

Arènes et Jardins de Cimiez, Avenue du Monastère, Nice, 📞 *08 92 68 36 22/08 92 39 21 92, www.nicejazz festival.fr*

A relaxed, family-friendly vibe marks out this week-long festival, in three stages, scattered around the beautiful Cimiez amphitheatre and gardens. Spectators are free to wander from concert to concert or grab a snack during performances. Recent stellar line-ups have included Keziah Jones, BB King and Tracy Chapman. Advance tickets are on sale at FNAC and Carrefour.

The Riviera Coastline is famed for its July jazz festivals; if you're a fan, **Jazz à Juan** (*www. jazzajuan.fr*) in July also attracts jazz and soul greats.

*July. **Adm** From 29€, children under 12 9 €–11€. **Credit** MC, V.*

Festival d'Art Pyrotechnique ★★

La Croisette, Cannes and Port Hercule, Monaco, www.festival-pyrotechnique-cannes.com and www.visitmonaco.com

Every summer, Cannes's La Croisette and Monaco's Port Hercule are lit up with the flashy spectacle of the International Fireworks Festival, completely free for spectators. There's an elastic 9:30pm start, depending on whether it's dark enough; relax at a neighbouring restaurant or café while you wait.

*July and Aug. **Adm** Free.*

Cities, Towns & Resorts

Antibes & Juan-les-Pins ★★★

Antibes tourist office: www.antibes juanlespins.com

Juan-les-Pins tourist office www. antibes-juanlespins.com

Interchangeable enough to share a website, these two resorts are the epitome of family-friendly fun. Juan-les-Pins has the best public, sandy beaches on the Riviera, while Antibes is famous for having been home to Picasso and for the young yachting crowd who hang out in its bars and restaurants. In 1923, the twin resorts became the Riviera's first summertime playground when the Grand Hôtel du Cap (now the Hôtel du Cap Eden-Roc) stayed open all year round, attracting guests as illustrious as Cole Porter and F. Scott Fitzgerald. If you come in mid-July, you'll hear blues in the air around La Pinède Gould during **Jazz à**

Juan (p. 62). The numerous theme parks on your doorstep include Europe's largest marine park, Marineland (p. 70).

Cagnes-sur-Mer & Villeneuve-Loubet

Cagnes-sur-Mer tourist office: 📞 04 93 20 61 64, **www.cagnes-tourisme. com**

Villeneuve-Loubet tourist office: 📞 04 92 02 66 16, **www.ot-villeneuve loubet.org**

The stretch of cheap, seaside resorts around Cagnes-sur-Mer and Villeneuve-Loubet has been dubbed Concrete-on-Sea by Anglophone locals.

This is not helped by the fact that the train line runs next to the sea at this point, so you have to find a rail-track crossing point every time you want to paddle.

While Cagnes-sur-Mer's star attraction is the Renoir Museum, Villeneuve-Loubet's Marina Baie des Anges stands out, with landmark apartments that curve back and forth like white, crested waves. Moreover, Villeneuve-Loubet is one of only 32 destinations in the country to have been awarded the official 'Station Kid' designation, meaning it's particularly family-friendly. This reasonably priced resort has some of the most family-friendly campsites on the Riviera (p. 87), while Labyrinthe de L'Aventure theme park and Canyon Forest rock and tree-climbing adventures are on your doorstep. Inland, you'll find the pretty, historic village from which the resort grew, complete with 12th-century castle.

Cannes ★★

Tourist office: 📞 04 93 39 24 53, **www.cannes-on-line.com**

With its film festival and its Belle Epoque architecture, Cannes is synonymous with old-style glamour. International tourism started here back in 1834, when British Lord Chancellor Lord Brougham moved to the then fishing village to enjoy the winter sunshine. The British aristocracy followed, as did palm-lined avenues, grand hotels and film stars' handprints, though the old town, Le Suquet, perched on its hill, remains a world apart, with bougainvillea-clad houses and winding lanes.

While Cannes certainly has its fair share of golden-tanned oldies, there's a crowd of beautiful young things who hang out in the pedestrianised streets around Rue Batéguier, while families have fun on its private sandy beaches with their children's play areas and on the mini-fairground rides and remote-control mini-motorboats near the Palais des Festivals. And when you want to get away from it all, the beautiful Îles des Lérins are a 15-minute boat-trip away (p. 67).

Monaco ★

Tourist office: 📞 377 92 16 61 16, **www.visitmonaco.com**

Monaco is the kind of toytown utopia where you won't find litter or graffiti; instead, there are Charles Garnier facades, shopping arcades selling authentic Renoirs, ubiquitous CCTV

CANNES

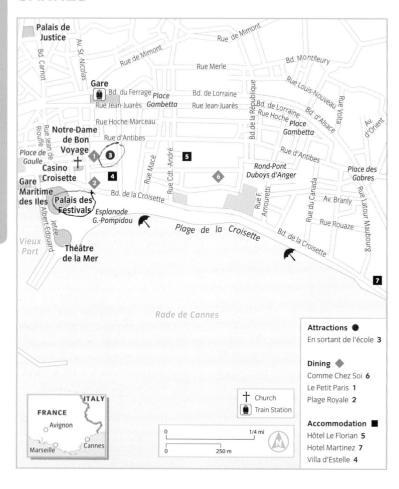

Palais de
Justice

Av. St-Nicolas

Bd. Carnot

Rue de Mimont

Rue de Mimont

Rue Merle

Bd. Montfleury

Rue Louis-Nouveau

Gare

Bd. du Ferrage Place

Rue Jean-Juarès Gambetta

Rue Jean-Juarès

Bd. de Lorraine

Bd. de la République

Bd. de Lorraine

Rue Hoche

Bd. d'Alsace

Rue Volta

Av. d'Orient

Rue Hoche-Marceau

Notre-Dame
de Bon
Voyage

Rue d'Antibes

Place
Gambetta

Rue Jean de Rouffe

Place de
Gaulle

Casino
Croisette

Rue d'Antibes

Rue Macé

Rue Cdt-André

1 **3**

5

6

Rond-Pont
Duboys d'Anger

Place des
Gabres

Rue Latour Maubourg

Gare
Maritime
des Iles

2

Palais des
Festivals

Bd. de la Croisette

Esplanade
G.-Pompidou

Rue F. Amouretti

Rue du Canada

Av. Branly

Rue Rouaze

Albert-Edouard

Jetée

Vieux
Port

Théâtre
de la Mer

Plage de la Croisette

Bd. de la Croisette

7

Rade de Cannes

ITALY

FRANCE

Avignon

Marseille

Cannes

† Church
🚂 Train Station

Attractions ●
En sortant de l'école **3**

Dining ◆
Comme Chez Soi **6**
Le Petit Paris **1**
Plage Royale **2**

Accommodation ■
Hôtel Le Florian **5**
Hotel Martinez **7**
Villa d'Estelle **4**

0	1/4 mi
0	250 m

cameras and steep streets linked by escalators and lifts. Like any modern city, it has too many high-rise apartment blocks—only here they have oak-panelled lifts, 24-hour porters and roof-top palm trees. It's a tax-free playground for Dior-clad billionaires sailing around on motor yachts with helipads. Yet it's also surprisingly suited to young families, with its immaculately tended public gardens with children's play areas, **Oceanographic Museum** (p. 73) and sandy beaches.

Nice ★★

Tourist office: 📞 *08 92 70 74 07,* ***www.nicetourism.com***

Vibrant Nice is France's fifth-largest city and the French Riviera's capital. For families visiting the Riviera, this freshly renovated city is a must for a day or an overnight trip.

The jutting peninsula of Saint-Jean–Cap-Ferrat is the p...
Riviera that most closely lives up to your imagination. This
paradise is a stamping ground for the likes of award-winning arc...
Lord (Norman) Foster and Microsoft billionaire Paul Allen, who live in
lavish villas behind high stone walls. Yet Saint-Jean port retains an
earthy charm, with its line of simple restaurants bordering the marina.
Kids will also enjoy treasure hunts at the Villa Ephrussi de Rothschild
(p. 74).

As well as inhaling the sea spray as you wander along the Promenade des Anglais and browsing the blooms in the world-famous flower market in Cours Saleya, you can see the carousel horses at the Hôtel Negresco and admire the burgundy-coloured houses around the Vieux Port. Best of all, there are many parks, from the botanical **Parc Phoenix** (📞 *04 92 29 77 00*) at the airport end of the Promenade des Anglais, with its musical fountains, duck pond and indoor dome with butterflies and reptiles, to the **Parc du Château** (p. 82), with waterfall and play areas. The city also brims with artistic talent—most notably, the Impressionists and post-Impressionists at the Beaux Arts museum and the contemporary stars at the MAMAC modern art museum.

You should avoid Nice's seedier side around the train station, and the outer suburbs with the exception of ravishing **Cimiez**, where Matisse used to live, and exclusive Mont Boron, where Elton John now resides.

Villefranche-sur-Mer & Beaulieu-sur-Mer ★ ★ ★

Villefranche-sur-Mer tourist office: Jardin François Binon, 📞 *04 93 01 73 68,* **www.villefranche-sur-mer.com**

Beaulieu-sur-Mer tourist office: **otbeaulieu.free.fr**

These seaside resorts east of Nice are more serene, more comely and more expensive than those to the west of the city. Dating back to Roman times, Villefranche-sur-Mer is a picturesque feast of *trompe l'oeil*-painted, apricot houses that curve around its deep, cobblestoned port. Its stately neighbour, Beaulieu-sur-Mer, is home to plush hotels: the exclusive La Réserve, founded by *New York Herald* owner Gordon Bennett, and the family-friendly **Royal Riviera** (p. 85).

There are fewer family-focused activities in these resorts than in many others, but children can have a go at making pottery at Greek **Villa Kérylos** (p. 71) and watch dolphins and whales off the Villefranche-sur-Mer coastline (p. 75).

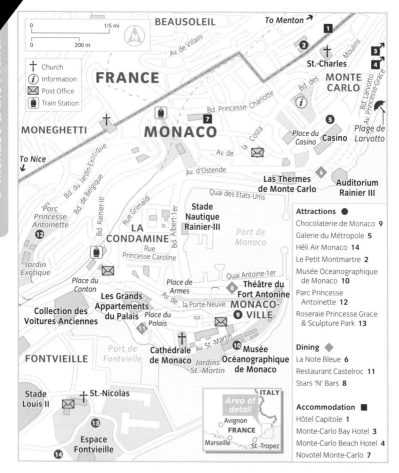

Attractions ●
Chocolaterie de Monaco **9**
Galerie du Métropole **5**
Héli Air Monaco **14**
Le Petit Montmartre **2**
Musée Oceanographique de Monaco **10**
Parc Princesse Antoinette **12**
Roseraie Princesse Grace & Sculpture Park **13**

Dining ◆
La Note Bleue **6**
Restaurant Castelroc **11**
Stars 'N' Bars **8**

Accommodation ■
Hôtel Capitole **1**
Monte-Carlo Bay Hotel **3**
Monte-Carlo Beach Hotel **4**
Novotel Monte-Carlo **7**

INSIDER TIP 》

If you're staying in Beaulieu-sur-Mer, make time for a stroll along the **Promenade Maurice Rouvier** from the Royal Riviera hotel to Saint-Jean port. Halfway along this coastal path you'll find the late David Niven's sugar-pink palace. It's a beautiful route for parents pushing buggies.

Natural Wonders & Spectacular Views

The Corniches ☆

These three minor roads offer unbeatable views of the Riviera. The low-lying **Basse Corniche** (N98) clings to the coastline, while the **Moyenne Corniche** (N7) passes Beausoleil, Eze and the Col de Villefranche. The highest is the **Grande Corniche** (D2564), which tunnels through

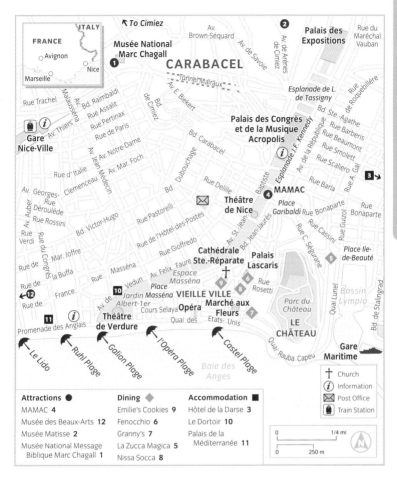

To Cimiez

FRANCE
Avignon
Marseille
Nice
ITALY

Musée National
Marc Chagall ❶

CARABACEL

Av. Brown-Séquard
Av. de Cimiez
Av. de Savoie

Palais des
Expositions ❷
Rue du
Maréchal
Vauban

Tunnel Malraux
Av. E. Biekert
Bd. de Cimiez

Rue Trachel
Malaussèna
Bd. Raimbaldi
Rue Assalit
Rue Pertinax
Rue de Paris
Av. Thiers

Esplanade de L.
de Tassigny
Rue de Roquebillère
Bd. Ste.-Agathe
Rue Barberis
Rue Beaumont
Rue Smolett
Rue Scaliero
Rue A. Gal

Gare
Nice-Ville

Bd. Carabacel
Av. Notre-Dame
Av. Jean Médecin
Rue d'Italie
Clemenceau
Av. Mar. Foch

Palais des Congrès
et de la Musique
Acropolis
Av. de la République
Esplanade J.F. Kennedy

Rue Barla

Rue Delille
Bd. Dubouchage

MAMAC ❹

❸

Av. Georges-
Clemenceau
Rue Déroulède
Av. Auber
Rue Rossini
Rue Verdi
Bd. Victor-Hugo

Théâtre
de Nice

Place
Garibaldi
Rue Bonaparte
Rue Bonaparte
Rue Guizol
Rue C. Ségurane
Rue Cassini

Place Ile-
de-Beauté ❺

Rue de la Buffa
Rue du Congrès
Mar. Joffre
Rue Pastorelli
Rue de l'Hôtel-des-Postes
Rue Gioffredo
Bd. Jean-Jaurès
Av. St.-Jean
Baptiste

Cathédrale
Ste.-Réparate ✝
Palais
Lascaris
Rue
Rosetti ❻

Bassin
Lympia

Rue de France
Masséna
Vedun
Av. Félix Faure
Espace
Masséna
Place
Masséna
Jardin Masséna ❿
Cours Selaya
Av. Albert-1er
VIEILLE VILLE
Opéra
Marché aux
Fleurs ❼
❽ ❾

Parc du
Château
LE
CHÂTEAU

Quai Lunel
Bd. de Stalingrad

Théâtre
de Verdure
Promenade des Anglais ⓫ ⓲
←⓬
Quai des
Etats-Unis
Quai Rauba Capeu

Gare
Maritime

Le Lido
Ruhl Plage
Galion Plage
l'Opéra Plage
Costel Plage
Baie des
Anges

✝ Church
ⓘ Information
✉ Post Office
🚂 Train Station

Attractions ●
MAMAC 4
Musée des Beaux-Arts 12
Musée Matisse 2
Musée National Message
Biblique Marc Chagall 1

Dining ◆
Emilie's Cookies 9
Fenocchio 6
Granny's 7
La Zucca Magica 5
Nissa Socca 8

Accommodation ■
Hôtel de la Darse 3
Le Dortoir 10
Palais de la
Méditerranée 11

0   1/4 mi
0   250 m

the cliffs and past Roquebrune and La Turbie. As you swerve around the bends of the Grande Corniche, you'll perhaps feel a Hitchcockian shudder to learn that Grace Kelly died here in 1982, on the same road that she zoomed along with Cary Grant in the 1955 film *To Catch a Thief*.

Îles des Lérins ★★★

Off Cannes (departures from quai Laubeuf opposite 1835 White Palm hotel). Île Saint-Honorat, 📞 04 92 99 54 00, **www.abbayedelerins.com**

You can enjoy a new perspective on the Cannes coastline from the four gorgeous Îles des Lérins out in the Med, only two of which are inhabited and can be visited: Île Ste. Marguerite and Île Saint-Honorat. Despite these islands' proximity to each other, island politics decrees that no boat trips visit both, so you have to choose.

The Best Beaches

Victims of their own success, beaches along the Riviera are always chock-a-block with sun worshippers. Yet what they have lost in emptiness, they have gained in restaurants, striped recliners and children's play areas. The best **public** beaches are the natural sand Blue Flag stretches at **Antibes–Juan-les-Pins**; others worth a detour are the pretty, sandy **Plage de Passable**, down a footpath from the village of Cap-Ferrat, and the sheltered and rarely crowded **Plage de Baie des Fourmis** in Beaulieu-sur-Mer.

Some private beaches have excellent family-friendly facilities, but you pay for the privilege. Most are open 9am to 6:30pm. Among the best are:

Cagnes-sur-Mer: Plage La Gougouline (**☎** *04 93 31 08 72, www.la-gougouline.com*) on Boulevard de la Plage in Cagnes-sur-Mer, with two swimming pools, a baby pool and a lifeguard. Admission: adults 12€; children up to 12 years 5€.

Cannes: Plage Royale (**☎** *04 93 38 22 00, www.plageroyale. com*) on Boulevard de la Croisette in Cannes, has a restaurant (p. 83), plus a sandy beach with a children's play area and summer watersports, swimming lessons and aqua-gym.

Cannes: Vegaluna Beach (**☎** *04 93 43 67 05, www.vegaluna. com*) on Cannes's Boulevard de La Croisette, with a children's play area and summer children's club and lifeguard. This sandy beach

History, literature and/or Leonardo DiCaprio fans love exploring *The Man in the Iron Mask*'s prison cell (see 'Who Was *The Man in the Iron Mask*?', p. 69) on the Île **Ste. Marguerite**, which is the main reason for visiting the Museum of the Sea, with its unexceptional archeological objects. There's also a partly restored royal fort.

Much of the island is accessible with a buggy, so it's worth delving further inland to find a leafy picnic spot (perhaps near Batéguier lake), although there are several restaurants/snack kiosks if you don't fancy bringing

your own food. You can also go paddling in the sea.

Owned by the Abbaye de Lérins monks, Île **Saint-Honorat** is smaller and arguably more beautiful.

An agapanthus-lined walkway leads to the 'modern' (actually 19th-century) monastery, while the ancient fortified monastery commands a rocky promontory. The monks produce reputed wines and a lethal green liqueur. This verdant haven of veneration and vineyards has less to attract toddlers, but it's a peaceful place to come with either a baby or older children. Note, however, that, unlike its sister island, its also offers watersports, swimming lessons and a free aqua-gym. Admission from 21€ to 25€ from July to mid-September; and 15€ from April to June and mid-September to October.

Juan-les-Pins: Les Pêcheurs (℡ *04 92 93 13 30*, *www. lespecheurs-lecap.com*) on Boulevard Maréchal Juin, a sandy beach with recliners, a swimwear shop and a great restaurant (p. 82).

Menton La Dolce Vita (℡ *04 93 35 44 50*, *www.plageladolce vita.com*) on Promenade de la Mer in Menton, boasting a restaurant, watersports and an indoor children's play area showing DVDs.

Monaco: La Note Bleue (℡ *377 93 50 05 02*, *www.lanotebleue. mc*) along Monaco's Plage du Larvotto, with recliners, a children's play area, table football and table tennis. This sandy beach also has an excellent restaurant (p. 84). In summer, there are bouncy castles. Two minutes away along **Larvotto Beach**, you'll find also find a kids' playground and trampolining. Admission from 28€–32€ for 2 people.

Nice: Neptune Beach (℡ *04 93 87 16 60*, *www.neptuneplage. com*), opposite the Hôtel Negresco on the Promenade des Anglais, a pebble beach with pedalos, a seawater pool for children and a supervised youngsters' play area (on a small sandy section). Admission 18€.

coastline is made up of rocks rather than sandy stretches. There are steep steps up from the landing stage, but the rest of the island is easily accessible with a buggy.

There's one self-service restaurant selling cold snacks.

Trans Côte d'Azur (for Île Sainte-Marguerite), ℡ *04 92 98 71 30,* *www.trans-cote-azur.com, daily* 7am–7pm June–Sept; daily 7am–6pm Oct and May, 7am–5pm Nov–Feb, Ticket 11.50€, children 5–10 6€. *Credit MC, V.*

Planaria (for Île Saint-Honorat), ℡ *04 92 98 71 38, www.cannes-iles delerins.com, May–Sept Mon–Sat 8:30am–5:30pm, Sun 7:30am–5:30pm; Oct–Apr Mon–Sat 8:30am–4:30pm, Sun 7:30am–4:30pm. Ticket 12€, children 5–10 6€. Credit MC, V.*

FUN FACT Who Was *The Man in the Iron Mask*?

Eminent scholars and writers from Alexandre Dumas and Voltaire to Victor Hugo have pondered over 'the prisoner whose name no-one knows, whose forehead no-one has seen, a living mystery, shadow, enigma, problem' (Victor Hugo). More than 60 names have been put forward, from Louis XIV's twin brother to playwright Molière, but the Iron Mask's identity remains unknown.

Neptune Beach, Nice

Aquaria & Animal Parks

La Petite Ferme du Far West ALL AGES

306 avenue Mozart, off RN 7, Antibes,
📞 08 92 30 06 06, www.marineland.fr

Ideal for toddlers and small children, this adventure farm is a bit scruffy round the edges, but yours will probably be too busy gazing at rabbits and horses or feeding the goats to notice. As well as pony rides, there's a puppet theatre and a face-painting parlour, but be prepared to queue. You can buy day-trip combination tickets with neighbouring theme park Marineland (this page).

Open *Daily 10am–7pm Apr–Aug, Wed, Sat and Sun 10am–6pm Feb–Sept and school holidays.* **Adm** *13€, children 3–12 from 10€.* **Credit** *AE, DC, MC, V.* **Amenities** ☕ 🅿 🛍 ♿

Marineland ⭐⭐⭐ ALL AGES

306 avenue Mozart, off RN 7, Antibes,
📞 08 92 30 06 06, www.marineland.fr

Europe's largest marine park is a not-to-be-missed family day out. This is not the place to explore animals in their natural environment, but the impressive spectacle of dolphins and sea lions somersaulting through the air or through hoops is a sure-fire winner for most children.

After you've watched the whale, sea lion and dolphin shows, you can admire the park's latest arrivals: two polar bears in a new 3.5€ million refrigerated home. Daring youngsters measuring over 1.2m can go on an accompanied wade into the dolphin tank to meet the dolphins (an extra 69€). Bring dry T-shirts for the whale show as those on the front row are sprayed with water.

You'll need at least half a day to visit Marineland, although there's plenty to entertain the family for a whole day out as the park is surrounded by its mini-empire of attractions (p. 76).

Open *Daily 10am–11pm July–Aug, daily 10am–7pm Apr–Sept, daily 10am–6pm mid-Feb–Mar and school holidays.* **Adm** *36€, children 3–12 from 28€.* **Credit** *AE, DC, MC, V.* **Amenities** ☕ 🅿 🛍 ♿

Natural Reserves, Parks & Gardens

Menton's Gardens

★ ★ ★ **ALL AGES**

Val Rahmeh, Avenue Saint-Jacques, 📞 *04 93 35 86 72; Serre de la Madone, Route de Gorbio,* 📞 *04 93 57 73 90/04 92 10 33 66; Jardin du Palais Carnolès, Avenue de la Madone,* 📞 *04 93 35 49 71.*

Menton is a true garden-lover's paradise. **Val Rahmeh** is a botanical garden with a beautiful lotus pond, specialising in rare, exotic species, and also has a grassy, buggy-friendly terrace where you can stroll.

Designed by Englishman Lawrence Johnston in the 1920s, *Serre de la Madone* is an impressive garden filled with nooks and crannies that are fun to explore, although those with young children will find all the steps tricky.

Children enjoy spotting both the kumquats and the contemporary sculptures at **Jardin du Palais Carnolès**. This citrus garden on Avenue de la Madone has wide walkways and plenty of park benches.

Roseraie Princesse Grace & Sculpture Park

★ **VALUE** **ALL AGES**

Fontvieille, Monaco, 📞 *377 98 98 22 77, access via Avenue des Guelfes/ Avenue des Papalins.*

This circular rose garden surrounded by shady park benches, a duck pond, children's play area and carousel is filled with the scent of 5,500 immaculately kept rose bushes from April to November. If you ask nicely, the gardeners with let you take home some of the discarded blooms that they are collecting in baskets. You can't take food into the rose garden; picnickers should head for the landscaped sculpture park that encircles it.

Open *Daily 9am–7pm Apr–Oct, daily 9am–6pm Nov–Mar.* **Adm** *Free.*

INSIDER TIP

Another family-friendly park in Monaco is **Parc Princesse Antoinette**, 54 bis boulevard du Jardin Exotique. As well as a children's playground and a 'mini Formule 1' circuit, there's a small farm with goats, sheep and rabbits that my kids love. This park is open all day 8:30am to 6pm.

Historic Buildings & Monuments

Villa Grecque Kérylos

★ **ALL AGES**

Impasse Gustave Eiffel, Beaulieu-sur-Mer, 📞 *04 93 01 01 44, www. villa-kerylos.com*

Born of the imaginative collaboration between two 20th-century Hellenists, this modern interpretation of an ancient Greek villa is a feast of mosaic-tiled walls, marble columns and even an extravagant sunken bath.

Expert potter Jean-Gabriel runs pottery workshops for children from 3 up every afternoon during school holidays, and every weekend the rest of the year; ask ahead and he'll bring one of his English-speaking colleagues to translate.

The Best Local Bowling «

2010 saw the much-anticipated opening of Ni Box (35 boulevard Louis II, Rond-point du Portier, ☏ *377 97 98 77 77, www.nibox.mc*) in Monaco. This trendy entertainment complex comes complete with bowling alley (with optional bumpers for kids), as well as a year-round rooftop skating rink, video games, discotheque and (seemingly self-contradictory) 'healthy' McDonalds.

Meanwhile, Riviera Loisirs Bowling (*www.rivieraloisirsbowling.com*) has three outlets on the Riviera that are great for keeping kids amused on a rainy day:

Antibes Bowling, 575 Première Avenue, Quartier Nova-Antipolis, Antibes, ☏ *04 92 91 70 30*, has 22 lanes, some equipped with inflatable tubes to make it easier for young kids. There are also video games, billiards table and a restaurant.

Cannes Bowling, 189 boulevard Francis Tonner, Cannes-La-Bocca, ☏ *04 93 47 02 25*, has 16 lanes, billiards table and a restaurant.

Nice Bowling, 5 esplanade Kennedy, Nice, ☏ *04 93 55 33 11*, has 24 lanes, billiards tables and a restaurant.

Note that buggies aren't allowed inside the villa. You can park near the town hall or by the casino.

Open *Daily 10am–6pm mid-Feb–June and Sept–mid-Nov and school holidays, daily 10am–7pm July and Aug, 2–6pm Mon–Fri and 10am–6pm Sat and Sun mid-Jan–mid-Feb and mid-Nov–Dec.* **Adm** *8.50€, children 7–17 6:30€, children under 7 free.* **Credit** *AE, MC, V.* **Amenities** 🛍

A good picnic spot after the Villa Grecque Kérylos is the **Square de Verdun** (next to the casino), with its children's playground and park benches.

Top Museums

Musée Matisse
⋆ ⋆ **VALUE** **ALL AGES**

164 avenue des Arènes de Cimiez, Nice, ☏ *04 93 53 40 53, www.musee-matisse-nice.org*

The great artist Henri Matisse (1869–1954) lived and died at this burgundy-red villa in Cimiez, where his vibrant paintings should appeal to just about every member of the family. My favourites are those inspired by Nice itself, which include the stormy *Tempête à Nice*, and the wildly colourful gouaches, almost childlike in their simplicity, with motifs of dancers, clowns, horses and more. Gory-minded youngsters, meanwhile, tend to be fascinated by the sculpture of a jaguar devouring a hare. After taking in some culture, you're free to explore the garden with its remains of a Roman amphitheatre. The museum has lifts to all floors.

You may also want to nip next door to the **Archaeological Museum** (☏ *04 93 81 59 57*), where you can discover the 2-hectare ruins of Roman town **Cemenelum**. It has the same opening hours as the Matisse Museum.

Open *Mon and Wed–Sun 10am–6pm exc. some public holidays.* **Adm** *free.* **Credit** *MC, V (minimum 8€).* **Amenities** 🛍

Musée National Message Biblique Marc Chagall
★ ★ ★ **VALUE** ALL AGES

36 avenue Docteur Ménard, Nice,
📞 *04 93 53 87 20/04 93 53 87 31,*
www.musee-chagall.fr

From violin-playing goats to floating lovers, monsters to fantastical human–animal hybrid figures, and horseback acrobats to roosters, Russian-born Chagall's brightly coloured paintings speak to all ages and are a great way to get younger children interested in art. Although the museum doesn't lay on anything special for children, older ones will enjoy the English-language video explaining Chagall's work, while you might like to devise a kind of artistic treasure hunt for younger ones by asking them to seek out some of the weird and wonderful objects that appear in the works.

Meanwhile, breastfeeding mums can find comfy seats in the dimly lit cinema room complete with stained-glass windows and painted grand piano. There's also a pretty garden where you'll find shady benches among the agapanthus and olive trees, as well as a café serving sandwiches, salads and ice creams.

Open *Mon and Wed–Sun 10am–6pm July–Sept, 10am–5pm Oct–June, exc. some public holidays.* **Adm** *7.50€, children under 20 free (free to all 1st Sun of month).* **Credit** *MC, V.* **Amenities** ☕ 🛍

Musée Oceanographique de Monaco ★ ★ ★ ALL AGES

Avenue Saint-Martin, Monaco-Ville,
📞 *377 93 15 36 00,* **www.oceano.mc**

Monaco's Oceanographic Museum has just celebrated its 100th anniversary. The highlight

Musée Matisse

[handwritten: PALOMA BEACH / 1 CHEMIN DE SAINT-]

A trip to Saint-Jean–Cap-Ferrat's **Villa Ephrussi de Rothschild** (📞 *04 93 01 33 09, www.villa-ephrussi.com*), our favourite Riviera palace. This Belle Epoque pink palazzo and its immaculate gardens will transport you back to the splendour of the Riviera's Golden Age, in the late 19th and early 20th centuries. While you soak in the extraordinary views, your children can explore its nine themed gardens, take part in the treasure hunts for children from 7 to 12 (available in English, and with a gift for children who can solve the riddle) or explore with the help of its audio-guides for older children. There is a coffee shop serving snacks and children's meals.

of this unmissable collection is the basement aquarium, a darkened sub-aquatic world of diaphanous moon jellies, circling sea bass and floaty seahorses (the latter keep my baby son Charlie entertained for hours). There's a sense of menace in the shark tank, but most fascinating, perhaps, is the Mediterranean section. Here you can learn all about the sea life literally on the museum's doorstep: that some species can change sex, for instance, or that the local flat lobster is known in French as the *cigale de la mer* (sea cicada) because of the noise it makes when it bashes its claws together.

Upstairs collections are more suited to older children: they comprise the objects amassed by Prince Albert I during the 28 research trips he made aboard his four yachts plus ethnographical items such as whalebone harpoons.

Don't miss the comical 18th-century diving suit or the whale skeleton.

Afterwards, head for the top-floor restaurant, with its excellent views and children's menu. Note that, although the museum has lifts, there are lots of buggy-unfriendly steps at the museum entrance, down to the loos and up to the restaurant. Handily for those who need to blow off some steam, the museum is next to the pretty **Jardin Saint-Martin**, with a children's play area.

Open Daily 9:30am–7:30pm July and Aug, 9:30am–7pm Apr–June and Sept, 10am–6pm Oct–Mar. *Adm* 13€, children 4–17 6.50€, children under 4 free. *Credit* MC, V. *Amenities* 🍴🛍

INSIDER TIP >>

Families can discover underwater treasures such as sea urchins and starfish around the Cap d'Antibes with **Visiobulle** (📞 *04 93 27 02 11, www.visiobulle. com*). This glass-bottomed boat

FUN FACT >> **Ronin**

The heart-pounding car chase in the Robert De Niro classic thriller *Ronin* was filmed in the streets around Nice's Vieux Port.

OSPICE SAINT JEAN -CAP FERR

Besides the Marc Chagall museum, other world-class art collection on the Cote d'Azur include **MAMAC**, a contemporary art museum on the Promenade des Arts, Nice (☎ *04 97 13 42 01, www.mamac-nice. org*), with lots of pop art and intriguing installations; Renoir's former home, **Musée Renoir**, 19 chemin des Collettes, Cagnes-sur-Mer (☎ *04 93 20 61 07*) and **Musée des Beaux-Arts**, 33 avenue des Baumettes, Nice (☎ *04 92 15 28 28, www.musee-beaux-arts-nice.org*), with its impressive collection of Impressionists, post-Impressionists and 20th-century artists. Two museums reflecting Picasso's attachment to the Côte d'Azur are the **Musée National Picasso**, Place de la Libération, Vallauris (☎ *04 93 64 71 83, www.musee-picasso-vallauris.fr*) and the recently renovated **Musée Picasso**, Château Grimaldi, Antibes (☎ *04 92 90 54 20).*

departs Ponton Courbet on Juan-les-Pins's Boulevard Guillaumont daily between April and September. Tickets cost 13€ for adults, 6.50€ for kids aged 2–11, free for kids under 2.

Child-friendly Tours

Dolphin & Whale Tour
☆ **ALL AGES**

ActiLoisirs, Gare Maritime, Villefranche-sur-Mer, ☎ *04 93 62 00 16/06 03 78 30 85, www.dauphin-mediterranee.com*

These unusual 4-hour boat-trips combine tourism with research to give you the chance to watch dolphins and whales in their natural environment. The French-speaking guide Philippe, a researcher on whale ethology for the University of the Sorbonne, navigates a route past the usual hideouts up to 35km off the coastline. You're most likely to see striped dolphins—on a recent trip we saw three different schools.

Sightings aren't guaranteed, although in several years of business they've never been without at least one sighting. Alternatively, you can actually go swimming with dolphins on a daylong trip, although the 300€-per-person price tag may put you off.

The sea can be choppy so, if in doubt, take a seasickness tablet before you leave. Make sure you phone to check on the day before the outing, as the schedule can change at the last minute according to the weather (particularly the wind). You need to arrive 30 minutes before departure time.

Open *9:30am and 1:30pm midweek departures mid-June–mid-Sept.* **Adm** *44€, children 2–12 30€, children under 2 free.* **Credit** *MC, V.*

Héli Air Monaco ☆ ☆ **ALL AGES**

Héliport de Monaco, Avenue des Ligures, Monaco, ☎ *377 92 05 00 50, www.heliairmonaco.net*

One unusual way to celebrate a family birthday is to treat your

heme park (p. 70) is surrounded by its own little
ns, including **Aquasplash** (with wave pools and water-
Ferme du Far West (p. 70) and **Adventure Golf**. You
combination (at Marineland's ticket booths) allowing access
40€ for adults, 31€ for kids aged 3–12, free for kids under 3.

Antib Avenue Mozart, Antibes, ☎ *04 93 33 68 03*, *www.azurpark. com*), opposite Marineland, with 30 rides and attractions, a restaurant and an ice cream parlour.

Labyrinthe de L'Aventure (2559 route de Grasse, Villeneuve-Loubet, ☎ *04 92 02 06 06*, *www.lelabyrinthedelaventure.com*), comprising 48 interactive games and adventures along a natural maze in the gardens of a 12th-century château, for children from 4 years. The same firm runs **Canyon Forest** (26 route de Grasse, ☎ *04 92 02 88 88*, *www.azur-aventures.com*), which offers rock- and tree-climbing adventures for children from 8 years, as well as **Pitchoun Forest** (next to Labyrinthe de L'Aventure), a junior version for kids from 3 years.

Koaland (Avenue de la Madone, Menton, ☎ *04 92 10 00 40*, *www.azurpark. com*), on the seaside in central Menton, is a small theme park with crazy golf, bouncy castles, mini go-karting, carousels, children's play areas and a snack bar. It's run by the firm behind Antibes Land and **Luna Park** (Palais des Expoitions, Nice, *www.azurpark.com*), a good rainy-day option since it's all-indoor, with 24 rides, including some especially for younger children.

children to their first helicopter flight. Héli Air Monaco organises *baptême* (baptism) flights for families, and will even provide a birthday cake if you ask in advance. The 10-minute bird's-eye tour covers 'Mer et Terre' (Sea and Land), whizzing over the Med to the Italian border and returning via the mountainous backcountry. At 60€ per person, it doesn't come cheap, but children will also be rewarded with a certificate and a Héli Air Monaco hat that makes a great souvenir. Those with toddlers under 2 are provided with a special harness.

Open Daily 8am–5:30pm. **Adm** from 60€ (four people minimum). **Credit** AE, MC, V.

INSIDER TIP »

Budding Murrays, Federers or Nadals can train up at tennis clubs in **Monte Carlo** (☎ *04 93 41 30 15*, *www.mccc.mc*) and **Cannes** (☎ *04 93 43 58 85*, *www.tennis-cannes.com*), with week-long courses for kids during the summer holidays.

Active Families

Ecole de Voile, Yacht Club d'Antibes ★★★ AGE 5 & UP

Plage du Ponteil, Boulevard James Wyllie, Antibes, ☎ 04 93 61 01 42, www.yc-antibes.net

With its enviable location overlooking Antibes's 16th-century ramparts, this sailing school organises 1-week beginners' sailing courses for children from 5 years (in Optimist dinghies from 5 years, catamarans from 12 years).

There are also windsurfing courses from 8 years up. Courses are popular and should be booked well in advance. Most coaches speak English.

Open *1-week summer courses 9:30am–noon and 2:30–5:30pm Mon–Fri (mornings only for children 5–6 years).* ***Adm*** *from 135€.* ***Credit*** *Cash only.*

Shopping

Chez Tom et Léa

9 rue de la Boucherie, Vieux Nice, ☎ 04 93 92 20 27

This diminutive toy and clothes shop in the crowded labyrinth of Vieux Nice has a mini-play area to keep children amused while you browse the colourful childrens' wear, wooden toys and accessories. Don't miss the cuddly animals

spilling out of a brightly painted, century-old boat retrieved from Villefranche-sur-Mer.

Open *Mon–Sat 10am–7pm Apr–Dec.* ***Credit*** *MC, V.* ***Amenities*** ⋀

Chocolaterie de Monaco

Place de la Visitation, Monaco, ☎ 377 97 97 88 88, www.chocolateriede monaco.com

Youngsters love the fantasy eggs and chocolate boxes shaped like rulers at this long-standing chocolate paradise in Monaco's old town—and so do the royals who live in the palace round the corner, who have given it their official seal of approval.

Open *Mon–Sat 9:30am–6:30pm.* ***Credit*** *MC, V.*

Comic Strips Café

4 rue James Close, Antibes, ☎ 04 93 34 91 40, www.comic-strips-cafe. com

A fun way for children to learn French is through comic books,

Little Tourist Trains

The cute little Petits Trains Touristiques you see trundling the streets of cities and towns all over France are a great way of seeing the sights with youngsters. Monaco's **Azur Express Tourist Train** (☎ *377 92 05 64 38*) departs from the Oceanographic Museum (p. 73) and makes a 30-minute tour, taking in the port, Monte Carlo and its palaces, the casino and more; commentary is available in English. You can pick up Nice's **Petit Train** (☎ *06 08 55 08 30, www.trainstouristiquesdenice. com*) on the Promenade des Anglais opposite Jardin Albert I; it tours the old town, the castle and the seafront, costing 9€ for adults and 4€ for kids under 9. Cannes's **Petit Train** (☎ *04 93 38 39 18, www. cannes-petit-train.com*) sets off from beside the Palais des Festivals and offers a choice of two routes or a combined 'Grand Tour' costing 10€ for adults, 5€ for kids aged 3–10. Again, commentary is available in English.

and there's no better place in Provence to find them than this bookshop in Old Antibes, specialising in *bandes dessinées* new and old, including classics such as *Astérix*. Some English translations are also available.

Open *Mon 2–7pm, Tues–Fri 10am–noon and 2–7pm, Sat 10am–7pm.* **Credit** *MC, V.*

En sortant de l'école ★★

18 rue Notre Dame, Cannes, 📞 *04 93 99 63 33*

Chock-a-block with toys, this archetypal treasure trove stocks eco-friendly wooden toys and mini-cars spilling out the door, mobiles vying for space on the ceiling and cuddly toys huddling on the shelves amidst musical boxes and kaleidoscopes.

Open *Mon–Sat 10am–8pm July–Aug, Mon–Sat 10am–7pm Sept–June.* **Credit** *AE, MC, V.*

Galerie du Métropole

17 avenue des Spélugues, Monaco, **www.metropoleshoppingcenter. com**

Smart children's shops sit cheek-by-jowl in this ultra-posh shopping centre next to the Hôtel Métropole, complete with marble floors and antique chandeliers. You can splash out on designer labels in **Ricriation** (📞 *377 97 70 84 12*), for children up to 16, and **Enfance** (📞 *377 93 30 00 82*), for youngsters up to 12.

Teenfactory (📞 *377 92 16 09 16*) sells trendy labels such as Levi's, Oxbow and Kookaï for tots to teens, while **Vilebrequin** (📞 *377 97 77 05 78*) has

multi-coloured swimming trunks for boys from 12.

Open *Mon–Sat roughly 10am–7:30pm, plus Sun 11am–7pm mid-July–mid-Aug.*

Pâtisserie Mesiano ★★

18 rue Barla, Nice, 📞 *04 93 55 37 74; 35 boulevard Marinoni, Beaulieu-sur-Mer,* 📞 *04 93 01 35 85*

Formerly known as Pâtisserie Lac, these twin pâtisseries have been taken over by master confectioner Patrick Mesiano. Years of pastry-chef experience at top hotels permeate his perfectly poised selection of pastries and chocolates. 'Our clients know good products [so] you can't cheat', says Mesiano. 'When we make a lemon tart, we freshly squeeze lemons (bought) from a local Provençal village market.'

Open *Mon, Tues, Thurs, Fri 9am–12:30pm and 3–7:30pm, Sat 9am–1pm and 3–7:30pm, Sun 9am–1pm and 4–7pm.* **Credit** *MC, V.*

Place Magenta ★

Nice

My favourite children's shops in Nice are clustered in the pretty streets off pedestrianised Place Magenta. Pepper tree-lined Rue Alphonse Karr is home to **Graine de Maman** (📞 *04 93 88 28 56*) specializing in clothes for pregnant mums and to **bébé inédit** (📞 *04 93 88 71 01*), where mums Brigitte and Linda will wow you with stunning designer clothes, jewellery and accessories for babies and toddlers. Around the corner, you'll find chic kids' clothes for tots to teens at **Annie**

Covered food and flower market: Forville market, Cannes mornings.

Fish market: Place Saint-François, Nice, Tues–Sun mornings.

Flower, fruit and vegetable market: Cours Saleya, Nice, Tues–Sun mornings.

Food and flower market: Jardin Binon, Villefranche-sur-Mer, Sat morning.

Food and flower market: Gare Routière and port, Menton, every morning.

Food and flower market: Quartier Carnolès, Roquebrune–Cap-Martin, every morning.

Fruit and vegetable market: Place d'Armes, Monaco, every morning.

Organic food market: Villeneuve-Loubet village, Wed and Sat mornings.

Provençal market: Place Massena, Antibes, Tues–Sun mornings.

Framboise (☎ *04 93 87 98 97*) on Rue Longchamp, at **Jacadi** (☎ *04 93 16 59 00*) and **IKKS** (☎ *04 93 87 42 01*) on Rue de la Liberté, and at **Petit Bateau** (☎ *04 93 83 05 00*) on Rue Masséna.

Open Mon–Sat roughly 10am–7pm, with break for lunch (usually 12:30–2:30pm). Credit MC, V.

Rue d'Antibes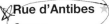

Cannes

Parallel to Boulevard de la Croisette, Cannes's smartest shopping street has all the upmarket children's brands loved by the French bourgeoisie. Down the far end, **Tartine et Chocolat** (no. 131, ☎ *04 93 68 18 09, www.tartine-et-chocolat.fr*) and **Jacadi** (no. 121, ☎ *04 93 99 37 73, www.jacadi.fr*) have the prettiest clothes and nursery accessories. In the middle, you'll find trendy clothes shops: **Catimini** (no. 56–66, ☎ *04 93 68 67 38, www.catimini.com*), catering for boys up to 14 and girls up to 16, and **IKKS Junior** (no. 77, ☎ *04 93 68 02 39*) for boys up to 14 and girls

up to 18 years. You can pick up a free gift at **Petit Bateau** (no. 50, ☎ *04 93 38 05 82, www.petitbateau.fr*), which has clothes for boys up to 18 years and girls up to 12. Toys and board games for all ages can be found at **Miny Jouets** (no. 28, ☎ *04 93 39 07 86*).

Open Mon–Sat roughly 10am–7pm, with break for lunch (usually 12:30–2:30pm). Credit MC, V.

FAMILY-FRIENDLY DINING

Nice & Around

The narrow streets of Vieux Nice are packed with snack bars selling *pan bagnat* (tuna Niçoise salad in a bap), crêpes and pasta, and restaurants offering local cuisine. As tourists flock to **Nissa Socca** (p. 81) for a taste of *socca* (6€), local families enjoy Niçoise cuisine at **Lu Fran Calin** (☎ *04 93 80 81 81*), newly relocated to Place Halle aux Herbes, where the outdoor terrace has plenty of room for buggies.

Nearby, the long-standing Niçoise restaurant **L'Escalinada** (☎ 04 93 62 11 71, *www.escalinada. fr*) on Rue Pairolière specialises in *beignets* (fritters) from 7€. In the celebrated Cours Saleya, you can grab open sandwiches and pastries at Belgian-style **Le Pain à Table** or spot film-star photos as you lunch on fish and wood-fired pizzas at **Le Safari** (☎ 04 93 80 18 44). Around the corner in Rue de la Préfecture, inexpensive local hangout **Emilie's Cookies** (p. 81) has opened a second venue.

Rue Dalpozzo is the place for Tex-Mex cuisine at reasonably priced **Texas City** (☎ 04 93 16 25 75, *www.texas-city-restaurant. com*), with its fun ambience and children's menus (7.50€), while the best hamburger and chips in Nice are found at **Frites City** (21 rue Delille, ☎ 04 93 85 13 61, *www.fritescity.com*). There's a branch of family-friendly restaurant **Hippopotamus** (☎ 04 93 92 42 77, *www.hippopotamus.fr*) on posh shopping street Avenue Félix Faure.

> **INSIDER TIP** ❯❯
>
> A good way to introduce your kids to Provençal cuisine is through food writer Rosa Jackson's Nice market tour and cooking class. See *www.petitsfarcis. com* for details.

MODERATE

La Pizzeria du Gourmet Italien ★★ FIND

Nouveau Port, Saint-Jean–Cap-Ferrat, ☎ *04 93 76 06 15, www.gourmet italien.com*

With its gingham tablecloths, red geraniums and view out over the yachts in the marina, this pizzeria is filled with local families even out of season. As with many family-run restaurants in Saint-Jean port, the homely cooking has changed little in 30 years of business. Delicious pasta, fish and wood-fired pizzas are the order of the day, including a list of specials—home-made lasagne is our family favourite.

Open *7–11pm Mon–Tues, noon–3pm and 7–11pm Wed–Sun July and Aug, noon–3pm and 7–11pm Tues–Sun Sept–June.* ***Main courses*** *13€–31€.* ***Credit*** *MC, V.*

> **INSIDER TIP** ❯❯
>
> Along Saint-Jean port, **Restaurant La Goélette** (☎ 04 93 76 14 38) is one of the few fish restaurants to offer a children's menu (costing 9.80€). Owner Jean-Pierre and his Portuguese wife Paola have been tempting diners with their *bouillabaisse* (p. 82) and its Spanish equivalent, *zarzuella*, for almost two decades.

INEXPENSIVE

Granny's ★ VALUE

5 place de l'Ancien Sénat, Nice, ☎ *06 14 25 10 92*

With tables spilling onto a pretty square, this informal crêperie serves Breton *galettes* and salads. Aptly for a restaurant named after Granny Smith apples, the sweet crepe with caramelised apples and cream is especially delicious. It's the best bet for a bargain-priced family lunch in Vieux Nice. Kids will enjoy

Recipe: *Socca*

Pancake-like socca is a Niçoise institution, and competition to make the best is stiff: among the contenders are **Chez René** at 1 rue Pairolière (📞 *04 93 85 95 67*), **Chez Pipo** at 13 rue Bavastro (📞 *04 93 55 88 82*) and **Nissa Socca** at 7 rue Sainte-Réparate (📞 *04 93 80 18 35*). If you fancy making this speciality yourself, here's the recipe:

250g chickpea flour
500ml water
2 tbsp olive oil
Salt
Pepper

Combine the water, flour and oil, then season with salt and pepper. Whisk well and pour through a strainer to remove lumps. Pour a thin layer onto a pre-greased baking sheet and leave for a few minutes, then place in a very hot oven (ideally a wood-fired oven). Pierce any bubbles with a fork as they appear. Leave until well browned, then sprinkle with freshly ground pepper, cut into squares and serve.

---

playing with the outdoor train set and exploring the neighbouring toy shop, **Atelier de Jouets**, run by the same Antibes family that run Granny's.

Open 8:30am–6:30pm daily exc. Wed. **Main courses** 3.50€–8:30€. **Credit** Cash only.

Emilie's Cookies ★★ FIND

1 rue de la Préfecture and 9 rue Alberti, Nice, 📞 *04 93 13 89 58,* **www.emiliescookies.com**

Young owners Emilie and Céline dreamed up the idea of opening a coffee shop while travelling in the US. The result is this all-day café where you can relax in armchairs with a bagel, quiche or sandwich chosen from a Beatles-themed menu—or a melt-in-the-mouth cookie baked before your eyes.

Open 8am–6:30pm Mon–Fri, 9am–6:30pm Sat. **Main courses** Lunch menus from 6.90€. **Credit** MC, V (10€ or over).

La Zucca Magica ★★ VALUE

4 bis quai Papacino, Nice, 📞 *04 93 56 25 27*

If vegetarian food tasted this good all over the world, I'd turn vegetarian. Set on the western side of Nice port, this pumpkin paradise—where children under 11 eat for free—is the eccentric creation of chef Marco, self-proclaimed King of Pumpkins.

Children will be intrigued by the year-round Hallowe'en decor of wall-to-wall pumpkins in every guise, and everyone will be wowed by simple but tasty flavours. Pasta and potato-based dishes whizz out of the hushed, candlelit open kitchen (an extra course or two is usually thrown in), with children able to pick and choose from the dishes they like.

Open 12:30–1:30pm and 7–10pm Tues–Sat. **Main courses** three-course ch menu 17€, four-course set *menu 29€, children under 11 e. **Credit** Cash only.*

Cannes & Around

Cannes has plenty of choice, from Michelin-starred cuisine along La Croisette to filled baguettes from Rue Meynadier's delicatessens. You'll find *bouillabaisse* galore around the Vieux Port, *cuisine de grand-mère* (grandma's cooking) on place du Suquet and posh Italian nosh around Rue du Commandant André.

The most family-friendly restaurants are the back-to-back private beach restaurants along Boulevard de la Croisette, where children can make sandcastles in the imported golden sand while they wait for their orders from the children's menus. The best are the sumptuous **Vegaluna Plage** (℡ 04 93 43 67 05, www.vegaluna.com), with kids' menu for 12€, **La Plage du Gray d'Albion** (℡ 04 92 99 79 79, www.lucienbarriere.com) and **Plage Royale** (p. 83).

EXPENSIVE

Comme Chez Soi ★★

4 rue Batéguier, Cannes, ℡ *04 93 38 20 65*

In the achingly trendy epicentre of Cannes occupied by the beautiful set lies this surprising oasis of Provençal style and French gastronomic cuisine. With its upholstered chairs and large comfy sofas, it truly makes you feel *comme chez soi* ('at home'). While you tuck into home-made bread, piping hot from the oven, chef Sophie Meissonnier conjures up culinary fantasies with foie gras, lobster and Simmental beef. Those in the know ring up 24 hours in advance to dine on Bresse roast chicken. For children up to 14, there is a Junior Menu with a choice of fish or meat with dessert and drink for 20€.

Open Tues–Sun 6pm–12:30am. **Main courses** from 24€. **Credit** AE, DC, MC, V.

Les Pêcheurs ★★★ FIND

10 boulevard Maréchal Juin, Cap d'Antibes, Juan-les-Pins, ℡ *04 92 93 13 30, www.lespecheurs-lecap.com*

Every time we have friends visiting, we come to this private beach resort: everything about the place is satisfying, from the car valet service as you arrive to the professional but easy-going staff and the comfy recliners to

---

TIP **Picnic with a View**

With its dreamy views over the Baie des Anges, the Parc du Château is a must for families visiting Nice, and is a great place for a picnic—you'll know it's time to eat when you hear the midday boom of the cannon installed in 1861 by the eccentric Sir Thomas Coventry More to remind his wife that it was lunchtime. Relax beside the château ruins or admire the man-made waterfall as your children climb on the rope web and dash around the play areas. If you don't fancy the hike up, there's a buggy-friendly lift beside the 16th-century Tour Bellanda, next to the Hôtel Suisse on Quai des États-Unis.

Barbajuans

This Monegasque recipe goes down well with youngsters. Half-moon-shaped *barbajuans* resemble fried ravioli filled with Swiss chard, spinach and ricotta cheese and make good snacks or starters accompanied with salad. The best *barbajuans* in Monaco are served at **Restaurant Castelroc** (☎ *377 93 30 36 68*) in the old town, with its enviable location overlooking the Prince's Palace.

To make *barbajuans* at home, visit the Media Gallery at *www.visitmonaco.com*, then scroll down to Recipes.

flop onto after lunch. You can even swim before lunch to work up an appetite, changing into your swimming gear (or a quick baby-change) in one of the beach huts. You eat your luxuriant lunch of grilled meat, fish and salads beneath a canopy of pine trees, with views over the Cap d'Antibes towards the Lérins islands (p. 67). Despite the stylish surroundings, no-one will mind if you lark about in the sea with your children as you wait for your food to arrive. Advance booking is recommended for restaurant and recliners in peak season.

Open Daily 10am–7pm May–Sept. *Main courses* 18€–40€. *Children's* menu 10€. *Credit* AE, DC, MC, V.

MODERATE

Plage Royale

Boulevard de la Croisette, Cannes, ☎ *04 93 38 22 00, www.plageroyale. com*

This beach restaurant along Cannes's famous La Croisette is a hassle-free place to bring children, who can play on the climbing frame as you relax on your blue-and-white-striped recliner. The menu offers a simple selection of salads, meat and fish, and there's a two-course children's menu. Don't miss the ice cream sundaes. It's only open for breakfast or lunch, except in July and August when the firework festival is on and evening meals are provided. Swimming lessons or water-skiing are available if you book in advance. You can hire recliners and parasols from 15€, and towels for 6.50€.

Open Daily 8–10:30am, noon–4:30pm (beach open 9am–7pm) Jan–Oct. *Main courses* 14€–26€. *Children's menu* 11€. *Credit* AE, DC, MC, V. *Amenities* 🍴

INSIDER TIP ≫

If you don't want to pay hotel breakfast prices in Cannes, grab a *pain au chocolat*, hot drink and freshly squeezed orange juice for 6.50€ at **Le Petit Paris** (☎ *04 93 38 88 60*) on Rue des Belges.

Monaco

Reasonably priced pizza and pasta restaurants line the pedestrianised streets of the old town, Monaco-Ville, while Larvotto beach is home to numerous family-friendly beach restaurants. Loftily priced gastronomic favourites include **Joël Robuchon** at the Hôtel Métropole (☎ 377 93 15 15 15).

MODERATE

La Note Bleue ★★

Plage du Larvotto, Avenue Princesse Grace, Monaco, ☎ *377 93 50 05 02,* **www.lanotebleue.mc**

With its hip furnishings and excellent cuisine, this beach restaurant is a cut above the rest in Monaco. The menu offers international flavours, from sushi and grilled fish to pasta and risotto. Next to the posh dining terrace is an informal dining area with bench seating that's usually filled with happy families, and youngsters are well catered for with children's menus, a play area and table football. During summer holidays, there are even bouncy castles.

Open Daily 9am–midnight mid-May–mid-Sept, 9am–5pm Mar–mid-May and mid-Sept–mid-Dec. **Main courses** *16€–30€. Children's menu 9€.* **Credit** *MC, V.* **Amenities** ⋀ 🖵

Stars 'N' Bars

6 quai Antoine 1er, Monaco, ☎ *377 97 97 95 95, www.starsnbars.com*

From families with babies to trendy teenagers, this American diner is always packed out with expats of all ages. You can watch the latest sports events on flatscreen TVs as you snack on run-of-the-mill fast food (Tex-Mex, pizzas, steaks or sandwiches), and there's a supervised

playroom for younger children (parental supervision is required for children under 2) and a video-game arcade for teenagers. As well as several floors of wall-to-wall sports memorabilia, the bar/restaurant has a large terrace overlooking Monaco port.

Open Daily 11am–midnight June–Sept, Tues–Sun 11am–midnight Oct–May. **Main courses** *9€–26€. Children's menu 11€.* **Credit** *AE, DC, MC, V.*

FAMILY-FRIENDLY ACCOMMODATION

A victim of its own success, the French Riviera is often packed out in summer months so it's best to book well in advance to secure reasonably priced accommodation anytime between May and September. Prices listed are often exclusive of VAT and breakfast.

Nice & Around

When it comes to living it up in style, it's hard to beat Riviera palaces such as the **Royal Riviera** in Saint-Jean–Cap-Ferrat (p. 85) or the **Palais de la Méditerranée** (☎ 04 92 14 77 00, **http://palais. concorde-hotels.com**) in Nice. Yet the French Riviera needn't come with a large price tag. Up-market Villefranche-sur-Mer offers surprisingly good value: in particular, the harbour-fronted **Hôtel de la Darse** (p. 85) and the friendly **Hôtel La Fiancée du Pirate** (☎ 04 93 76 67 40, www.fianceedupirate.com), with pool and double rooms with ocean views from 95€. For a little more money, you can stay at the bang-in-the-centre **Hôtel Welcome** (📞 *04 93 76 27 62*, **www. welcomehotel.com**), loved by film-maker Jean Cocteau (double rooms with sea view from 108€). Nice's new B&B, **Le Dortoir** (📞 *04 93 88 93 63*, **www.ledortoir. net**) on Rue Paradis, is already filling its spacious yet competitively priced suites (from 100€) with trendy families.

VERY EXPENSIVE

Royal Riviera ★ ★ ★

3 avenue Jean Monnet, Saint-Jean–Cap-Ferrat, 📞 *04 93 76 31 00*, **www. royal-riviera.com**

This is my favourite luxury family-friendly hotel along the Riviera. It's not just the swish furnishings and location that do it for us, but also the welcoming staff. Rooms in the main hotel have the bonus of sea views, but the bedrooms and bathrooms in the recently built Orangerie are more generously sized. Children under 14 stay free if sharing a

Royal Riviera

Deluxe Room or Suite with their parents. You can fit two extra beds in a Junior Suite, but you'll be more comfortable if you book one of the 16 interconnecting rooms. Children are provided with mini-slippers, dressing gown, flannel and teddy bear on arrival, and while you're being pampered at the spa, they can enjoy table tennis and water-skiing lessons. Both the gastronomic restaurant and the simpler, poolside restaurant have children's menus. Not surprisingly, the hotel is filled with happy, well-heeled families.

TIP ⟫ The Best Riviera Ice Cream Stops ⟨

In Monaco, stop off at the **Le Café de Paris** (📞 *377 98 06 36 36*) to spy on the Aston Martins parked in the Place du Casino as you down the principality's best sundaes. In Cannes, the top spot is **Gilles Vilfeu** 📞 *04 93 39 26 87*) on Rue des États-Unis, which serves up more than 40 flavours including sorbets. In Nice, masterful ice cream maker **Fenocchio** (📞 *04 93 62 88 80*, **www. fenocchio.fr**) in Place Rossetti and in Rue de la Poissonerie is an institution, though its icy crown is under threat from newcomers serving home-made ice cream, including **Crema di Gelato** (📞 *04 93 54 10 32*) in Rue de la Préfecture.

…s 96. **Rates** *Doubles from …, Junior Suites from 715€. …sed Dec–mid-Jan.* **Credit** *AE, …C, MC, V.* **Amenities** **In room**

INEXPENSIVE

Hôtel de la Darse ★ VALUE

Port de la Darse, 32 avenue du Général de Gaulle, Villefranche-sur-Mer, 04 93 01 72 54, ***www.hoteldeladarse.com***

With its wonderful location overlooking the famous Port de la Darse, this simple hotel offers exceptional value. Families can choose from comfortably furnished doubles, triples and a quad with balconies overlooking the port; ask for a refurbished one if you want air-conditioning. The original proprietors, who've owned the hotel since 1925, took control of the day-to-day management several years ago, and spend each winter refurbishing. Only breakfast is served, but there are several restaurants close by. Alas, there's no lift. Toddlers can enjoy the nearby children's play area.

Rooms *21.* **Rates** *Doubles from 57€, triples from 79€, quads from 89€. Cot free, extra bed 13€. Breakfast 8€, children 2–10 4€. Closed mid-Nov–mid-Feb.* **Credit** *AE, MC, V.* **In room**

Cannes & Around

If you're wanting to splash out on a night or two in one of the seafront grand hotels along La Croisette, try the swanky **Hotel Martinez** (*04 92 98 73 00,* ***www.hotel-martinez.com***), with its piano bar and Cannes's largest private beach. While mum enjoys some time at the spa, tots to teens are entertained at the summertime children's club. Children under 12 stay free when sharing their parents' room.

INSIDER TIP

Avoid staying in **Cannes** during the film festival: hotels and restaurants double their prices, festival films are reserved for industry folk, and you'll usually only spot celebrities on their 30-second whisk up the red carpet.

INEXPENSIVE

Hôtel Le Florian VALUE

8 rue de Commandant André, Cannes, 04 93 39 24 82, ***www.hotel-leflorian.com***

A no-frills hotel in the trendiest street in Cannes, the Florian is a godsend for travellers on a budget, run by the same family since 1958. The small rooms are plainly furnished but clean and air-conditioned, and there are also furnished studios and one-bedroom apartments that can be rented by the week. Rooms overlooking the school can be noisy during the day but are quiet at night.

Rooms *20 rooms, 11 apartments.* **Rates** *Doubles from 65€, studios from 350€ per week, one-bedroom apartment from 450€ per week. Cot free, extra bed 10€.* **Credit** *AE, DC, MC, V.* **In room**

Villa d'Estelle ★★★ FIND

12–14 rue des Belges, Cannes, 04 92 98 44 48, ***www.villadestelle.com***

One of Cannes's best-kept secrets, this apartment-hotel more than makes up for a lack of sea views (except from the four-bedroom penthouse suite) with reasonable prices and convenient location minutes from La Croisette. Along with tasteful, neutral decor, this 19th-century hotel has a plunge pool and an independently owned, self-service sushi restaurant. Each of its apartments has an American-style kitchen with microwave, washing machine and dishwasher. Options for families range from studio apartments (with double bed and sofa-bed) to three-bedroom apartments. Most have communicating doors, too. We'd recommend choosing an apartment in the new building, as they have fresher, more contemporary decor.

Apartments 23. *Rates* Studio apartments 135€, or 95€ per night for 3-night stay. Cot/extra bed 12€ per night, 25€ per week-long stay.

Credit AE, DC, MC, V. *Amenities* 🖼 ⁛⁛ *In room* ☒ 🖳 ⎕

INSIDER TIP

Bargain-hunters will love the diminutive **La Jabotte** (📞 04 93 61 45 89, *www.jabotte.com*), overlooking sandy Salis beach on the Cap d'Antibes, within walking distance of Antibes old town and 10km from Cannes. Its 10 comfortable rooms (including one family room) start at 69€ per night and are scattered around a mimosa-strewn patio.

Monaco & Around

The best luxury Monaco hotels for affluent families are the **Monte-Carlo Bay Hotel** (📞 377 98 06 02 00, *www.montecarlobay. com*), with rooms from 325€, and its sister the **Monte-Carlo Beach Hotel** (📞 04 93 28 66 66, *www.monte-carlo-beach.com*), with rooms from 310€. Set in 10

TIP The Best Campsites on the Riviera

Camping du Pylone (📞 04 93 74 94 70, *www.campingdupylone.com*) on Avenue du Pylone in Antibes has a pool, children's pool, restaurant, supermarket and bakery. Located 200m from Marineland theme park, it also offers volleyball, football, table tennis and games nights. Tent/caravan pitches per night start at 25.50€ for two adults and two kids under 8.

Les Cigales (📞 04 93 49 23 53, *www.lescigales.com*) on Avenue de la Mer in Mandelieu-La-Napoule offers mobile homes and studios for up to six people. Less than 1km from the sea, it too has a pool, children's pool, snack bar, playground, table football and table tennis. Weekly rentals for mobile homes start at 360€.

Camping Parc Montana Le Sourire (📞 04 93 20 96 11, *www.camping-parcsaintjames.com*) on Route de Grasse in Villeneuve-Loubet lets mobile homes for up to eight people (from 305€ per week). Although 4km from the sea, this camping village has play areas, a pool, table tennis, minigolf and a restaurant (open mid-May to mid-September).

For a Rainy Day ‹‹

What better way for kids to spend a rainy day than painting pottery?
Portrait artist Prune organises workshops for kids from 3 years old on Wednesday and Saturdays at her diminutive art studio on the edge of Monaco (Saint-Charles underground car park is just opposite on Boulevard de France). While parents relax at a streetside café or grab a snack at neighbouring Chez Pascal restaurant, kids will be busy painting or creating a 3D sculpture of their hands. **Le Petit Montmartre** (06 15 01 79 83, *www.petit-montmartre.com*) is at 17 boulevard Général Leclerc, Beausoleil. Afterwards, take a no. 2 bus from nearby bus stop La Crémaillère straight to Monaco Ville on the rock. From here, it's a 5-minute walk to the **Oceanographic Museum** (p. 73), where you can enjoy the subterranean aquarium before grabbing a snack at one of the Old Town's numerous pizza and pasta restaurants.

acres of gardens, the Monte-Carlo Bay has a children's club, children's paddling pool and sandy-bottomed lagoon. A 5-minute walk from Monaco in Roquebrune–Cap-Martin, the Monte-Carlo Beach curves around a sheltered bay and has a private landing stage, Olympic-sized pool and watersports club.

A cheaper alternative in central Monte Carlo is the recently opened **Novotel Monte-Carlo** (377 99 99 83 00, *www.novotel. com*), with comfortable rooms from 180€ per night and pool, while the simply furnished **Hôtel Capitole** (04 93 28 65 65, *www. hotel-capitole.fr*) in Beausoleil (yet within 500m of Monte Carlo's casino) is also worth a look; double rooms cost from 88€ per night. Self-catering families should also check out apartment-hotel **Eza Vista** (04 97 07 80 80) in Eze.

La Croisette, Cannes

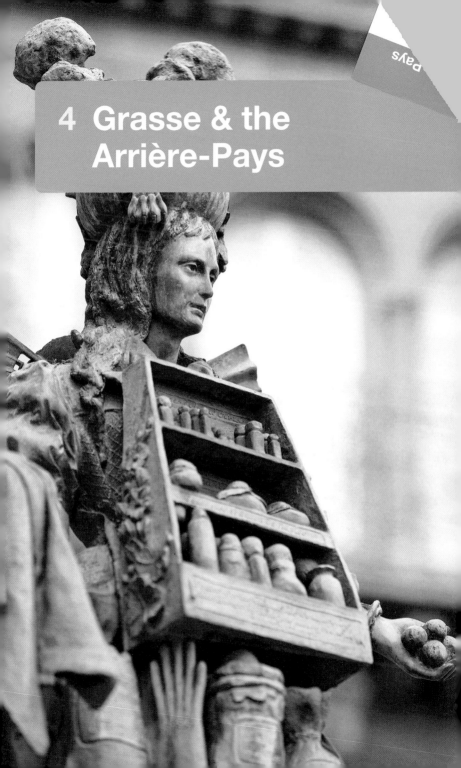

4 Grasse & the Arrière-Pays

GRASSE & THE ARRIÈRE-PAYS

Attractions ●	Musée International de	Scénoparc **5**	Le Pigeot **23**
Auron **1**	la Parfumerie **32**	Trophée d'Auguste **8**	Le Tilleul **10**
Buggy Cross **21**	Paintball 06 **14**	Valberg **3**	Les Terraillers **18**
Confiserie Florian **20**	Parc Départemental	Vallée des Merveilles	
Fondation Maeght **13**	de la Brague **19**	by 4WD **6**	**Accommodation** ■
Gorges de Saorge **7**	Parc Départemental	Verrerie de Biot **17**	Auberge de la Vignette
Graine & Ficelle **9**	de la Valmasque **22**		Haute **33**
Grottes de St.-Cézaire **34**	Parc National du Mercantour **4**	**Dining** ◆	Auberge de Tourrettes **31**
Isola 2000 **2**	Parfumerie Molinard **29**	Brittain's Restaurant **24**	Clos des Cyprès **26**
		Café des Musées **28**	Hôtel de Mougins **25**
		Crêperie des Arts **16**	Le Hameau **12**
		La Taverne Provençale **15**	Orion Bed & Breakfast **11**
		Le New Punjab **30**	Parc des Monges **27**

urving behind the glamorous Riviera coastline, the Arrière-Pays ('back-country') is a world apart, full of old farmhouses with metre-thick stone walls draped in bougainvillea, pastis-drinking locals playing *pétanque* in shaded courtyards, and medieval hilltop villages that drew Picasso, Chagall, Matisse and D. H. Lawrence to their light-drenched, cobbled streets. What these villages have lost in 'petiteness', they have gained in world-class art, Michelin-starred cuisine and plentiful activities to keep your children from boredom.

The region greeted the new decade with the re-opening of two of its best museums. The newly refurbished Fondation Maeght in St.-Paul de Vence is once again wowing art-lovers with a legendary collection of 20th-century art, while architect Frédéric Jung's 5-year facelift has transformed the International Perfume Museum in Grasse into a sweet-smelling haven for children, complete with interactive tours, buggies for toddlers and a supervised play area.

Less pastoral and more populated than other Provence landscapes, the Riviera's back-country will appeal to families who like to combine countryside with year-round convenience. You can design your own perfume in Grasse, watch glass-blowing in Biot, go gourmand in Mougins and cook up a storm in Le Pont du Loup and St.-Jeannet. Yet when you want to be far from the crowds, you're within an hour's drive of remote, alpine pastures in the Alpes-Maritimes hinterland, with its gorges, *grottes* (caves) and mountain goats.

VISITOR INFORMATION

The French Riviera Regional Tourism Committee runs the website **www.cotedazur-tourisme. com**, with useful information on attractions and events as well as a practical guide to help you prepare for your stay. Other useful resources for parents staying on the Côte d'Azur include **http:// kidookid.com** and **www.familyfirst. fr**, which both provide information in English on events, activities, shopping and childcare.

Getting There

By Plane For flights to the nearest airport, Nice, see p. 57.

By Train For Eurostar/TGVs to Antibes, Cannes and Nice, see p. 58. TER local trains run from Cannes to Biot (15 minutes) and to Grasse (30 minutes) via Mouans-Sartoux and from Nice to Tende via villages in the Niçois Arrière-Pays, including Peille, Peillon and Sospel.

By Car See p. 34.

Orientation

The A8 runs along the coastline from the Italian border near Menton, past Nice and Cannes and into the Var. From this main artery, smaller roads run into the Arrière-Pays. There's a turning at Cannes onto the N85 (commonly known to locals as La Pénétrante) towards Mougins and Grasse, at Cagnes-sur-Mer onto the N7 towards Vence, and near Nice onto the N202 heading up towards the ski resorts and the Alpes de Haute-Provence. Meanwhile, the picturesque D2210 (roughly parallel to the A8) runs from Grasse through back-country hills towards Vence. Major restaurants, hotels and attractions in the back-country are usually well signposted.

Getting Around

Bus services run from Nice Airport to Grasse, Vence and Sophia Antipolis and to ski resorts in the Azure Alps; see **www.nice.aeroport.fr** for details.

Families staying in central Grasse, Mouans-Sartoux or Biot will be able to reach many attractions by train. Vence, Valbonne and Mougins are well equipped with food stores and newsagents selling English-language newspapers for families who just want to chill out at their villa, but you'll need a **car** if you plan to explore the region further. Villages such as Peille, Peillon and Sospel have direct train links to Nice and to the Mercantour National Park, but you'll still need a car to access most places. For car hire at Nice Airport and at major stations on the Riviera, see p. 92. Local tourist offices can recommend local bus services, taxis and bike-hire firms.

For those looking to rent a car, **Budget** (℡ *04 93 87 45 37*), **Europcar** (℡ *08 25 82 90 21*) and **Avis** (℡ *08 20 61 16 31*) can be found beside the train station in Nice. Hertz (***www.hertz.co.uk***) and Europcar (***www.europcar. co.uk***) also have city-centre locations in Antibes, Cannes, Grasse and Nice.

WHAT TO SEE & DO

Children's Top 10 Attractions

❶ **Listening** to the stalactite xylophone at the Saint-Cézaire caves (p. 96).

❷ **Designing** your own perfume at Molinard (p. 102).

❸ **Exploring** prehistoric rock engravings by 4WD in the Vallée des Merveilles (p. 103).

❹ **Quad-biking** in the dust at Mougins's Buggy Cross (p. 104).

❺ **Spotting** bronze figures in the Fondation Maeght's Giacometti courtyard (p. 99).

❻ **Tasting** hand-made sweets at the Florian factory (p. 100).

❼ **Swimming** the rapids at the Gorges de Daluis (p. 101).

❽ **Climbing** iron-rung ladders in the Mercantour National Park (p. 103).

Fast Facts: Grasse

Banks: HSBC (℡ *04 92 42 30 00*), 22 place aux Aires, Grasse.
Hospitals: Centre Hospitalier de Grasse (℡ *04 93 09 52 11*, ***www.ch-grasse1.fr***) on Chemin de Clavary runs a 24-hour emergency service.
Internet Cafés: Player's Café (℡ *04 93 12 05 00*), 3 bis rue d'Opio in Valbonne, is open Monday to Friday 10am to 1pm and 2:30 to 8pm, and Saturday 10am to 1pm.
Pharmacies: You'll find chemists in central Grasse at 28 place aux Aires and 11 boulevard du Jeu de Ballon. After-hours pharmacies operate on a rota basis—the rota is posted on each pharmacy's door.
Post Offices: La Poste (℡ *08 00 00 90 42*), 9 boulevard Fragonard in Grasse.
Shopping: See p. 105 and, for markets, p. 106.

Grasse

9 Snowboarding with the children's ski club at Isola 2000 (p. 104).

10 Sleeping in a *Jungle Book* tree house at the Orion Bed & Breakfast (p. 113).

Child-friendly Events & Entertainment

Throughout the year, the backcountry villages host festivals where you can pick up local produce and join in with the villagers' fun. The best places to keep track of what's coming up are *www.cotedazur-tourisme.com*, with listings of almost 4,000 events, and *http://videgreniers06.free.fr*, with information on local *brocantes* (bric-a-brac fairs).

Fêtes Florales ★★★

Grasse, ☎ 04 97 05 57 90, www.ville-grasse.fr

France's perfume capital, Grasse is the place to come for flower festivals. Each May, the town is permeated with the smell of 50,000 cut roses for the **Expo Rose** festival, and rose-strewn events are scattered around the town, from the Palais des Congrès to the Musée Villa Jean-Honoré Fragonard. In Cours Honoré Cresp, a rose-infused market sells everything from candles to chocolates. Each August, the **Jasmine Festival** celebrates the start of the jasmine harvest with flower parades and a 'Miss Jasmine' competition.

*May and Aug. **Adm** Expo Rose: 5€, children 6–12 3€. Jasmine Festival: see Grasse tourist board website (www.ville-grasse.fr) for adm prices Mid-July–mid-Aug. **Adm** Evening performance: from 16€; child 3–12 from 13€. Zoo visit: 2€. **Credit** AE, DC, MC, V. **Amenities** ☕ 🅿 ♿*

Enfantillages ★★

Le Pré des Arts, Valbonne, ☎ 04 93 12 32 30

Face-painting, pottery classes and magic workshops are the

English-language Cinemas

For English-language films, look for the 'VO' (version originale) symbol. For current listings, see the cinema's own website or *www.angloinfo.com*.

Cinéma Casino, 30 avenue Henri Isnard, Vence, ☎ *08 92 89 28 92*.

La Strada, 201 route de Cannes, Mouans-Sartoux, ☎ *04 92 92 20 13/08 92 89 28 92*.

Le Studio, 15 boulevard Jeu-de-Ballon, Grasse, ☎ *04 93 40 17 10/08 92 68 27 45*.

Les Visiteurs du Soir, Salle des Fêtes, Espace de la Vignasse, Valbonne, ☎ *04 93 12 91 88/08 92 89 28 92*, *www.lesvisiteursdusoir.com*.

order of the day during this weekend children's festival. Events are held at Le Pré des Arts concert hall and at co-sponsor Île aux Trésors, the local toy library in Place Méjane. Films and theatrical performances are in French, but the puppet theatre and animated films are generally enjoyable even to children who don't speak the language.

1st weekend in Dec. **Adm** *Free.* **Amenities** P ♿

Towns & Villages

Grasse ★★

Tourist office: ☎ *04 93 36 66 66, www.ville-grasse.fr*

You can smell the jasmine soaps as you browse the shops with their ochre facades along the narrow streets of Grasse. France's perfume capital, long a back-country hideaway for queens and coronets, has never been picture-postcard perfect, but after being sidelined in the 1970s and 1980s as investment concentrated on the coastline, it's now back in fashion. A recently restored train link with Cannes brings day-trippers seeking respite from the beach, and well-informed gourmets flock to **La Bastide St. Antoine** (p. 108) for Jacques Chibois's Michelin-starred cuisine. Artists' studios, interior decor shops and estate agents are springing up in freshly painted buildings around the old-town centre. As well as the town's perfume factories and museums, families can discover nearby *grottes* (caves) and gorges.

Mougins ★★★

Tourist office: ☎ *04 93 75 87 67, www.mougins-coteazur.org*

This picturesque hilltop village has expanded into one of the mainstays of the Arrière-Pays. It's chock-a-block with gastronomic restaurants that together hold several Michelin stars, from the long-established **Moulin de Mougins** to relative newcomer **Le Candille**. But it's also a foodie heaven for self-catering families, with the best fish shop (**Poissonerie Develay**, ☎ *04 93 75 23 66*) and the best

Getting Rid of the Smell

The French craze for perfume began in 16th-century Grasse, when the town's leather-makers devised a way of concealing the unpleasant odour of animal hides with fragrance. When the influential royal Catherine de' Medici was given a pair of perfumed gloves, courtiers rushed to follow suit. The town subsequently became renowned for perfume, as is alluringly depicted in Patrick Süskind's dark novel and film, *Perfume* (for adults only), most of which was actually shot in Barcelona.

---

butcher (**Boucherie Lerda,** ☏ *04 93 90 01 81*) in the region. Located midway between the glamorous Cannes coastline and the perfumed hills of Grasse, it's also a good place for family-friendly activities such as quad-biking and horse-riding, and boasts an antique-car museum.

Valbonne & Biot ★★

Valbonne tourist office: ☏ *04 93 12 34 50, www.tourisme-valbonne.com*

Biot tourist office: ☏ *04 93 65 78 00, www.biot.fr*

These photogenic medieval villages combine as a hub for the 30,000-strong international community working at the nearby technology park, Sophia-Antipolis. Valbonne is so Anglophone that it has an English bookshop (p. 106), a British grocery store (p. 105 and p. 94) and an English-language cinema. Biot defines itself by its bubble-strewn glassware and by the fact that 20th-century Cubist painter **Fernand Léger** lived and worked here. Both villages are very popular bases for families, with child-friendly fêtes, attractions and nearby parks.

Vence ★

Tourist office: ☏ *04 93 58 06 38, www.vence.fr*

Overlooked in favour of its photogenic sister, Saint-Paul de Vence, Vence is the Arrière-Pays's second town after Grasse. A popular stopover for many pre-eminent 20th-century artists and writers, this cathedral town has neat streets and flower beds that speak of quiet prosperity. Among its tranquil charms are riding on the place du Grand Jardin's carousel and wandering through the pedestrianised streets of the medieval old town. You can enjoy spotting **Marc Chagall's** mosaic in the cathedral, **D. H. Lawrence's** grave plaque in the cemetery (although he was later cremated) and **Matisse's Chapelle du Rosaire.**

Vence provides a convenient gateway for families to explore the gorge-dotted valleys of La Tinée and La Vésubie.

One of the back-country's most exclusive and priciest places to stay, the neighbouring *village perché* (hilltop village) of **Saint-Paul de Vence ★★★** (tourist office: ☏ *04 93 32 86 95, www.saint-pauldevence.com*) is

Villages Perchés (Hilltop Villages)

The Riviera's back-country is famed for its villages perchés—hilltop villages that include overrated **Saint-Paul de Vence**, with its art galleries; **Gourdon**, with its Le Nôtre-designed château gardens; **Sainte-Agnès**, with its eagle's-nest views; **La Turbie**, with its impressive Trophée des Alpes monument (p. 99); and archetypal **Peillon**, with its gastronomic Auberge de la Madone restaurant. **Hilltop Cabris** (tourist office: ☏ *04 93 60 55 63,* *http://cabris.chez-alice.fr*) is one of the back-country's hidden gems. In the hills behind Grasse, this immaculate village is bursting with places to feast on Provençal cuisine and dramatic Riviera panoramas. For the best views, climb up to the cypress-shaded gravel courtyard beside the 10th-century château ruins. From here you can see all the way from the jutting coastline of Cap-Ferrat to the Saint-Cassien lake.

St.-Paul de Vence

home to artists' workshops and to the exalted Fondation Maeght (p. 99). It is worth making the journey here for the narrow cobbled streets and artists' studios, although it may not be suitable for buggies.

Natural Wonders & Spectacular Views

Grottes de St.-Cézaire ★★
FIND

1481 Route des Grottes, Saint-Cézaire-sur-Siagne, ☏ *04 93 60 22 35,* *www.lesgrottesdesaintcezaire.fr*

These caves are at their most beautiful when it rains, making them the perfect wet-weather destination, but they are also an ideal place to seek a bit of cool relief on a hot day. Six million years old, they are a dazzling combination of rich-red iron oxide, marble-cream limestone and chocolate-coloured rock. Children will have fun spotting bizarre shapes in the waxwork-like concretions: can you see death skulls or jellyfish? My daughter Alexandra was captivated by the eerie sound of the stalactite xylophone that our guide played for us. Wear warm clothing and flat shoes, and take a harness for babies, since there are 123 steps which get slippery in wet weather (there are stair rails). And beware the rust-red rock stains if you're wearing light-coloured clothing.

Open Daily 10:30am–6:30pm June–Aug, daily 10:30am–noon and 2–5:30pm Sept–May. Closed Dec–Jan. **Adm** 7€, children 13–18 5.50€, 6–12 4€. **Credit** AE, DC, MC, V. **Amenities** 🅿 🛍 🍴

Aquaria & Animal Parks

Graine & Ficelle ★ ★ ★ GREEN

670 chemin des Collets, Saint-Jeannet, 5km northeast of Vence, 📞 06 85 08 15 64, **www.graine-ficelle.com**

This diminutive farm in the dandelion-strewn hills behind Vence is a bucolic paradise for young children, with donkeys to feed, baby rabbits to coo over, and a chicken run. The best time to come is weekend brunch, when Parisian exile Isabella cooks up a vegetarian storm using produce from her organic vegetable patch, which you can enjoy at convivial communal tables with baby lambs darting around your legs. There are low tables and chairs for children, and drawing materials to keep them amused. Isabella also organises cookery classes and activity days for children. For all visits, make sure you book in advance and bring cash.

Rabbits at Graine & Ficelle

Da Vinci's Code hits Provence?

Da Vinci Code addicts may be interested to know that Biot was once an HQ for the Knights Templar.

---

*Open Daily by reservation in advance only, by phone or e-mail (**E: graine. ficelle@wanadoo.fr**). **Adm** Weekend brunch and farm visit 35€ (exc. wine), children under 12 19€. Farm visit adults 11€, children under 12 8€. **Credit** Cash only.*

Nature Reserves, Parks & Gardens

Parc Départemental de la Brague

RD604 from Valbonne, RD4 from Biot, RD103 or RD198 from Sophia Antipolis

Listen out for warblers and field-fares amid the waterfalls and aromatic Mediterranean plants at this park that follows the meandering path of the Brague river between Biot and Valbonne. You'll find parking and picnic tables off *routes départementales* (minor roads) 604, 4 and 198. Avoid the lower part of the river near Sophia Antipolis, where detergents have begun to pollute the water.

Amenities ♿ ☂

Parc Départemental de la Valmasque ★ FIND

RD35 from Mougins to Valbonne, RD103 from Valbonne, RD135 from Vallauris

Covering 561 hectares of parkland stretching from Valbonne to Mougins, La Valmasque Park is an inviting place for families. You can spot wild boar or foxes

as you walk or bike around the oak and pine forests and open prairies, which host more than 60 bird species; or admire Font Merle lake, which overflows with summer-flowering lotus. There are children's play areas, bird-watching hides and picnic tables aplenty, and the place is easily accessible, with car parks spread along the RD35 Route de la Valmasque near Sophia Antipolis.

Amenities ♿ ☂ ⅄

Parc National du Mercantour
★★★

www.mercantour.eu

Forming the lungs of southern France, this 70,000-hectare national park stretching for 75km is a sparsely populated haven for endangered fauna and flora, including wild orchids, bearded vultures and golden eagles. You can enjoy skiing (see 'Active Families', p. 104) and watersports (p. 101), or pay a visit to the **Vallée des Merveilles** (p. 103) or **Scénoparc** (p. 104).

> **INSIDER TIP**
>
> Between June and September, a scenic way of getting to the Mercantour National Park is aboard the **Train des Merveilles** (☎ 04 93 04 92 05, *www.tendemer veilles.com*), which runs daily at 9am from Nice SNCF station to

the town of Tende in under 2 hours with an onboard tour guide (English-language guides are available). Return journeys cost 22.60€ with several daily afternoon departures from Tende.

Historic Monuments

Trophée d'Auguste ★

Avenue Albert 1er, La Turbie, 📞 *04 93 41 20 84,* ***www.la-turbie.monuments-nationaux.fr***

Commonly known as the Trophée des Alpes, this extraordinary Roman monument rises above La Turbie like an unlikely crown. Dating back to the 6th century BC, the trophy was originally 49m (160 ft) high and topped by a statue of Emperor Octavius Augustus. With just the pedestal remaining, you can only wonder at the grandeur of the original statue; however, the miniature replica in the museum should help to fire your imagination. In the mid-20th century, several buildings were destroyed

to make space for the garden that surrounds the trophy, which is a good place to wait with a buggy if you don't fancy the climb up to the viewing point for some bird's-eye coastline views.

Open *Tues–Sun 9:30am–1pm and 2:30–6:30pm mid-May–mid-Sept, 10am–1:30pm and 2:30–5:30pm mid-Sept–mid-May.* ***Adm*** *5€, under 18s free.* ***Credit*** *Cash only.* ***Amenities*** 🅿 🔒

Top Museums

Fondation Maeght ★★★

Saint-Paul de Vence, 📞 *04 93 32 81 63,* ***www.fondation-maeght.com***

If you visit just one art museum during your trip, make it the freshly refurbished Fondation Maeght. The brainchild of art dealers Aimé and Marguerite Maeght, this private foundation has a vast collection of 20th-century works by Marc Chagall (p. 102), Henri Matisse, Pierre Bonnard and other artists who lived and worked on the sun-drenched Riviera. It's best to visit on a sunny day, as the gardens are filled with sculptures and pools. Children love exploring the garden rooms, from Joan Miró's labyrinth to Alberto Giacometti's courtyard of bronze figures and Georges Braque's mosaic pool.

There are several staircases and no lift, so it's worth bringing a baby harness. Note that you'll often find the car park below the museum full, but there are usually spaces in the one next to it.

Trophée d'Auguste

Contemporary art gallery, Fondation maeght

Open *Daily 10am–7pm July–Sept, 10am–6pm Oct–June.* **Adm** *11€, children 10–18 9€, under 10s free.* **Credit** *AE, DC, MC, V.*

INSIDER TIP ⟫

Let your kids (from 8 up) release their energy with a paintball session in the forested hills near Saint-Paul de Vence's Fondation Maeght with **Paintball 06** (📞 04 93 58 95 90, **www.paintball06. fr**). It's 30€ for a 2-hour discovery session for kids 8–12.

Musée International de la Parfumerie ★★

2 boulevard du Jeu de Ballon, Grasse, 📞 *04 97 05 58 00,* **www. museesdegrasse.com**

Looking splendid after its 5-year facelift, overseen by celebrated architect Frédéric Jung, Grasse's new Perfume Museum boasts kids' interactive tours and a supervised play area. Older children may enjoy discovering ancient Egyptian embalming vases or learning about the process of perfume-making in a laboratory filled with copper perfume distillers and decanting jars. Younger ones should head straight to the greenhouse where they can sniff raw perfume materials such as jasmine, bergamot and vanilla. During the school holidays, there are 2-hour perfume workshops for kids every Monday afternoon.

The perfume museum works well for a day trip in combination with the **Fragonard** perfume factory next door or **Parfumerie Molinard** (p. 102) where kids can design their own perfume. If you're coming by car, park in the multi-storey car park with a lift beneath Cours Honoré Cresp.

Open *Daily 10am–7pm May–Aug (until 9pm Sat), daily 11am–6pm Apr, Mon and Wed–Sun 11am–6pm Oct–Mar; closed Nov.* **Adm** *3€, under 18s free. 2-hour family workshops July–Aug Mon 2:30–4:30pm 6€.* **Credit** *MC, V.* **Amenities** 🛒

With their waterfalls and jaw-dropping descents, the Alpe
Maritimes's gorges are a must-see. While it's worth the trip for the
views alone, adventurous families can also enjoy sports such as rafting
(from 6 to 8 years), canyoning and Via Ferrata (p. 106).

Most accessible are the **Gorges du Loup** in the hills behind Grasse.
From more than 1,220m (4,000 ft) above sea level, the 45km Loup river
cascades through waterfalls such as the **Cascade de Courmes and
Cascades des Demoiselles** and erodes rock into striking formations
like the **Saut du Loup**. The Gorges du Loup are a popular point for
aquatic hiking and canyoning (*06 86 66 35 49, www.loisirs-explorer.
com/destination-nature*). The pure, fish-laden waters of the Roya river
flow through the **Gorges de Saorge** near watersports mecca Breil-sur-
Roya, where you can try canyoning, kayaking, rafting, canoeing or tubing
with **Roya Evasion** (*04 93 04 91 46, www.royaevasion.com*) or **Mat &
Eau** (*06 81 56 21 56/06 83 18 48 74, www.mat-et-eau.com*).

The **Gorges du Cians and Gorges de Daluis** in the Vallée de la
Tinée are dramatic, with their paper-cut narrowness and burnished red-
ness. Nicknamed the Little Colorado Niçois, the Gorges de Daluis are
idyllic for watersports in springtime, when the waters are higher. Watersports are offered by **Les Eskimos à l'Eau** (*06 11 38 02 82, www.
eskimosaleau.com*) and **Eau Vive Evasion** (*04 92 83 38 09, www.
eau-vive-evasion.com*), include rafting, hot dog, kayaking, aquatic hiking and rapids swimming.

Arts & Crafts

✦ Confiserie Florian ★★★

*Le Pont du Loup, Tourrettes-sur-Loup,
04 93 59 32 91, www.confiserie
florian.com*

A must for children of all ages
who've read Roald Dahl's *Charlie and the Chocolate Factory*, this
working sweet factory produces
organic sweets and chocolates
infused with Provençal flowers
and fruits using traditional 19th-
century recipes. As well as visiting the sweet museum for its
ancient sweet recipes and cooking utensils, you can look
around the factory floor, where
workers crystallise violet, sub-
merge clementines in syrup and
hand-dip fruit into orange-
coloured chocolate.

At the foot of the famous Pont
du Loup ('Wolf's Bridge'), there's
a sweet-smelling, Mediterranean
garden. Its benches are handy for
baby-changes or just relaxing
and admiring the rocky vista.

*Open Daily 9am–6:30pm Jan–Sept
and Dec; factory visits 9am–noon and
2–6pm Jan–Sept and Dec. Closed
Oct–Nov. Adm Free. Credit MC, V.
Amenities* P ▮

Flying Firefighters

When the heat sizzles and the wind blows in summertime Provence, one discarded cigarette butt can start a raging forest fire. This is when *Canadairs* (sea planes) come into action. You can see these planes swooping down on the Lac Saint-Cassien to fill their bellies with water before dowsing the flames of local wildfires.

Next door to Confiserie Florian, kids over 8 can try their hand at making chocolate desserts with English-speaking Parisian chef Yves Terrillon at **L'Atelier de la Cuisine des Fleurs** (04 92 11 06 94). Two-hour cookery classes on Wednesday afternoons cost 25€.

Parfumerie Molinard ★ ★ ★
AGE 4 & UP

60 boulevard Victor Hugo, Grasse, 04 92 42 33 11, *www.molinard. com*

Stuck for something to do on a rainy day? Children 4 and up can take part in a 30-minute perfume-making workshop at this 19th-century factory. Trainee alchemists mix their own perfumes with the help of charming, English-speaking Céline—who's a mum herself. For 28€, children come away with a diploma and a 30ml bottle of their personally designed perfume. Kids over 12 can sign up for a 90-minute in-depth workshop, choosing up to a dozen essences from a collection of around 100 *eau de parfum* smells. Their formula joins an archive of 15,000 secret formulas, so they can re-order their perfume whenever they want. A 5-minute walk from the town centre, the perfumery has a four-storey car park without a lift, and there is street parking opposite.

Open *Daily 9:30am–7pm July–Aug, Mon–Fri 9:30am–6:30pm. Workshops by advance booking.* **Adm** *30-minute*

Chagall Comes to Notting Hill

Older children may connect artist Marc Chagall with the film *Notting Hill*, in which the celebrated actress Anna (Julia Roberts) spots a poster of Chagall's painting *La Mariée* (*The Bride*, 1950) on travel-bookshop owner William's (Hugh Grant) wall. Commenting on the painting's floating wedding couple with a violin-playing goat, Anna says: 'It feels like how being in love should be. Floating through a dark sky . . . Happiness wouldn't be happiness without a violin-playing goat.'

Famous for animated and heavily symbolic artworks that mingle romanticism with religion, Russian-born Chagall (1887–1985) lived and died in Saint-Paul de Vence. Fans can see more of his work in Cimiez (p. 73).

Traditional glassmaking in Biot

workshop for children over 4 28€ (children under 12 must be accompanied by an adult, to a maximum of three per adult); 90-minute workshop for children 12–18 and adults 40€. **Credit** *AE, DC, MC, V.* **Amenities** 🅿🔒

Verrerie de Biot ★★

Chemin des Combes, Biot, ☎ 04 93 65 03 00, www.verreriebiot.com

This working glass factory could do with a lick of paint, but the sight of four old men in shorts and sandals blowing on molten glass down the end of long metal pipes is great entertainment for all the family. Somehow this Dad's Army of glassmaking manages to produce glassware of surprising beauty and complexity. Afterwards, you can buy the famous bubble-strewn glassware, visit the glass eco-museum and contemporary glass gallery, or grab a snack at the café (with children's menu).

Open Mon–Sat 9:30am–8pm, Sun and bank holidays 10:30am–1:30pm and 2:30–7:30pm May–Sept, Mon–Sat 9:30am–6pm, Sun and bank holidays 10:30am–1:30pm and 2:30–6:30pm Oct–Apr. **Adm** *Free.* **Credit** *AE, MC, V.* **Amenities** 🅿🔒🛍

Child-friendly Tours

Vallée des Merveilles by 4WD
★★★

Panza Merveilles, Tende, ☎ 04 93 04 73 21/06 07 58 37 19, www.panzamerveilles.com

A great (and easy) way to tour the Vallée des Merveilles in the Mercantour National Park is by 4WD, especially if you want to avoid hours of walking with young children. Guide Franck Panza (or one of his English-speaking colleagues, all official Mercantour National Park *accompagnateurs*) drives you through alpine pastures dotted with wild orchids and along bumpy, military routes (nicknamed 'rock-and-roll routes' by locals) towards a sparser, snow-lined landscape. From here, it's only a short walk to Europe's largest collection of prehistoric rock engravings. We loved our visit here: while my children cooed over rabbit-like marmots, my husband and I stared at ancient pictograms scratched into reddish slate and listened to Franck's stories about the fiercely independent Vallée de la Roya people. The best month to come is June, when the rhododendrons are out in force. Pick-up is available from Tende train station.

Open June–Sept, advance booking required. **Adm** *70€ for the day, children 8–14 35€.* **Credit** *Cash only.*

INSIDER TIP ▶

In the depths of the **Mercantour National Park** (p. 103), the reintroduction of wolves, which began in 1992, has sparked fierce debate between ecologists and shepherds. Listen to the divided

Skiing in the Azure Alps

If you're in the region in winter, make the most of the multifaceted Alpes-Maritimes by skiing in the Azure Alps. With 135 slopes, making it the largest ski area in the Alpes-Maritimes, attractive **Auron** (*www.auron.com*) is ideal for young families and favours advanced skiers more than Isola. There's a crèche for children from 6 months to 6 years and a ski school for kids from 3 to 7 years.

A 1970s concrete confection, **Isola 2000** (*www.isola2000.com*), is the newest and highest resort with the best range of slopes for beginners to intermediates; facilities include 22 ski lifts, a funicular railway and a water park. It's good for those with pre-teens, as there's a kids' snowboarding club and a ski school for children from 4 to 6 years. There's also a crèche for toddlers from 15 months to 4 years. Both Auron and Isola 2000 offer summer pursuits such as cycling, horse-riding, paintballing and trampolining.

Alternatively, easily accessible **Valberg** (*www.valberg.com*) is best suited to intermediate skiers and snowboarders. There's a crèche for kids from 6 months to 6 years and a snow school for children from 3 years.

If you don't want the hassle of driving, the best budget option is to get there by bus. **Santa Azur** (*04 93 85 34 06, www.santa-azur.com*) organises a ski-bus (from 30€ including 1-day ski pass) from Nice to both Auron and Isola 2000 in 2 hours, while **ANT Tourisme** (*04 92 29 88 86, www.ant-tourisme.com*) has shuttles from Nice to Valberg in 2½ hours. For wealthy high-flyers, there's a speedier helicopter option from Nice to Auron, Isola 2000 and Valberg with **Héli Air Monaco** (*377 97 77 32 20, www.heliairmonaco.com*).

opinions and see the wolf-packs for yourself on a trip to **Scénoparc** (*04 93 02 33 69, www.alpha-loup.com*) in Saint-Martin Vésubie. English-speaking tours and audioguides are available. Tickets cost 12€ for adults, 10€ for kids up to 12 years, and are free for those under 4 years.

Active Families

Buggy Cross ★ AGE 5 & UP

909 chemin Font du Currault, Mougins, 04 93 69 02 74/06 12 82 07 13, *www.buggycross.fr*

Boys and tomboys 5 or over have a ball biking in the dust at Buggy Cross, spinning quad-bikes and mini-motorbikes (ranging from 50cc to 125cc) around three tyre-protected tracks. There's a small terrace where you can relax over a drink while you watch your budding Button or Hamilton in action.

Note that Buggy Cross is next door to **Mougins riding school** (04 93 45 75 81), so you can organise a multi-activity afternoon.

Vallee des Merveilles

*Open Wed, Sat and Sun 11am–dusk (daily 11am–dusk public and school holidays). **Adm** over 5s from 10€ for 10-minute slot on 50cc motorbike or quad-bike. **Credit** Cash only. **Amenities*** ☕ ⓟ

Shopping

Brittain's Home Stores

Forum roundabout, 1913 route de Cannes, Valbonne, at junction of D3 and D103, ☎ 04 93 42 01 70, www.brittains-stores.com

If you find your children clamouring for a jam doughnut or Heinz beans, head to this grocery store set up by the eponymous John and Caroline Brittain

in 2004—it's stacked from floor to ceiling with British favourites, from steak-and-onion pasties to Walkers crisps and classic ale. It's also a good place to buy freshly-made sandwiches and salads (weekdays only) for a picnic lunch. They've now opened up a restaurant nearby (p. 109).

*Open Mon–Sat 9am–6:30pm. **Credit** MC, V. **Amenities** ⓟ*

Cerise

31 boulevard du Jeu de Ballon, Grasse, ☎ 04 93 36 30 20

Situated on a palm-lined avenue in central Grasse, Cerise has been selling French-designed

TIP ▶ Little Tourist Train ◀

Foot-weary families can jump on the Fragonard motorised petit train (☎ 06 07 75 63 60, *www.petits-trains.com*) for a 40-minute trip around central Grasse. Trains depart from Cours Honoré Cresp between 11am and 5pm daily, May to September.

Iron Bars & Pot-holes

If you'd like to try climbing with older children, check out Via Ferrata – a form of rock climbing along iron-rung ladders that allows beginners to scale dramatic rock faces usually only accessible to experts. Similar iron rungs were used in World War I to move Italian troops through the mountain range between Italy and Austria.

Two bases that offer Via Ferrata, both in the Mercantour National Park, are **Roya Evasion** (℡ *04 93 04 91 46, www.royaevasion.com*) in Breuil-sur-Roya, for children over 14, and **Escapade** (℡ *04 93 03 31 32, www.guidescapade.com*) in Saint-Martin de Vésubie, for children 10 or over. Meanwhile, near Caille, **Lou Païs** (℡ *04 93 60 34 51, www.lou-pais. com*) offers kids 10 or over the world's first subterranean Via Ferrata, where you scale cave ceilings and explore stalagmites and stalactites.

children's clothes for ages up to 18 for more than 30 years, from swimming costumes to socks.

Open *Tues–Sat 9:30am–12:30pm, 3–7pm.* **Credit** *MC, V.*

English Book Centre ★

12 rue Alexis Julien, Valbonne Vieux Village, ℡ *04 93 12 21 42, www. englishbookcentre.com*

This is a good place to pick up a copy of the sing-along CD *French on the Move for Kids*, to get your children into the holiday mood, or to inspire your taste buds by treating yourself to

Jacques Chibois's *Provence Harvest*. As well as adults' and children's books, it sells children's DVDs and games.

Open *Tues–Sat 9:30am–1pm, 3–6:30pm.* **Credit** *MC, V.*

Fragonard ★★

20 boulevard Fragonard, Grasse, ℡ *04 93 36 44 65, www.fragonard.com*

Smell the *fleur d'oranger* bath gel and treat yourself to other luscious toiletries at factory prices at this shop next to the historic Fragonard factory. Junior customers won't go away

TIP ▶ The Area's Best Markets

Clothes & food market: Place des Arcades, Valbonne, Fri morning.
Flower & vegetable market: Place aux Aires, Grasse, Tues–Sun mornings.
Flower & vegetable market: Place du Gaulle, Biot, Tues morning.
Flower, fruit and vegetable market: Place du Grand Jardin and Place Surian, Vence, Tues–Sun mornings.
Local produce market: Place du Marché, Sospel, Sun morning.
Organic food market: Place du Centenaire, Peymeinade, Mon morning.
Provençal market: Grand Pré, Saint-Vallier de Thiey, Sun morning.

empty-handed—there are special duck soaps and children's fragrances, including *Eau des Fées* ('fairy water') for girls and *Eau des Aventuriers* ('adventurers' water') for boys.

At nearby **Fragonard Maison** (2 rue Amiral de Grasse, ☏ 04 93 40 12 04). you'll find cute embroidered toy bags and cuddly toys.

Open *Daily 9am–6pm Feb–Oct, daily 9am–12:30pm and 2–6pm Nov–Jan.* ***Credit*** *MC, V.*

JouéClub

42–44 avenue Foch, Vence, ☏ 04 93 58 51 36, www.joueclub.com

This branch of the French toy chain sells all the latest educational toys and board games for children, and is also well-stocked with everything from Doudou et Compagnie teddy bears to inflatable pool toys and skateboards.

Open *Tues–Sat 9am–12:30pm, 3–7pm.* ***Credit*** *AE, MC, V.*

FAMILY-FRIENDLY DINING

Grasse, Mougins & Around

Café des Arcades (☏ 04 93 12 00 06) in Valbonne offers family-friendly dining in the pretty, pedestrianised Place des Arcades, where kids can run around as you dine, while Cabris has several restaurants overlooking a kids' playground, including the moderately priced **Le Flambeau** (☏ 04 93 60 61 00) on Rue Frédéric Mistral, with Provençal and Italian cuisine. In Grasse, we recommend **La Grignote** (☏ 04 93 09 91 45) in Place aux Aires and **Café des Musées** (p. 109) as the most reliable reasonably priced options in central Grasse.

Gastronomic restaurants for a romantic night away from the kids include Jacques Chibois's

Provencal Produce

Michelin two-starred **Bastide St. Antoine** (📞 *04 93 70 94 94, www.jacques-chibois.com*) in Grasse, the idyllic **Auberge du Vieux Château** (📞 *04 93 60 50 12, www.aubergeduvieuxchateau. com*) in Cabris and the famous **Moulin de Mougins** (📞 *04 93 75 78 24, www.moulin-mougins.com*), where new chef Sébastien Chambru now offers cookery classes for kids on Wednesday afternoons.

EXPENSIVE

Les Terraillers ★★★

11 chemin Neuf, Biot, 📞 *04 93 65 01 59, www.lesterraillers.com*

If you'd like to give your children their first taste of Michelin-starred cuisine, this is the place to do it. Less formal than some of its starred compatriots, this family-run restaurant offers sophisticated yet robust French cuisine. From the mouth-watering cheese dome and the knowledgeable sommelier Geraldine, to the tea trolley with its pots of fresh herbs for you to concoct your own blend, the key to its success is in the detail. Children up to 10 years choose their own three-course menu for 25€.

Open Mon–Tues and Fri–Sun noon–2pm and 7:30–10pm; closed Nov. ***Main courses*** *39€–45€; three-course lunch menu from 39€.* ***Credit*** *AE, MC, V.*

MODERATE

★ La Taverne Provençale ★★★ MOMENT

Place de l'Église, Gourdon, 📞 *04 93 09 68 22*

We often bring friends to this long-standing restaurant. It serves *cuisine de grand-mère* ('grandma's cooking') infused with Provençal flavours, amid gingham tablecloths and photo-genic views reaching as far as the Cannes coast. There's a two-course children's menu including a drink, but little ones might prefer to choose from the wide selection of pizzas. Ask for a table on the edge of the terrace for the best views, and bring an extra layer as temperatures drop at this altitude.

Open Daily noon–2:30pm and 7–10:30pm July–Aug, 12–2:30pm Mar–June and Sept–mid-Nov. Closed mid-Nov–Jan. ***Main courses*** *10€–27€. Children's menu 11.50€.* ***Credit*** *MC, V.*

Le Pigeot ★★ FIND

16 rue Alexis-Julien, Valbonne Vieux Village, 📞 *04 93 12 17 53*

The sweet-and-savoury flavours of Moroccan cuisine appeal to many children, especially my daughter Alexandra who gorges on couscous and sultanas when we visit. There's no children's menu, but portions are ample, so you can easily share three dishes between four. This popular haunt has a rich North African decor with hand-painted furniture and half-height chairs that suit children. If you have young ones who are liable to run around, book a table on the ground floor rather than up the stone steps on the mezzanine.

Open Daily 7:30–10pm June–Aug, Wed–Fri and Sun noon–1:30pm and 7:30–10pm, Mon–Tues and Sat 7:30–

The Olive Tree

From tourist-brochure photos to tablecloth designs, the gnarled branches and silvery leaves of the olive tree are often used to symbolise southern France. This adaptable tree survives unrivalled heat and neglect. Its green and black fruit is used to make *tapenade* (olive paste) and olive oil, while its wood is hand-crafted into chopping boards and corkscrews. Appreciated since Roman times, when olive trees were reserved for burning on the altars of the gods, the olive tree is still a protected species in France.

10pm Sept–May. *Main courses* 16€–27€. *Credit* AE, MC, V.

INSIDER TIP ▶▶

Families longing for a full English breakfast, a cream tea with scones or fish and chips (15€) may find that **Brittain's Restaurant** (& *04 93 12 03 97, www.brittains-restaurant.com*), on the outskirts of Valbonne, hits the spot. Those who can't imagine a holiday without a good curry should go to reasonably priced **Le New Punjab** (& *04 93 36 16 03*) in Rue des Fabreries (just off Place aux Aires) in Grasse. My daughter likes the creamy chicken korma and naan breads. They also do take-outs and deliveries.

INEXPENSIVE

Café des Musées

1 rue Ossola, Grasse, & *04 92 60 99 00*

Wedged between museums, this diminutive café is the ideal place to stop off for a *croque-monsieur* or to grab a morning coffee and croissant. The menu offers a good selection of salads, but locals tend to opt for the hot *plat du jour* (daily special). For

dessert, try the home-made tarts that wait temptingly in a glass cabinet. The small outside terrace fills up quickly at lunchtime in summer months, so arrive early. New mums may dislike trekking to the outside loo, where there's no room for baby changes.

Open Mon–Fri 8:30am–7pm, Sat and Sun 9am–7pm Apr–Oct; Mon–Fri 8:30am–6pm, Sat 9am–6pm Nov–Mar. *Main courses* 8.80€–12€. *Credit* MC, V.

INSIDER TIP ▶▶

A scenic, and easily accessible, picnic spot is **La Valmasque park** (p. 98), with its lotus-scattered lake and play areas.

Vence & Around

A good bet for family dining is **Tourrettes-sur-Loup,** with a range of cuisine for all taste buds, from Provençal to Mexican.

The most famous names for gastronomic cuisine around Vence are Michelin-starred **Le Saint-Martin** (& *04 93 58 02 02, www.chateau-st-martin.com*) on Avenue des Templiers on the

An Ice Cream Stop

With its hand-crafted ice cream in flavours ranging from Malaga to orange-carrot, **Les Comptoirs Coffédis** (04 93 24 60 39) in pedestrianised Place Clémenceau in Vence serves the back-country's best ice cream.

outskirts of Vence, and **La Colombe d'Or** (04 93 32 80 02, *www.la-colombe-dor.com*) in Saint-Paul de Vence's Place du Général de Gaulle, with a surprisingly earthy menu that belies its decor of priceless artworks and celebrity clientele.

Scattered around Saint-Paul de Vence are a number of tourist restaurants serving reasonably priced, family-friendly fare: we'd recommend **Le Caruso** (04 93 24 36 47) on Montée de la Castre near the church for pizzas, and **Malabar** (04 93 32 60 14) on the outer Rempart Ouest for hamburgers and ice creams.

❋ Le Tilleul ★ ★

Place du Tilleul, Saint-Paul de Vence, 04 93 32 80 36, *www.letilleul-saintpaul.com*

Le Tilleul is our favourite restaurant in Saint-Paul de Vence, its tables scattered on a pretty cobbled square shaded by a gnarled linden tree. Chef Stéphane Marie dreams up delicious French cuisine accompanied by a well-chosen wine menu. Kids choose between ham with pasta or chips. It's perfect for families juggling kids' meal-times, as it's open during the afternoon serving home-made sandwiches, Belgian waffles and ice cream. On

chilly days in spring and autumn, blankets are provided for outdoor diners.

Open *Daily noon–10:30pm* **Main courses** *14.50€–29€.* **Credit** *MC, V.*

One of our family favourites in Tourrettes-sur-Loup, the **Crêperie des Arts** (04 93 24 08 31) in Route de Vence, has changed ownership. Let's hope they keep the *steak-haché* filled Obélix savoury crepe on the menu.

FAMILY-FRIENDLY ACCOMMODATION

Grasse, Mougins & Around

Hôtel de Mougins ★ ★

205 avenue du Golf, Mougins, 04 92 92 17 07, *www.hotel-de-mougins. com*

Hôtel de Mougins combines the Provençal chic of an 18th-century *bastide* with the creature comforts of a full-service hotel. Pretty bedrooms and suites (all with terraces or balconies overlooking the garden) are housed in the old *bastide*, as well as in four recently built *mas* scattered around the lush Mediterranean garden. Gastronomic fare is served all year round at Le Jardin restaurant, where new Italian chef Alessio

Recipe: Courgette-blossom Fritters

Most children love this southern French dish. Here's how to make it at home:

- Courgette flowers
- 150g flour
- 250ml cold milk
- 2 eggs, separated
- Salt, pepper, parsley
- Vegetable oil

First make up the batter by combining the flour, milk and two egg yolks. Then beat the egg whites until stiff and fold them into the batter. Season with finely chopped parsley, salt and pepper. Dip your courgette flowers into the batter and fry them two at a time in sizzling oil. Remove them when they are lightly golden and serve immediately.

Giove serves up rich Mediterranean flavours. The hotel also offers in-room massages, you can enjoy a game of pétanque, or even book on one of their cookery courses. During the summer you can also enjoy informal lunchtime snacks at the Pool House.

Rooms 51. **Rates** Doubles from 195€, two connecting rooms for four from 430€, extra bed 50€. **Credit** MC, V. **Amenities** 📶 🍸 📺 💷 🖥 🍴 🖼

MODERATE

Clos des Cyprès ★ ★

87 chemin des Canebiers, Grasse, 📞 04 93 40 44 23, **www.closdes cypres.fr**

Avoid the ragged hotels in Grasse town centre in favour of this B&B a 10-minute drive away: with its rough dry-stone walling and hectares of wild-flower fields, it offers a slice of *vieux Provence*. Owners Pierre-André and Anne-Marie have carefully restored the 19th-century farmhouse with traditional lime-based paint, red hexagonal floor tiles and stylish pastel interiors. Rooms Narcisse and Jasmin both fit an additional bed comfortably. Lunch and dinner aren't provided, but you can use the BBQ and eat at one of the tables dotted around the garden. Keep an eye on your children around the pool, as it's only partly fenced off. If Clos des Cyprès is booked up, another local B&B worth trying is **La Surprise** (📞 06 77 86 86 38, **www.lasurprise.co.uk**) in Magagnosc.

Rooms 5. **Rates** Doubles from 80€, two adjoining rooms for four from 160€, extra bed 40€. **Credit** MC, V. **Amenities** 📺 🛏 🖥

INEXPENSIVE

Parc des Monges ★

635 chemin du Gabre, Auribeau sur Siagne, 📞 04 93 60 91 71, **www. parcdesmonges.com**

On the riverfront below the *village perché* of Auribeau-sur-Siagne lies this well-landscaped

Down on the Farm

Get back in touch with nature with a stay on a farm. Our favourite farm B&B is **Graine & Ficelle** (📞 *06 85 08 15 64, www.graine-ficelle. com*), with its stylish, rustic bedrooms and newly appointed eco-lodges.

Alternatively, if you're looking for a luxurious alternative to a real farm, try the eccentric hotel **Auberge de la Vignette Haute** (📞 *04 93 42 20 01, www.vignettehaute.com*), with its spacious rooms filled with antiques and richly coloured fabrics; the restaurant houses a glass-fronted stable where farm animals graze beside you as you dine.

campsite with its winter-flowering mimosa and summer-flowering oleander. Everything is spotlessly clean, from the cream-and-green paintwork of its chalets to the communal washing facilities. The site offers four-person mobile homes and five-person chalets for weekly rental (or 3 nights minimum out of high season) and camping/caravan sites for single-night stays. Mobile homes and chalets have wooden terraces, bathrooms and well-equipped kitchens; mobile homes also have cooker ventilation systems and separate toilets. Families are well catered for with a children's play area, table tennis, a *pétanque* court and a well-barricaded outdoor pool with a baby pool. You'll need to bring your own sheets, and organise a bank transfer in advance if you don't want to pay in cash.

Rooms *15 mobile homes and chalets, plus camping/caravan sites.* **Open** *Apr–Sept.* **Rates** *Four-person mobile homes from 400€ per week, camping/caravanning from 16.90€ for two adults, caravan/tent and car, then child over 7 4.10€, child under 7 from 3.50€.* **Credit** *Cash or bank*

transfer only. **Amenities** 🛎 💻 ∧ 🖼 ♀ ⚡ **In room** ☒ 🛏

INSIDER TIP
Families staying near Valbonne can enjoy day-pass access to the pool and sports facilities at **Club Med** (📞 *04 93 09 71 53, www. clubmed.fr*) in Opio. Tickets cost 90€ for adults, 70€ for kids aged 12–17, 50€ for kids from 4–11 and are free for those under 4 years. The restaurant also serves buffet lunch.

Vence & Around

MODERATE

Auberge de Tourrettes

11 route de Grasse, Tourrettes-sur-Loup, 📞 *04 93 59 30 05, www. aubergedetourrettes.fr*

Along the main street of violet village Tourrettes-sur-Loup, this stylish inn offers a convenient base for families to explore the back-country. Double bedrooms fit an extra cot, or there are two family suites, each with one double bedroom and a twin bedroom that can fit up to three single beds. The first-floor Suite Sureau has a gorgeous private

The *Mas* & the *Mistral*

The mas (farmhouse) presides across rural Provence and the Riviera back-country. Metre-thick stone walls, shuttered windows and triple-edged, terracotta-tiled roofs were built to resist the whistling *mistral* wind and the blistering summer sun. Much over-used nowadays by estate agents, the term *mas* traditionally referred to a low, rectangular farmhouse where families shared the same roof with sheep, doves and even silkworms.

terrace (choose a first-floor room if you don't fancy a long climb up the stairs). Another major selling point is its tearoom, with large windows overlooking the beautiful valley, serving simple food from cooked breakfasts and midday bruschettas and salads to tea-time muffins. There isn't a pool, alas, but you can chill out in the herb garden with deck-chairs aplenty.

Rooms 8. **Rates** *Doubles 110€, suites for four 240€; rates include breakfast.* **Credit** *AE, MC, V.* **Amenities** ☕ 🖥 **In room** 🖥 🗂

Le Hameau ★★★ VALUE

528 route de la Colle, outskirts of Saint-Paul de Vence, 📞 04 93 32 80 24, www.le-hameau.com

Set in a garden of citrus trees and jasmine, this is our favourite address in Saint-Paul de Vence. They've been in business for over 40 years, so clearly we're not the only fans—perhaps it's the reasonable prices in this unreasonably priced area that keep guests coming back. The converted 18th-century stables are reminiscent of haciendas, with their white-washed walls,

but interiors have a distinctly Provençal flavour: flowered *boutis* (quilts) and heavy wooden furniture predominate. Every one of its 17 air-conditioned rooms and 'apartments' is different; if you want to self-cater, no. 15 actually *is* an apartment, with a kitchen. For those with toddlers, I'd recommend the ground-floor rooms, to avoid winding staircases.

As well as an infinity pool, you can enjoy the use of a spa with a sauna, hammam (Turkish bath) and Jacuzzi. In summer, there are breakfast buffets on the flower-strewn terrace and lunch-time snacks around the pool.

Rooms 17. **Rates** *Doubles from 150€; family suites from 270€, extra bed 30€.* **Credit** *AE, MC, V.* **Amenities** 📶 🖥 📶 📷 🔒 🎤 **In room** A/C ✖ 📶 🗂 📺 🗂

Orion Bed & Breakfast ★★
GREEN

Impasse des Peupliers, 2436 chemin du Malvan, 10-minute drive from old village, Saint-Paul de Vence, 📞 04 93 24 87 51/06 75 45 18 64, www.orionbb.com

With its tree-houses named after Rudyard Kipling characters, the

The Cicada's Song

The humming of cigales (cicadas) is synonymous with the Provençal summer. Male *cigales* only buzz when the temperature reaches 20°C. So when you hear their summertime mating call, you know it's time to laze around on your terrace drinking pastis, with fresh lemonade for the children.

Orion is an eco-friendly children's paradise: natural fabrics are used in the tree-houses, which are scattered around the forested garden, and the outdoor pool is filtered through stones and aquatic plants. Owner Diane and her daughter Aina are charming hosts who speak fluent English. Children will love the trampoline, while adults will find the communal microwave, fridge and kitchenware useful.

There are two special family tree-houses: Colonel Hathi with two bedrooms and a double-sized shower, and the linked King Louie with a double bed and Mowgli with twin beds. If you prefer *terra firma*, there's a two-bed house with fully equipped kitchen. There's a 3-night minimum stay, with only week-long rentals during peak season. Note: the pool isn't fenced.

Rooms 5. **Rates** *four-person family tree-house for 3-night weekend or four-night midweek stay from 800€; rates include breakfast.* **Amenities** ▭ ⊥ ☴ ▭ *In room* @

Tree house at Orion Bed & Breakfast

5 The Western Côte & Inland Var

THE WESTERN CÔTE & INLAND VAR

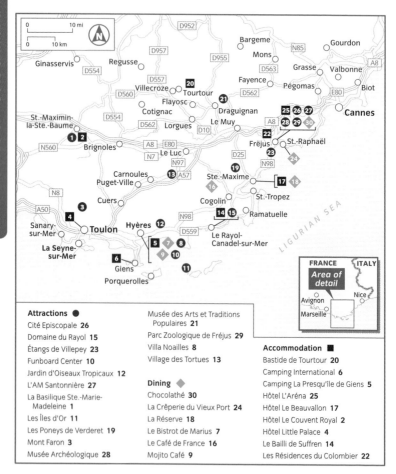

Attractions ●
Cité Episcopale **26**
Domaine du Rayol **15**
Étangs de Villepey **23**
Funboard Center **10**
Jardin d'Oiseaux Tropicaux **12**
L'AM Santonnière **27**
La Basilique Ste.-Marie-
  Madeleine **1**
Les Îles d'Or **11**
Les Poneys de Verderet **19**
Mont Faron **3**
Musée Archéologique **28**

Musée des Arts et Traditions
  Populaires **21**
Parc Zoologique de Fréjus **29**
Villa Noailles **8**
Village des Tortues **13**

Dining ◆
Chocolathé **30**
La Crêperie du Vieux Port **24**
La Réserve **18**
Le Bistrot de Marius **7**
Le Café de France **16**
Mojito Café **9**

Accommodation ■
Bastide de Tourtour **20**
Camping International **6**
Camping La Presqu'île de Giens **5**
Hôtel L'Aréna **25**
Hôtel Le Beauvallon **17**
Hôtel Le Couvent Royal **2**
Hôtel Little Palace **4**
Le Bailli de Suffren **14**
Les Résidences du Colombier **22**

From the Blue Flag beaches of the Western Côte to the forested
inland hills, the Var is a region of opposites. Day trippers dream
of Brigitte Bardot as they tan on Ramatuelle's star-studded beaches,
while locals produce cut flowers, honey and chestnuts in sleepy pro-
vincial towns. World champions windsurf on the Giens Peninsula as
fishermen darn sardine nets in Sanary-sur-Mer. Ancient and modern
lie cheek-by-jowl in Roman Fréjus where its 1st century AD amphitheatre now has a 21st-century glass-panelled counterpart designed by
Jean-Michel Wilmotte. Most of the 6,000 sq km of verdant inland
Var is little visited by the kitten heels and super-yacht owners that
crowd the St.-Tropez peninsula all summer long. Yet, come October,
designer boutiques and chic restaurants shut up shop, leaving this former fishing village to hibernate in peace.

Its capital city, Toulon, may leave you unimpressed, but the Western Côte is scattered with undiscovered beaches, child-friendly resorts and endless watersports that make it perfect for family beach holidays. When you've had your fill of beach fun, head inland to explore mimosa-strewn hilltop villages such as Bormes-les-Mimosas, Ramatuelle and Grimaud. Many Var towns hold *bravades* (acts of defiance): these festivals give an insight into local people who are grateful to their ancestors for defending their land from invasion over the centuries.

VISITOR INFORMATION

For general information and an overview of this multifaceted region, pay a visit to the website of **Var Tourism** (*www.tourismevar. com*). Families staying near Fréjus will find *www.kidookid.com* a useful English-language reference for activities and childcare advice.

Getting There

By Air Eastern resorts such as St.-Raphael and Fréjus are within easy reach of **Nice Airport** (📞 04 89 88 98 28, *www.nice.aeroport.fr*), (p. 58). The Central Var is best served by **Toulon-Hyères International Airport** (📞 08 25 01 83 87, *www.toulon-hyeres.aeroport.fr*), about 3km south of Hyères and 23km east of Toulon. **Ryanair** (p. 29) runs direct flights from London Stansted. Flight time is about 2 hours. For a wider choice of flight options, **Marseille** airport is a practical option for Western Var resorts. See p. 143.

By Train Anyone concerned about their carbon footprint can take the train from London to Toulon in about 7 hours and to St.-Raphaël in about 8: you take the Eurostar from St. Pancras to Lille or Paris, then catch a TGV. Contact Rail Europe (p. 32) for timetables and prices.

By Car See p. 30.

Orientation

The A57/A8 motorway runs inland from Toulon to St.-Raphaël, providing a quick route from one to the other and easy access to places in the inland Var, including Gonfaron (p. 125) and Brignoles. Alternatively, you can take the more picturesque, but often heavily congested, D559 (starting and ending on the N98) along the coast from Toulon to Ste.-Maxime.

Getting Around

The Var's coastal towns are well connected by train (except for St.-Tropez and Ste. -Maxime), bus and boat. However, services to inland Var villages are less frequent and can be erratic. For bus timetables, contact **Sodetrav** (📞 08 25 00 06 50, *www.sodetrav. fr*); for regional train timetables, see *www.ter-sncf.com*.

Companies offering car hire at the airport and train station include EasyCar and Alamo (p. 36).

The Saint

Born in Pisa, Torpes was a Roman citizen who converted to Christianity under St. Paul. He was beheaded for refusing to give up his faith, and his corpse was put in a boat that eventually washed up on the shores of what was subsequently named St.-Tropez after him.

WHAT TO SEE & DO

Children's Top 10 Attractions

❶ **Arriving** by boat in St.-Tropez (p. 121) from neighbouring Ste. -Maxime or Fréjus.

❷ **Sunning** yourself on the cleanest and most beautiful beaches in the South of France (p. 125).

❸ **Riding** pure-bred Arab horses in the forested Massif de Maures (p. 123).

❹ **Taking** a cable car up Mont Faron for a breathtaking view (p. 124).

❺ **Learning** about tortoises and donkeys in Gonfaron (p. 125).

❻ **Exploring** the heavenly Îles d'Or (p. 126).

Fast Facts: St.-Tropez, St.-Raphaël & Fréjus

Banks: **HSBC** is at 39 rue François Sibilli, St.-Tropez, and 71 boulevard d'Alsace, St.-Raphaël; **Barclays** is at 68 place de la Porte d'Hermès, Port Fréjus.

Hospitals: Hôpital de St.-Tropez (☎ 04 98 12 50 00) on RD559 in Gassin, and the **Centre Hospitalier Intercommunal Fréjus St.-Raphaël** (☎ 04 94 40 21 21, www.chi-frejus-saint-raphael.fr), 240 chemin de St.-Lambert, Fréjus, both have 24-hour emergency service.

Internet Cafés: **Kreatik Café** (☎ 04 94 49 20 14), Rue Pierre Curie, St.-Tropez, is open Monday to Saturday 10am to 12:30pm and 2:30 to 6pm. **Cyber-Sp@ce** (☎ 04 94 82 29 90), 104 chemin de la Lauve les Impérators, St.-Raphaël, is open Monday to Thursday 10am to 7pm, Friday 10am to 10pm, Saturday 2 to10pm.

Pharmacies: There are chemists at 9 quai de Suffren, St.-Tropez; 62 rue du Général de Gaulle, Fréjus; 846 boulevard de la Mer, Port Fréjus; and 33 rue Alphonse Karr, St.-Raphaël.

Post Offices: Post offices are located at Place Alphonse Celli, St.-Tropez; Avenue Victor Hugo, St.-Raphaël; 75 rue de la Juiverie, Fréjus Old Town; and Place de la République, Fréjus Plage.

Shopping: See p. 131 and, for markets, p. 133.

English-language Cinemas

For English-language films, look for the 'VO' (version originale) symbol. For current listings, see **www.angloinfo.com**.

Cinéma Lido, Rue Amiral Baux, St.-Raphaël, ☏ *08 92 68 69 28.*

Eldorado, Boulevardbld Gabriel Peri, Draguignan, ☏ *08 92 68 00 71.*

L'Olbia, Rue du Soldat Bellon, Hyères, ☏ *08 92 89 28 92.*

Le Cinéma, Cours de la République, Lorgues, ☏ *08 92 68 05 92.*

Le Pagnol, Carré Léon Gaumont, 107 route du Plan de la Tour, Ste. -Maxime, ☏ *08 92 68 72 12/04 94 43 26 10.*

Le Royal, 2 rue du Docteur Jean Bertholet, Toulon, ☏ *08 92 89 28 92.*

❼ Viewing Roman finds and ruins in Fréjus (p. 121).

❽ Checking out the fish in St.-Raphaël's market (p. 121).

❾ Watching dolphins off the coast of Fréjus (p. 121).

❿ Windsurfing or kayaking around the Giens peninsula (p. 126).

Child-friendly Events & Entertainment

Mimosa Festival ★

Bormes-les-Mimosas (www. bormeslesmimosas.com), Le Rayol-Canadel (www.lerayolcanadel.fr), Ste.-Maxime (www.ste-maxime. com), St.-Raphaël (☏ 04 94 19 52 52, www.saint-raphael.com)

A native of Australia, the mimosa has been celebrated every year since it was introduced to the southern French coast in the 19th century. Between January and March, resorts along the Var coastline hold week-long festivals to honour this sunny member of the acacia family, heralding the end of winter. Events include the election of 'Miss Mimosa', a themed carnival parade, markets, exhibitions and guided tours (on foot or by coach) to see the flowers in all their glory. Don't leave without buying mimosa-flavoured sweets or cordial.

*Jan–Mar. **Adm** Free.*

Fête de la Bravade

St.-Tropez, ☏ 08 92 68 48 28, www. ot-saint-tropez.com

Many towns in Provence have a *bravade* ('act of defiance') in their event calendar. Arguably the biggest and best is the one that takes place in St.-Tropez in May, in celebration of the Tropezian army who protected the port from invaders during the Renaissance. Men dress up in old-fashioned military uniforms and women in Provençal costumes to march through the streets firing muskets, playing whistles and banging drums (it's definitely not for the sensitive of hearing). After plenty of singing and dancing, the festival ends with a Mass to celebrate St.

Tropez (in English, Torpes) himself, whose effigy is carried through the streets.

May. **Adm** *Free.*

Fête des Enfants ★★

Hyères, ☎ *04 94 00 78 82, www. hyeres-tourisme.com*

If you're in the region at Christmas, there's nowhere better to bring your children than Hyères, where the streets are filled with entertainment including puppet shows and dancing displays, to accompany the traditional Christmas market. There are also film screenings, performances of musicals, and workshops in photography, fashion, dance and circus skills, and more. Even if you don't speak French, you'll enjoy soaking up the atmosphere, especially given that all events are free.

Last 2 weeks Dec. **Adm** *Free.*

Cities, Towns & Resorts

Draguignan

Tourist office: ☎ *04 94 50 16 20, www.dracenie.com*

The former capital of the Var has a somewhat down-at-heel feel, although the grand *sous-préfecture* (town hall) and elegant town houses give the old town a faded charm. Apart from climbing the 17th-century clock tower, with its table-top views and the **Musée des Arts et Traditions Populaires** (☎ *04 94 47 05 72*), there's not much for families to see in central Draguignan. However, the surrounding countryside offers plenty to explore, from the

intriguing **Pierre de la Fée** dolmen (p. 130) to numerous picturesque villages, including restaurant-rich **Flayosc** (p. 137), medieval **Tourtour** and **Villecroze** for its troglodyte caves.

Hyères ★

Tourist office: ☎ *04 94 00 78 24, www.hyeres-tourisme.com*

Provence's most southerly resort is where tourism in the South of France began, after well-heeled but consumptive visitors, including Queen Victoria, wintered here in the 18th century. Temperate and palm-filled Hyères has plenty to offer families, particularly if you love watersports. But first take a gander at the old town: wander around the cobbled streets with their plethora of health food shops, admire the 19th-century villas and have lunch in quaint Place Massillon, then hike uphill to the Mediterranean gardens of Parc Ste.-Claire and Parc St.-Bernard (p. 128) for staggering views over the Var coast.

No trip to Hyères would be complete without a boat trip to the nearby **Îles d'Or** (p. 126), known for their tranquillity, beauty and diving. Sporty families will also love the **Giens peninsula**, famous for its windsurfing, its **Blue Flag beaches** and 'double tombolo'—two 4km strips of land, with an interior marsh.

Ste. -Maxime and St.-Tropez ★★

Ste. -Maxime tourist office: ☎ *04 94 55 75 55, www.ste-maxime.com*

St.-Tropez tourist office: ☎ *08 92 68 48 28, www.ot-saint-tropez.com*

Parc St. Bernard, Hyeres

These two towns sitting opposite each other across the Bay of St.-Tropez epitomise the glamour of the Côte d'Azur. Mimosa-strewn **Ste. -Maxime** is the calmer half of the desirable duo. Endless Blue Flag beaches such as the famed **La Nartelle** and **Plage des Eléphants** (p. 124), as well as excellent restaurants, kids' play areas, merry-go-rounds and summer trampolines make it a good option for a seaside sojourn. Along La Croisette, the **Jardin Botanique** is also worth a visit. Sadly, the main coastal route into St.-Tropez runs along the seafront in Ste. -Maxime—avoid this busy road by opting for the **Bâteaux Verts** (see below) that offer a 20-minute boat service into central St.-Tropez.

Neighbouring **St.-Tropez** is in a league of its own. Its narrow streets are chock-a-block with chic shops and restaurants where day trippers mingle with the rich, the famous and the designer-clad. It's worth a visit just to goggle at the super-yachts backed into the picturesque quayside harbour or gaze toward the Alps from the 17th-century **citadelle**. Unlike some of its summer visitors, the pastel-painted village of St.-Tropez is remarkably unspoilt—town planners keep a very tight eye on development.

Even though some places come with a large price tag, savvy families can enjoy St.-Tropez without maxing out the credit card. Theme parks such as **Azur Parc** and **Aqualand** (p. 129) are nearby, while culture vultures will love the **Musée de l'Annonciade** (p. 129). Neither resort has a train station so best access is by boat, car, bus or—for the well-heeled only—helicopter.

INSIDER TIP ≫

Driving to St.-Tropez between April and September is insanity— you'll spend hours in traffic jams. Your best option is to take the boat from St.-Raphaël to St.-Tropez (04 94 95 17 46, *www. tmr-saintraphael.com*) or between Ste. -Maxime and four other ports including St.-Tropez (04 94 49 29 39, *www. bateauxverts.com*)—a trip that children will love. Although it's busy, Saturday (market day) is a good time to visit.

St.-Raphaël and Fréjus ★★★

St.-Raphaël tourist office: 04 94 19 52 52, *www.saint-raphael.com*

Fréjus tourist office: 04 94 51 83 83, *www.frejus.fr*

ST.-TROPEZ

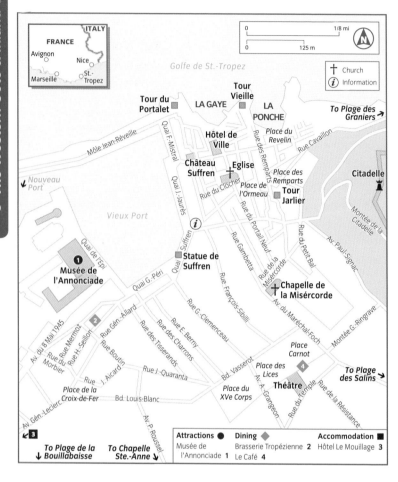

Golfe de St.-Tropez

FRANCE
ITALY
Avignon
Nice
Marseille
St.-Tropez

† Church
ⓘ Information

Tour Vieille
Tour du Portalet
LA GAYE
LA PONCHE

To Plage des Graniers →

Môle Jean-Réveille
Place du Revelin
Hôtel de Ville
Rue Cavaillon

Nouveau Port

Quai F.-Mistral

Château Suffren
Eglise
Place des Remparts
Citadelle

Rue du Clocher
Place de l'Ormeau
Tour Jarlier

Quai J.-Jaurès

Vieux Port

Rue du Portail Neuf
Montée de la Citadelle

ⓘ

Rue du Petit Bal

Quai de l'Épi

Statue de Suffren

Quai Suffren

Rue Gambetta

Av. Paul-Signac

Musée de l'Annonciade

Quai G.-Péri

Rue F.-Sibilli

Rue de la Miséricorde

Chapelle de la Misércorde

Av. du Maréchal-Foch

Rue G.-Clemenceau

Av. du 8 Mai 1945
Rue Rue Mermoz
Rue Gén.-Allard

Rue H.-Seillon
Rue des Tisserands
Rue des Charrons

Place Carnot

Montée G.-Ringrave

Rue du Morbier
Rue Boutin
Bd. Vasserot

Place des Lices

To Plage des Salins →

Rue J. Aicard
Rue J.-Quaranta

Place du XVe Corps
Théâtre

Rue A.-Grangeon

Rue du Temple
Rue de la Résistance

Place de la Croix-de-Fer
Bd. Louis-Blanc

Av. Gén.-Leclerc
Av. P. Roussel

To Plage de la Bouillabaisse ↓
To Chapelle Ste.-Anne ↓

Attractions ●	Dining ◆	Accommodation ■
Musée de l'Annonciade 1	Brasserie Tropézienne 2	Hôtel Le Mouillage 3
	Le Café 4	

Seventies-style apartment blocks have marred these affordable seaside resorts, but few can argue with their spectacular natural resources: numerous sandy beaches and a backdrop of the red-hued Estérel mountain range. Coupled with their plethora of sea- and land-based activities and their close proximity to the glittering French Riviera (Cannes is a 30-minute train ride away), Fréjus and St.-Raphaël are very popular with families.

Gaul's oldest Roman city, **Fréjus**, is dotted with impressive Roman remains, and the pretty old town is home to well-priced art galleries (following a successful local government makeover replacing dodgy bars with subsidised artists' studios). Families can enjoy the smart seafront with its numerous roundabouts and rides. The upscale neighbourhood of **St.-Aygulf** is a great base for enjoying top family attractions such as the Var's largest activity park, **Base Nature**, theme parks **Aqualand** and **Luna Park** (p. 76) and the **Étangs de Villepey** nature reserve (p. 126).

Neighbour **St-Raphaël** is a shadow of its turn-of-the-20th-century glory, when it was the exclusive watering hole for France's literati. Nowadays it's best known for its **Santa Lucia Marina** (the third-largest on the Riviera) and for shopping. You can enjoy exploring the numerous kids' shops (p. 131) and the lively daily **Marché République** food market.

Toulon OVERRATED

Tourist office: 📞 *04 94 18 53 00,* **www.toulontourisme.com**

This major naval base, the Var's capital, has cleaned up its act considerably since the demise of the Front National-led council, but it's still not the most attractive place to spend precious holiday time. Aside from the port with its tourist train and boat trips, the real reason to come here is to take the cable car up Mont Faron (p. 124) for views, walks and a zoo.

Natural Wonders & Spectacular Views

Massif de Maures ★

Stretching from Hyères to Fréjus and covering around 1,350 sq km, the Massif de Maures, with forests in the north and *maquis* scrubland undergrowth in the drier south, has plenty to interest families. Active types will find that there's plenty of scope for walking, cycling and horse-riding, and everyone should make time to stop off in the peaceful village of **Collobrières** (tourist office: 📞 *04 94 48 08 00,* **www. collobrieres.fr**), which has a thriving chestnut-growing and cork-production industry, and makes a good base for discovering the inland Massif. Afterwards, travel north on the winding D39 to the area's highest point, **Notre-Dame des Anges** (780m), to take in the panoramic views and the chapel. From here, continue north towards the N97 and **Gonfaron**—home of the **Tortoise Village** and a flying-donkey legend (p. 126).

Whistle-stop Villages

Flower-strewn, hilltop villages abound near the coastline; among the most celebrated are **Bormes-les-Mimosas, Ramatuelle** and **Grimaud.** Further inland, few villages can match the imposing position of **Mons,** perched 820m (2,700 ft) above sea level. Although it's a trek, you'll be rewarded with to-die-for views over forested hills towards the Riviera coastline. It's also the perfect place for a family Sunday lunch, at **Lou San Bastian** (p. 136).

Plage d'Argent, Porquorelles

Mont Faron ★★

For far-reaching views over the port of Toulon and the Var coast, visit this 480m chalk hill—children love the 10-minute ride up in the **cable car** (☏ *04 94 92 68 25*, *www.telepherique-faron.com*) from Boulevard Amiral Vence (the fainthearted can drive, although the hairpin bends might prove just as nerve-jangling). First stop at the top has to be the **zoo** (☏ *04 94 88 07 89*), which specialises in breeding big cats. In summer, a horse-drawn cart is on hand to take you from the cable car to the zoo. Save money by buying a combined ticket for Mont Faron's cable car and zoo, at 12.50€ for adults and 8.50€ for children aged 4 to 10.

For military enthusiasts, there are also 19th-century forts and the **Museum of Provence Landings** (☏ *04 94 88 08 09*). There are plenty of spots for a picnic under the Aleppo pines; **Le Panoramique**

restaurant (☏ *04 94 88 08 00*) is a good alternative for lunch.

Aquaria & Animal Parks

Jardin d'Oiseaux Tropicaux ★

RD559, La Londe, between Hyères and Bormes-les-Mimosas, ☏ *04 94 35 02 15*, *www.jotropico.org*

The 6-hectare Tropical Bird Garden is home to more exotic plants and birds than you could shake a bamboo stick at, including some 600 species of plants and trees. As you wander through the fresh-smelling forest, cactus-rich Mexican garden and palm grove, you can admire parrots from the Pacific, ibis from Africa, and jabirus, the tallest flying birds in South America. Allow about half a day for a visit.

Open *Daily 9:30am–7pm June–Sept, daily 2–6pm Feb–May and Oct, Wed, Sat and Sun 2–5pm Nov–Jan.* ***Adm*** *9€, children 2–12 5€.* ***Credit*** *MC, V.* ***Amenities*** 🏕️ 🍴

The Best Beaches

The Western Côte offers many beautiful Blue Flag beaches, but you'll have to head west of Le Lavandou to avoid the crowds. The most family-friendly include:

Plage d'Argent, Porquerolles island, Hyères (Blue Flag). A short walk from the village, this Caribbean-esque public, white-sand beach is reputedly the most beautiful in southern France.

Plage de la Nartelle, Ste.-Maxime (Blue Flag). A supervised sandy beach with public and private areas.

Plage des Jumeaux, Route de l'Epi, Ramatuelle (04 94 55 21 80). A family-friendly private beach on the Ramatuelle peninsula, with a restaurant, shop and playground.

Plage du Dramont, RD559, St.-Raphaël. One of the main sites of the 1944 Provence Landings, this public pebble beach has watersports and a restaurant.

Parc Zoologique de Fréjus

 04 98 11 37 37, www.zoo-frejus. com

With the closure of Cap-Ferrat Zoo, local families are thronging to Fréjus as the next-best thing. Several animals from Cap-Ferrat are being re-homed here and a new lions' den and monkey house are currently under construction. This safari-style zoo is very spread out, so it's best to visit by car.

Open Daily 10am–6pm June–Aug, daily 10am–5pm Mar–May and Sept–Oct, daily 10:30am–4:30pm Nov–Feb. **Adm** adults 14€, children 3–9 9.50€, children under 3 free. **Credit** MC, V. **Amenities** ⚲ 📷 ♀

Village des Tortues ★★

Quartier des plaines, Gonfaron, 04 94 78 26 41, www.villagetortues.com

Do you know what a tortoise looks like underneath its shell? How long do the babies take to hatch? You can find out the answers to these questions and more from a volunteer guide or

from the audiovisual display at Tortoise Village, a specialist sanctuary on the edge of the **Massif de Maures** (p. 123). As well as being a breeding centre for the threatened **Hermann tortoise**, the last land tortoise in France, the 2-hectare park is a refuge for sick or abandoned tortoises; walking around the shady paths, you'll see more than 2,500 of the creatures nesting, incubating, being nursed or bathing in the pools. For 30€ you can pick one to sponsor.

Open Daily 9am–7pm Mar–Sept; daily 9am–6pm Oct–Feb **Adm** 10€, children 5–16 6€ (discounted entry if you buy on the website). **Credit** MC, V. **Amenities** 📷 ⚲ ⚲ 📷 ♀

Natural Reserves, Parks & Gardens

Domaine du Rayol ★ FIND

Avenue des Belges, Le Rayol-Canadel, 04 98 04 44 00, www. domainedurayol.org

FUN FACT ⟩⟩ **Flying Donkeys...** ⟨⟨

Legend has it that a donkey flew down a ravine near Gonfaron in the 17th century—and the event, the Fête de l'Ane, is still celebrated here every March.

Dense forest, exotic flowers, waves crashing on the shore and the occasional cry from an unidentified bird—you could almost be in an episode of *Lost*. Families could easily spend half a day exploring the grounds of this waterside 19th-century villa, which has gardens devoted to flora from the Mediterranean, South Africa, Australia, California and Chile. Although guided tours are only available in French, there's English-language information to help you find your way around. As well as a year-long event and workshop calendar, from June to September there's a 'marine garden' to explore wearing the snorkel and flippers provided (ages 8 and up; booking required). The café with its home-made quiches is a good spot for lunch.

Open *Daily 9:30am–7:30pm July and Aug, 9:30am–6:30pm Apr–June, Sept and Oct, 9:30am–5:30pm Nov–Mar.* ***Adm*** *9€, children aged 6–18 6€, children under 6 free, family ticket 19€.* ***Credit*** *MC, V.* ***Amenities*** 🅿 🛍

Étangs de Villepey ★ VALUE

Off RN98 west of Fréjus, www. frejus.fr

Known as the 'Petite Camargue Varoise', these 260 hectares of marshland are a haven for migrating birds, and you can follow the footpaths (or hide in the hide), picking out flamingos, egrets and ducks from over 250 species that visit here. It's especially busy during March and September. When you've had enough of wildlife, there's always the beach of St.-Aygulf or the Var's largest activity park, **Base Nature** (📞 *04 94 51 91 10*), next door; entry is free, although entry to the swimming pool costs 3€.

Open *Daily dawn till dusk.* ***Adm*** *Free.*

Les Îles d'Or ★★

Off coast of Hyères, www.hyeres-tourisme.com

These three small islands are a world away from the glitz and glamour of the Côte d'Azur, but their fine sandy beaches, Caribbean-clear waters and multitude of activities make them a must-visit. Each island has its own personality. **Porquerolles** is the largest and most developed, with 54km of signposted paths for cycling or walking, white sandy beaches and several hotels and restaurants of variable quality (we recommend taking a picnic instead). It's just a 20-minute boat ride from La Tour Fondue at the tip of the **Giens peninsula** (see *www.tlv-tvm.com*). Neighbouring **Port Cros** is the smallest, wildest and most mountainous of the islands, and also a diver's paradise. In 1963 it became Europe's first **national park,**

Lire & Learn

The Var has a rich history in children's literature. Little Prince author Antoine de St.-Exupéry had a home in Agar in St.-Raphaël, and you can admire a fountain monument to the boy-hero there. Meanwhile, the privately owned **Île d'Or,** off Dramont beach, was immortalised by *Tin Tin* creator **Hergé** in **L'Île Noire**. **Ste.-Maxime** was the birthplace of bedtime favourite *Babar the Elephant*, created here in the 1930s by resident **Jean de Brunhoff**—in *Babar's Travels* you'll see one of the village's beaches, now known as Plage des Eléphants.

incorporating a maritime zone (Porquerolles is similarly protected), and you can sign up for a 40-minute accompanied or self-guided underwater discovery trail. The **Île du Levant** is most famous for its naturist resort, Heliopolis, but 90% of the island is a military base and no-go area.

Historic Buildings & Monuments

Cité Episcopale ★

58 rue du Cardinal Fleury, Fréjus, 📞 *04 94 51 26 30, www.frejus.fr*

In the heart of Fréjus old town, the bishop's palace, a compact collection of rosy religious buildings, is worth an hour or so of anyone's time. The octagonal baptistery dates from the 5th century, making it the oldest in France—notice the small door where disciples entered and the larger door where they exited after being baptised. Make sure to look up as you walk around 'ye ancient Cloister' to spy the 14th-century paintings of fantastical beasts, then buy a monster-themed colouring book from the

little shop. The adjacent archaeology museum (p. 128) is unmissable, and the coolness of the cathedral on a hot day is worth its weight in ecumenical silver. Stop for a drink in the little square when you've finished.

Open *Daily 9am–6:30pm June–Sept, Tues–Sun 9am–noon and 2–5pm Oct–May.* **Adm** *5€, under 25s free.* **Amenities** *Guided tours (in French). Disabled access.* **Credit** *MC, V.*

La Basilique Ste.-Marie-Madeleine ★ VALUE

St.-Maximin-la-Ste. -Baume, 📞 *04 94 59 84 59, www.lesamisdela basilique.com*

Da Vinci Code addicts will enjoy exploring the mystery of Mary Magdalene's remains at this imposing Gothic basilica. In the crypt lies a finely grained marble sarcophagus that many believe is the genuine tomb of this saintly sinner; the book suggests it's beneath the glass pyramid at the Louvre in Paris.

There's parking nearby, but it's difficult to find spaces on market days (Wednesdays). Just opposite the basilica, **La Table en Provence** (📞 *04 94 59 84 61*) is

TIP **Park Life**

Although a small town, Hyères (p. 120) has three parks of note: **Parc Olbius Riquier**, with a minizoo, pony rides, wandering peacocks and a playground; **Parc St.-Bernard**, at the foot of Villa Noailles (p. 128), with wonderful coastline views; and **Parc Ste. Claire**, the former home of American writer Edith Wharton (1862–1937). Entry to all three parks is free.

the perfect stop for ice creams and simple snacks.
Open *Daily 9:30am–6pm.* ***Adm*** *Free.*

Villa Noailles ★ VALUE

Montée de Noailles, Hyères, ☎ *04 98 08 01 98,* ***www.villanoailles-hyeres. com***

In a town with a Templar tower and a ruined castle, it comes as a bit of a shock to stumble across this **Cubist** villa (although you'll have to climb up a steep hill to get here). Designed by Robert Mallet-Stevens for aristo Charles Noailles in the 1920s, the villa played host in its heyday to avant-garde luminaries such as Jean Cocteau and Man Ray, who made a film here in 1929. Although only open to the public for rotating design, fashion and photography exhibitions (check the website or phone in advance), the villa still adheres to its artsy past, hosting the **International Festival of Fashion and Photography** every May, and acting as one of the venues for the December **Children's Festival** (p. 120). Even if you can't go inside, the gardens (Parc St.-Bernard; p. 128) are worth a look for the views alone. The tourist office organises guided tours in English.

Open *During exhibitions only; visit website or call ahead for details.* ***Adm*** *Free.*

> **INSIDER TIP**
>
> Fit in a trip to the **Musée des Arts et Traditions Populaires** (☎ *04 94 47 05 72*) in central Draguignan. Set within a pretty 18th-century town house in the old town, this well-designed ethnographic museum charts the history of Provençal life through reconstructions and audio-visual guides. Open Tuesday to Saturday; entry is free for kids up to 18 (3.50€ for adults).

Top Museums

Musée Archéologique ★★
FIND

Place Calvini, Fréjus, ☎ *04 94 52 15 78,* ***www.frejus.fr***

Small but perfectly formed, this little archaeology museum, part of the **Cité Episcopale** (p. 127), displays some exceptional Roman-era finds from the environs. Pride of place goes to the **double-headed Hermes**: dating from 1st century AD and dug up in 1970, it is now the emblem of Fréjus—where else can you spot it around town? Opposite you'll see a complete mosaic of a panther taken from a Roman house, and in the next room are scale

TIP ▶ The Best Theme Parks ◀

Aqualand (*www.aqualand.fr*), Quartier Le Capou, RN98, Fréjus (📞 *04 94 51 82 51*), and also at Route Plan de la Tour, CD25, Ste.-Maxime (📞 *04 94 55 54 54*), provides water-based fun for all. The park in Ste.-Maxime is more suitable for families with younger children. Both parks are open daily from mid-June to early September. Tickets cost 25 € for adults, 18.50€ for kids age 3–-12 and are free for kids under 3.

Azur Park (📞 *04 94 56 48 39*, *www.azurpark.com*), off N98, Carrefour de la Four, near St.-Tropez. As well as more than 28 attractions, there's an 18-hole golf course, dinosaurs and a wood-fired grill restaurant. It's open every evening from April to September; entry is free with discount passes for multiple rides from 10€.

Kiddy Parc (📞 *04 94 57 68 93*, *www.kiddyparc.com*), Avenue de l'Aéroport, Hyères. Go-karts, minimotos, inflatables, swimming pools and a minifarm should keep 2- to –12- year-olds happy here for an afternoon. The park is open all year with tickets for kids aged 2 years and above from 13.90€; accompanying adults go free. There's also a funfair at nearby **Magic World** (📞 *04 94 38 51 03*).

Le Jardin de César et Léonie (📞 *04 94 45 11 43/06 86 87 82 36*, *www. cesar-et-leonie.fr*), 721 chemin du Jas de la Paro, Le Muy. This theme park offers nature-based fun, including botanical workshops, tree-top adventures and horse or donkey treks in the heart of the Massif de Maures. Open from April to October, the theme park offers entry passes from 19.50€ for adults and 15€ for kids under 12.

---

models of a Roman house and the old port of Fréjus.

Open Tues–Sun 9:30am–12:30pm and 2–6pm mid-Apr–mid-Oct, 9:30am–12:30pm and 2–5pm mid-Oct–mid-Apr. **Adm** Adults 4.60€, accompanied children under 12 free. **Credit** Cash only.

Musée de l'Annonciade ★★

Place Grammont, St.-Tropez, 📞 04 94 17 84 10, www.ot-saint-tropez.com

When you've gorged on ice cream from **Barbarac** (p. 136), gazed wistfully at the super-yachts and fought your way through the crowds, seek some solace in the airy 16th-century Annonciade chapel. With world-class paintings by Braque, Dufy, Matisse and Seurat, this temple of 20th-century art should be on everyone's 'to do' list. The best thing about it is that it allows you to see St.-Tropez itself depicted through the decades in all its golden glory—thanks to painter Paul Signac, who installed himself here in 1892, the village became a honey-pot for avant-garde artists. Look out for the still life by underrated and overlooked Suzanne Vala-don, mother of Maurice Utrillo. If you don't want to be followed around by guards, it's best to put toddlers in buggies.

Open Daily 10am–noon and 2–6pm July–Sept, Wed–Mon 10am–noon and 2–6pm Oct–June. **Adm** Adults

The Fairy & the Fiancé

The Pierre de la Fée (fairy stone) dolmen near Draguignan is an extraordinarily large Neolithic (2,500–2,000 BC) stone table supported by columns that weigh more than 20 tonnes and contain bone fragments. Legend tells that a fairy, disguised as a shepherdess, seduced a young man and accepted his wedding proposal on the condition that he made her a table from three huge stones. After toiling long and hard to manoeuvre two stones, the young man couldn't budge the third. The fairy used her magical powers to help lift the third stone into place, whereupon the young man realised that he was condemned to die for loving one of greater talent (try explaining that to the children). He died and was turned to stone.

You'll find the Pierre de la Fée on Route de Montferrat on the outskirts of Draguignan, about 1½km from the centre.

5€, children under 12 free. **Credit** *Cash only.* **Amenities** 🛍

INSIDER TIP ≫

A **Fréjus Pass** gives you entry to five sites including the town's archaeology museum, local history museum and amphitheatre. It costs 4.60€ for adults, 3.10€ for children aged 12–18, pensioners and family groups, and is valid for 7 days.

Arts & Crafts

L'AM Santonnière ★★
AGE 7 & UP

73 rue de Bausset, Fréjus, 📞 04 93 45 48 90/06 80 83 00 34 **www. santondeprovence.com**

You'll have seen plenty of these little clay figures on your travels around Provence, but this is the only place you'll be able to design and sculpt your own (or anything else that takes your fancy), during 2-hour workshops (in French) for adults and children.

Open Wed and Sat 3–6:30pm. **Workshop** *Adults 25€, children 7–15 20€.* **Credit** *Cash only.*

Active Families

Funboard Center ★★
AGE 7 & UP

Route de l'Almanarre, Hyères, 📞 04 94 57 95 33, **www.funboardcenter. com**

Almanarre beach on the windy Giens peninsula is a world-famous spot for wind- and kite-surfing, and the perfect place for children to learn from the experts. Run by a world champion, this watersports centre offers private, group and week-long courses for young and old. You can also rent kayaks to explore the coast *en famille*.

Open Daily 9am–6pm. **Rates** *Beginner's week-long course, 150€, individual lesson in English 45€ (1 hour).* **Credit** *Cash only.*

Hand-decorated santons

INSIDER TIP >

Set in the Massif des Maures countryside near Ste. -Maxime, **Les Poneys de Verderet** (📞 06 83 34 87 66, *www. leverderet.ffe.com*) is a great place to come horse-riding. Highly qualified instructor Valérie Lacaze offers 20-minute pony rides for tots (7€) or hour-long lessons for kids over 6 (20€). You'll need to wear long trousers and sturdy shoes.

Shopping

Caribou Nature ★★

1 passage du Peyron, next to Marché République in Vieille Ville, St.-Raphäel, 📞 04 94 40 54 28, www. caribounature.com

Filled to the gills with traditional wooden toys, Caribou Nature is the kind of toyshop I'd love to have around the corner. The last time I visited, I came back laden with puzzles, mobiles and a wooden train set for my kids. The **Marché République**—the

town's best morning food market—is next door.

Open Tues–Sat 9:30am–12:30pm 3–7pm (plus some Sun and Mon mornings during school holidays). Credit MC, V.

INSIDER TIP >

St.-Raphaël has two other good children's shops. Buy toys and games from **Au Pays des Merveilles** (115 rue Jules Barbier, 📞 04 94 95 24 66) and clothes from **Du Pareil au Même** (148 rue Jean Aicard, 📞 04 94 17 26 14).

Confiserie Azuréenne

Boulevard Koenig, Collobrières, 📞 04 94 48 07 20, www.confiserie azureenne.com

The inland Var village of Collobrières is best known for its chestnut production: about 900 hectares of trees yield about 600 tonnes every October, a harvest that is celebrated with a festival. This little museum-shop honours the shiny brown chestnut in

Little Tourist Trains

Le Petit Train de Pignes (☎ 06 13 21 68 42) in **Ste.-Maxime** takes you on 40-minute trips to the top of Sémaphore hill for sweeping views over the Bay of St.-Tropez. In July and August, you can enjoy moonlit trips from 9pm to midnight. Another little train (☎ 04 94 97 22 85, **www.art-concept.net/petit-train-grimaud**) runs from Port Grimaud to the pretty *village perché* of **Grimaud,** one of the oldest villages in the Maures, which is much more fun than driving. In **Toulon**, learn all about the city's naval history on the little train that leaves from the port (☎ 06 20 77 44 43). It's a 25-minute journey each way. Tickets cost 6.50€ for adults and 3.50€ for kids.

all its states: in jam, nougat, ice cream and, of course, as *marrons glacés*. You can shop online, and try out recipes too.

Open *Daily 9:30am–12:30pm and 2–6:30pm.* **Credit** *MC, V.*

K Jacques ★

25 rue Allard, St.-Tropez, ☎ *04 94 54 83 63,* **www.kjacques.com**

Although Atelier Rondini claims to be the first shop in St.-Tropez that sold *la sandale tropézienne*, this shop stocks a bigger and more attractive selection of the gladiator-like sandals favoured by the fashion elite. Expect to pay at least 100€ for the smallest child's pair.

Open *Daily 10am–12:30pm and 3–7pm mid-Mar–Sept.* **Credit** *MC, V.*

Maison de la Tarte ★★ FIND

33 rue Jean-Jaurès, Fréjus, ☎ *04 94 51 17 34*

This tart shop is a feast for the senses—you'll barely be able to tear yourself away from the window display, though you'll need to if you want to sample a slice

of one of the 12 varieties, including banana and chocolate or fig. It's also a convenient place to pick up a morning croissant or baguette.

Open *Mon–Sat 6am–7pm.* **Credit** *Cash only.*

So

3 place St.-François de Paule, Fréjus, ☎ *06 11 54 14 24*

This colourful and wacky little shop in the old town sells own-range designer togs for adults and children, as well as a stylish line in home decor.

Open *Tues–Sat 10am–noon and 3–6:30pm.* **Credit** *Cash only.*

FAMILY-FRIENDLY DINING

Fréjus & St.-Raphaël

Head to Rue Sieyès in Fréjus to stock up on picnic items: melt-in-the-mouth cheeses from **Mon Fromager** (☎ 04 94 40 67 99) or spit-roast chickens and Paella from **Maison Belu** (☎ 04 94 51 39 66).

The Best Local Markets

Fish market: Vieux Port, St.-Raphaël, every morning.

Fish, food & flower market: Rue Fernand Bessy, Ste.-Maxime, every morning (except Mon during winter).

Food market: Place de la Poste, St.-Aygulf, Fréjus, Tues and Sat mornings.

General market: Place des Lices, St.-Tropez, Tues and Sat mornings.

Organic food market: Place Vicomtesse de Noailles, Hyères, Tues, Thurs and Sat mornings.

Provençal market: Place de la République, Flayosc, Mon morning.

Self-catering families can also pick up fresh pasta and sauces from **La Boîte à Pâtes** (✆ 04 94 17 37 63) next door.

Chocolathé ★ ★ VALUE TEAROOM

19 rue Général de Gaulle, Fréjus, ✆ *04 94 83 00 71*

With its contemporary chocolate-and-cream decor, Chocolathé is the place to go for a reasonably priced snack. It opened in 2009 as a **teahouse** serving 26 types of tea, but young Parisian owner Cécile soon expanded the menu.

There's now a tasty selection of paninis, salads and *croque monsieur*, plus a hot dish of the day. She even imports coffee from Big Train (the manufacturer that supplies Starbucks). While Cécile busies herself in the kitchen preparing our lunch, my daughter Alexandra and I eye up the glass cookie jars lined along the counter. Every family-friendly detail is considered, from the baby-changing facilities in the spacious toilets to the 4€ kids' menu.

Open *Mon–Sat 8am–7pm (plus some Sun afternoons during school holidays).* **Main courses** *10.50€–16€, children's menu 4€–7.50€.* **Credit** *MC, V.* **Amenities** 🚼 ♿

La Crêperie du Vieux Port ★ ★ CRÊPERIE

20 cours Guilbaud, St.-Raphaël, ✆ *04 94 19 44 88*

This local family favourite makes the perfect pit-stop after a walk around the harbour. You can choose from more than 20 pancake fillings. My daughter likes the one filled with a beefburger and crème fraîche. There's no children's menu, but the kitchen will prepare small portions by request, or don't mind if little ones share. There's plenty of room for buggies.

Open *Daily noon–midnight May–Oct.* **Main courses** *8€–17€.* **Credit** *MC, V.*

Ste.-Maxime, St-Tropez & Around

In Ste. -Maxime's pedestrianised old centre, you'll find everything you need for a quick snack. On Rue Paul Bert, **Le Grangousier** (✆ 04 94 96 54 00) sells filled baguettes, quiches, pizza slices

And God Created . . . a Heavenly Tart

Who'd have thought that sponge filled with custard could taste so good? As well as falling in love with St.-Tropez (and director Roger Vadim) during the filming of *And God Created Woman* in 1956, Brigitte Bardot developed a taste for local baker Alexandre Micka's Polish cream cake. Her suggestion to name it after the village was accepted and *la tarte tropézienne* was born. The recipe is top-secret, but you can buy the cakes from the shops of the same name at 9 boulevard Louis Blanc or 36 rue Georges Clémenceau in St.-Tropez, plus in branches in lots of other towns (see **www.tarte-tropezienne.com**).

and paella, while **Rotisserie du Marché** (℡ *04 94 96 58 52*), on Montée de l'Epagneul near the *marché couvert*, offers an impressive selection of spit-roast meats from cured ham to quail and spare ribs.

Overlooking the yachts along St.-Tropez's Quai Jean Jaurès is the ubiquitous people-watching café **Sénéquier**, while the **Crêperie Bretonne** (℡ *04 94 97 48 53*) in nearby Quai Frédéric Mistral provides an easy pit-stop with kids. The restaurant-lined Place des Lices has a couple of good snack vans. As you eat paninis from **La Baraque** and ice creams from established **Glaces Alfred**, you can watch locals playing *pétanque* and your kids playing on the merry-go-round. Gastronomic restaurants for a night away from the kids include celebrity-starred **Spoon-Byblos** (℡ *04 94 56 68 00*, *www.byblos. com*, menus from 89€) on Avenue Paul Signac and Michelin-starred **Résidence de la Pinède** (℡ *04 94 55 91 00*, *www.residencepinede. com*, menus from 95€) overlooking Plage de la Bouillabaisse.

MODERATE

La Réserve ★★ FIND

8 place Victor Hugo, Ste.-Maxime, ℡ *04 94 96 18 32*

Step into the Provençal countryside. In its third generation of business, this restaurant is like a home from home for many Ste.-Maxime locals. Comfortable chairs are covered in beige and red cushions, while menus hang from a large tree trunk in the middle of the room. Specialities from different French regions include *fondue bourguignonne* (beef fondue), *homard du vivier* (fresh lobster) and *bouillabaisse* (fish and seafood stew). A kids' Junior Menu is available.

Open May–Sept noon–2pm and 7–10:30pm daily, Oct–Apr noon–2pm and 7–10pm daily. **Main courses** *Menus from 21€, children's menu 12€.* **Credit** *AE, MC, V.*

Le Café ★

Place des Lices, St.-Tropez, ℡ *04 94 97 44 69,* **www.lecafe.fr**

There is an amazing number of cafés and restaurants in this little town—but with everyone packed shoulder-to-shoulder, deciding

Dine & Doze

Two of the most beautiful places to stay in the inland Var are **Chez Bruno** (📞 *04 94 85 93 93*, *www.restaurantbruno.com*, double rooms from 100€, truffle menus from 65€) in Lorgues and Alain Ducasse's **Hostellerie de l'Abbaye de la Celle** (📞 *04 98 05 14 14*, *www.abbaye-celle.com*, double rooms from 250€) in La Celle. Both boast well-renowned chefs: Bruno is the Var's king of truffles, while Ducasse's Michelin-starred cuisine (with menus from 40€) is famous across France and beyond. The posh cuisine means that these places work best for older families, although both places offer excellent children's menus on request.

Dining on the shaded, outdoor terrace of either restaurant is guaranteed to be a holiday highlight. While the Hostellerie de l'Abbaye de la Celle has a lovely pool and organic vegetable garden to explore, Chez Bruno is simply a restaurant with rooms.

---

where to go isn't easy. A friend told me, 'you can take anyone to Le Café', and he was right. You'll find all ages and nationalities in this traditional yet trendy place on the main square, and children have plenty of room to run around once the market stall-holders have packed up—so long as they don't disturb the *pétanque* matches. The Mediterranean menu includes pasta, grilled meat, fish and salads. An 18€ lunch menu (two courses plus coffee) is good value, and there's a 12€ kids' menu. Don't miss the tarte tropézienne for dessert.

Open Daily noon–2:30pm and 7–11pm. ***Main courses*** 12€–34€, kids' menu up to 10 years 12 €. ***Credit*** MC, V.

Le Café de France ★★

Place Neuve, Grimaud, 📞 *04 94 43 20 05*

The best thing about Le Café de France is its location in the heart of the Var's best-looking village. My family and I were serenaded by a Spanish guitar player during a recent idyllic lunch at this family-run restaurant. The à la carte menu doesn't come cheap, but portions are generous and you can always opt for the three-course menu at 25€ instead. There's also a kids' menu at 9.50€. While adults savour their *cassolette du pêcheur* (seafood casserole in puff pastry) on the shaded terrace, kids can run around the village square from where Grimaud's little tourist train departs.

Open Apr–Sept daily noon–2:30pm and 7–10:30pm, Oct–Mar phone to check as opening hours vary. ***Main courses*** 19€–35€, menus from 25€, kids' menu 9.50€. ***Credit*** MC, V.

INEXPENSIVE

Brasserie Tropézienne ★
VALUE

10 rue Henri Seillon, St.-Tropez. 📞 *04 94 97 01 65*

Behind the Capitainerie du Port, Brasserie Tropézienne is one of the secret addresses of St.-Tropez. Locals have been coming to this all-day brasserie, run by

TIP ## The Best Ice Cream

Barbarac (04 94 97 67 83) at 2 rue Général Allard in St-Tropez is unrivalled for delicious ice cream: among the flavours we recommend are white chocolate and black cherry (Amarena).

You'll find lip-smacking lavender, fig and plum sorbets at **Claude Ré** (04 94 65 28 41) at 10 rue de Limans in **Hyères** (near Hôtel du Portalet), which also specialises in regional biscuits.

Alsace-born Pascal, for 17 years. The no-nonsense menu includes steaks, salads, pasta, pizzas and simple snacks such as *croque madame*. Interestingly, jugs of wine starting at 4.50€ are cheaper than bottled water at 5€.

Open Daily July–Aug 7am–3am, Sept 7am–1:30am, Oct–June 7am–4pm. **Main courses** 5€–19.50€. **Credit** AE, MC, V.

Toulon & Hyères

MODERATE

Le Bistrot de Marius ★ FIND

1 place Massillon, Hyères, 04 94 35 88 38, www.bistrotdemarius.fr

Situated in the crumbling, cobbled old town, next to the 12th-century Templar tower, this restaurant serves the tastiest food in Hyères. It's prettiest at night, when tea lights flicker in the gentle breeze, but you'll eat well any time. You'll find all the regional favourites, including fish, grills and desserts such as *crème caramel*, all of them top-notch. Children under 12 even have their own two-course gourmet menu for 11€. The square is small and packed with tables so there's not much room for running around.

Open Wed–Sun 12:30–2:30pm and 7:30–10:30pm, daily in July and Aug.

Main courses 9.50€–44€, menus from 19€, kids' menu 11€. **Credit** MC, V.

INEXPENSIVE

Mojito Café CUBAN

9 avenue Docteur Robin, Port La Gavine, Hyères, 04 94 57 36 15

The good-value Cuban food, including tapas and grills, served here provides a refreshing change from the samey Provençal menus served in the sea of restaurants surrounding the harbour. As well as a two-course children's menu at 8.20€, there's a large TV screen for match-watching.

Open Tues–Sun noon–2:30pm and 8pm–midnight. **Main courses** from 11€, children's menu 8.20€. **Credit** MC, V.

The Inland Var

The inland Var boasts photogenic hilltop villages that are chock-a-block with restaurants. One such panoramic village is Mons, where gourmand families should head to reasonably priced **Lou San Bastian** (04 94 76 95 71) in Place St.-Sébastien, with its geranium-strewn terrace and tasty Provençal cuisine.

Another village for enjoying jaw-dropping views is Tourtour, where you'll be well fed for 20€

at **La Farigoulette** (📞 *04 94 70 57 37*) on Place des Ormeaux. For a posh dinner without the kids, **La Table** (📞 *04 94 70 55 95, www.la table.fr*) is one of the Var's best-kept gastronomic secrets.

If you're staying near Draguignan, head out to Flayosc, where you can glimpse bustling village life while taking your pick from Provençal to Vietnamese cuisine. With their excellent French menus (from *24€*) and Provençal decor, **L'Oustaou** (📞 *04 94 70 42 69*) on Place Joseph Brémond and **La Fleur de Thym** (📞 *04 94 50 31 53, menus from 29€*) on Boulevard Jean Moulin are class acts. However, kids may prefer the table football and children's menus at snack bars around Place de la République.

FAMILY-FRIENDLY ACCOMMODATION

Fréjus & St.-Raphaël

Some of the most desirable neighbourhoods around the twin seaside resorts include the **Valescure** pine forest near St.-Raphaël, and **St.-Aygulf** on the outskirts of Fréjus. **Port Fréjus** seafront is a convenient spot for watersports, while **Port Grimaud** has a good selection of holiday villages.

INEXPENSIVE

Hôtel L'Aréna ★

139–145 rue du Général de Gaulle, Fréjus, 📞 *04 94 17 09 40, www. hotel-frejus-arena.com*

On the doorstep of the old centre, this friendly hotel provides a handy base for a few days of exploring Fréjus on foot. Decorated throughout in a Provençal ochre palate, the double rooms are small, so opt for larger triples or quads (with one double bed and a twin-bedded mezzanine for kids). In summer, the excellent *table d'hôte* dinner is served on a terracotta-paved terrace. It's next to the train station, but bedrooms are well soundproofed and background noise by the enclosed pool is muted by leafy palms.

Rooms 39. Rates Doubles from 85€, triples from 100€, quads from 125€. Cot free, extra bed 25€. Closed November. Credit AE, MC, V. Amenities ▼ ☐ 🗿 🖾 ¶¶ In room A/C @ 🗂

Picnics with a View

If you're in **Hyères**, buy yummy sandwiches and cakes from **Pâtisserie Blonna** (📞 *04 94 35 35 92*) on Place Georges Clemenceau before getting the boat over to Porquerolles—a picnic on the **Plage d'Argent** (p. 125) is much better than an expensive, mediocre meal in one of the island's few restaurants.

In **Ste.-Maxime**, head for the grassy tip of the **Pointe des Sardinaux**, a pine forest with Roman fishpond remains, armed with supplies from **Claude Pierrugues** (📞 *04 94 49 17 71*) in Avenue de Lattre de Tasigny.

Surrounded by pine forest near Fréjus, **Les Résidences du Colombier** (℡ *04 77 56 66 09*, *www.vacances-ulvf.com*) is a good option for a budget break. This holiday village has 24 Provençal-style, self-catering *gîtes* and a kids' club (4–12 years) during school holidays. Full-board, week-long stays per person cost from 320€ for adults, from 204€ for kids aged 6–12, from 160€ for kids aged 3–5 and are free for kids under 3.

Ste-Maxime, St-Tropez & Around

Families in the know head to **Hôtel Le Mouillage** (see below)—a smart exception to St.-Tropez's often overpriced hotels. Next door, **Pastis Hôtel** (℡ *04 98 12 56 50, www.pastis-st-tropez.com*, doubles from 200€) is perfect for well-heeled families. Looking fit for a double-page spread in *World of Interiors*, this nine-room boutique hotel is surprisingly family-friendly, with spacious rooms and a heated saltwater pool. In nearby Ste.-Maxime, twin hotels **Les Santolines** (℡ *04 94 96 31 34, www.hotel-la-croisette.com*, doubles from 75€) and **La Croisette** (℡ *04 94 96 17 75*, doubles from 80€) are reasonably priced options. The best rooms for a longer stay are the two-room family suites (not to be confused with the standard quadruple rooms that don't have air-conditioning) and self-catering apartments for up to seven (new at La Croisette in 2010). Meanwhile, the best-value chain hotel in

Ste.-Maxime is the privately owned **Best Western Montfleuri** (℡ *04 94 55 75 10*, doubles from 45€). The smiling staff and good location means this hotel is quickly booked up.

Our favourite Belle Epoque palace on the Western Côte, the family-friendly **Hôtel Le Beauvallon** (℡ *04 94 55 78 88*, *www. lebeauvallon.com*), re-opens in summer 2011 following a top-to-toe renovation. Meanwhile, families can already enjoy its swanky new beach club, **Beauvallon sur Mer**.

EXPENSIVE

Le Bailli de Suffren ★★

Avenue des Américains, Le Rayol-Canadel-sur-Mer, ℡ 04 98 04 47 00, www.lebaillidesuffren.com

Next to the lush **Domaine du Rayol** gardens (p. 125), this plush four-star is ideal for a pampered family holiday at the water's edge. As well as 55 Junior Suites in the main building, there are 19 stylish self-catering apartments for four to six people. There's not much to do here apart from lie by the pool (not accessible to self-catering guests) or on the small beach, but you're close to **St.-Tropez** if you get cabin fever. The gourmet restaurant (with children's menu) can be hit-and-miss, but the beach and terrace restaurants are both excellent.

Rooms 72. Rates Suites 198€–487€, apartments 416€–1,498€ per week. Extra bed 50€. Cot free. Breakfast 24€, children aged 3–11 17€. Credit

AE, MC, V. *Amenities* 🏃 🍴 📻 🖥
In room A/C ❌ 🗄

Hôtel Le Mouillage FIND VALUE

Port du Pilon, St.-Tropez, 📞 *04 94 97 53 19, www.hotelmouillage.fr*

Overlooking Bouillabaisse beach, this remarkably priced hotel is a 5-minute walk from shops and a 10-minute drive from celebrity-studded Pampelonne. Charming owners Jean-Claude and Pascale Pepino have a flair for interior design: rooms with private terraces are decorated around Southern themes. Trickling fountains lull you beside the pool and on the verdant terrace with its rattan sofas. Free on-site parking is another bonus.

Rooms 10. Rates Doubles from 100€, triples from 130€. Cot 20€, extra bed 40€. Closed mid-Nov–mid-Dec and Jan. Credit AE, MC, V. Amenities 🍷 🅿 🖥 *In room* A/C 🖥 🍴 🗄 🗄

Toulon & Hyères

The outskirts around Hyères are very built-up, so the best option for accommodation is the Giens peninsula—a world-famous spot for wind- and kite-surfing: sporty kids will be in paradise.

Camping La Presqu'île de Giens ★★

153 route de la Madrague, Giens, Hyères, 📞 *04 94 58 22 86, www.camping-giens.com*

With its spectacular location on the tip of the Giens peninsula, this three-star campsite is a haven for watersports enthusiasts—although there's no swimming pool, you're surrounded by Blue Flag beaches, including the famous Almanarre (p. 130) just 800m away. The site has well-equipped chalets and mobile homes that sleep four to six, as well as pitches for those with their own tourers or tents. There's more than enough to occupy children, including an on-site playground, boat trips to nearby Porquerolles (p. 126) or a visit to Kiddy Parc (p. 129).

Rooms 150 chalets and mobile homes. Rates 238€–1,022€ per week. Credit MC, V. Amenities 🍷 🍴 🛍

Families who'd prefer a campsite with a swimming pool should check out Camping International (📞 04 94 58 90 16, www.international-giens.com) as a nearby alternative to Camping La Presqu'île de Giens. A four-person mobile home costs from 335€ per week.

Hôtel Little Palace ★ FIND

6 rue Berthelot, Toulon, 📞 *04 94 92 26 62, www.hotel-littlepalace.com*

If you need to stay in Toulon overnight or for a few days, you won't find a better place than this. The hotel was recently bought and beautifully made over in the Provençal style by a retired teacher from Brittany, whose daughter and son-in-law own the Grand Hotel Dauphiné just opposite. As well as triple rooms for families, there is a new self-catering apartment with fully equipped kitchen next door.

Down on the Farm

A wonderful way to make the most of the Var countryside is to stay in an eco-*gîte* at **Beaugensiers Farm** (04 94 48 94 44, *www.laferme debeaugensiers.com*), about 20 minutes north of Toulon and Hyères on the RD554. A five-person *gîte* costs from 380€ per week. Families who speak some French will be able to enjoy midweek workshops on everything from bee-keeping to recycling and butter-making. If you're staying nearby, you can come to **feed and pet the animals** on Sunday afternoons (2 to 6pm). Another unusual way to spend your holiday is on an ostrich farm. **Maxim Autruches** (04 94 96 75 30, four-person *gîte* from 470€ per week) near Ste.-Maxime has four fully equipped but basic *gîtes* with a swimming pool and tennis court. Just think of the omelettes.

There are some downsides: only some rooms have air-conditioning, and there are four floors but **no lift**.

Rooms 23. **Rates** Doubles from 49€, triples from 72€, suites from 82€, apartment from 120€. Breakfast 9€. **Credit** MC, V. **Amenities** 🖥 **In room** A/C 🗋

The Inland Var

MODERATE

Hôtel Le Couvent Royal ★★
VALUE

Place Jean Salusse, St.-Maximin-La-Ste.-Baume, 04 94 86 55 66, *www.hotelfp-saintmaximin.com*

One of Provence's finest Gothic monuments, this **12th-century former monastery** has been converted into a hotel. Furnishings don't live up to the grandeur of the surroundings and rooms aren't air-conditioned, but prices reflect that. There's not enough to keep children entertained for long stays, but it's a good place to stop over if you want to explore the inland Var. Ask for a room overlooking the cloisters, and consider splashing out on a Deluxe room: the larger ones in La Cordaire wing fit a couple of extra beds at a squash. The smaller bedrooms in the North wing are the prettiest, with their exposed stone. The stone-vaulted chapterhouse houses a restaurant offering children's menus and a bar with a flatscreen TV. Nearby activities include riding, golf and quad-biking.

Rooms 66. **Rates** Doubles from 140€, deluxe from 225€. Extra bed 20€, breakfast 13€. **Credit** AE, MC, V. **Amenities** 🍽 **In room** 🖥 🗋

INSIDER TIP ➤

View-seekers will love the **Bastide de Tourtour** (04 98 10 54 20, *www.bastidedetourtour. com*, doubles from 150€). The interior decor is rather fusty, but gazing down on three Côte d'Azur regions over an evening drink in the loggia (Prestige rooms only) leaves an indelible memory.

6 Marseille & Aix-en-Provence

MARSEILLE & AIX-EN-PROVENCE

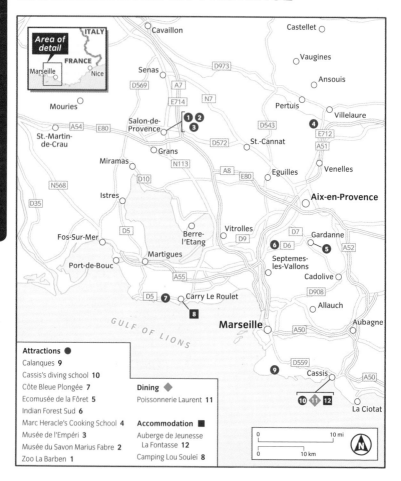

Attractions ●
Calanques **9**
Cassis's diving school **10**
Côte Bleue Plongée **7**
Ecomusée de la Fôret **5**
Indian Forest Sud **6**
Marc Heracle's Cooking School **4**
Musée de l'Empéri **3**
Musée du Savon Marius Fabre **2**
Zoo La Barben **1**

Dining ◆
Poissonnerie Laurent **11**

Accommodation ■
Auberge de Jeunesse
  La Fontasse **12**
Camping Lou Souleï **8**

ordered by the Camargue marshlands to the west and the
Var's family-friendly seaside resorts to the east, this region is
a tale of two cities: Aix-en-Provence and Marseille. While both have
impressive architectural heritage and a strong cultural agenda, their
fates diverged long ago. With its vibrant student life and café society,
the Roman spa town of Aix is a mecca for sun-seeking literati and the
pampered bourgeoisie.

France's vibrant second, and oldest, city, on the other hand, has been
marred by a scary criminal reputation. All this is set to change as a result
of Euroméditerranée—Europe's largest urban-regeneration project.
By 2013, Marseille's port will be home to trendy dock-warehouse con-
versions and modernist landmarks including Zaha Hadid's 29-storey
glass tower, film director Luc Besson's multiplex cinema and a Rudy

Riccioti-designed Museum of European and Mediterranean Civilisations—along with a new tramway and rail terminal. Property investors are beginning to realise that Marseille could be the next Barcelona.

This reasonably priced corner of the festive South will appeal most to art-loving families on a budget, and is ideal for year-round city-and-seaside breaks. You can gaze at the white-cliffed Calanques in Cassis; follow in the footsteps of Cézanne in Aix; taste Med-caught fish in harbourside settings in Marseille; and learn about France's military history in Salon-de-Provence. Wherever you are, you will get the chance to glimpse the soul of Provence.

VISITOR INFORMATION

All the cities, towns and villages in this chapter are in the **Bouches du Rhône** département. For general information on the area, see *www.visitprovence.com*. Another useful resource for parents exploring Marseille and Aix-en-Provence is *http://marseille.citizenkid.com*, which has information (in French) on family-friendly events, shopping and childcare.

Getting There

By Air Marseille-Provence Airport (*www.mrsairport.com*) is within 20 minutes' drive of both Marseille and Aix-en-Provence. France's third-largest airport is well served by airlines with connecting flights from most UK airports. There are also direct flights with British Airways from London Gatwick, with easyJet from London Gatwick and Bristol, and with Ryanair from Dublin and London Stansted. Flights from London take just under 2 hours.

By Train You can get to Marseille or Aix from London in under 7 hours, taking a Eurostar from St. Pancras, then changing in Lille or Paris. Tickets are available from Rail Europe (p. 32); standard fares start at £109 return for adults and £94 for children 4 and over.

By Car See p. 34.

Orientation

The A54 from Salon joins the A7 and then the A8 to reach Aix. Then the A51, which becomes the A7, takes you from Aix to Marseille, and vice versa.

The D559 runs inland from Marseille to Cassis, and the D568 goes from Marseille to the Côte Bleue, where you can take the D5 towards Carry-le-Rouet and Sausset-les-Pins, along the coast.

Getting Around

If you're exploring the area by public transport, it's best to base yourself in Marseille or Aix. Buses are fairly frequent; you can

Fast Facts: Aix-en-Provence & Marseille

Banks: In Aix-en-Provence: HSBC, 10 place Jeanne d'Arc. In Marseille: HSBC is located at 11 bis rue St. Ferréol, and Barclays at 112–114 rue de Rome.

Hospitals: In Aix-en-Provence, Centre Hospitalier du Pays d'Aix (℡ *04 42 33 90 28, www.ch-aix.fr*) on Avenue des Tamaris has a 24-hour emergency service. Hôpital de la Timone (℡ *04 91 38 00 00, www. ap-hm.fr*), 264 rue St. Pierre in Marseille, specialises in pediatric emergencies.

Internet Cafés: LoGiDrake (℡ *04 92 34 47 88*), at 36 place Miollis in Aix-en-Provence, is open Monday to Friday 8am to 8pm, Saturday 11am to midnight and Sunday 2 to 10pm. Marseille's Net Process (℡ *04 91 34 75 71*), 8 rue du Bosquet, is open Monday to Saturday 9:30am to midnight, Sunday 1pm to midnight.

Pharmacies: There are three pharmacies along Cours Mirabeau in Aix-en-Provence; there are almost 400 pharmacies all over Marseille including 122 rue de Rome.

Post Offices: In Place de l'Hôtel de Ville, Aix-en-Provence; and in Marseille at 50 rue de Rome and 1 cours Jean Ballard.

Shopping: See p. 159 and, for markets, p. 160.

peruse timetables at *www.lepilote. com* (in French), although it's generally better to visit the bus station in person to get details. Train information for the Provence Alpes Côte d'Azur (aka PACA) region can be found at *www.ter-sncf.com*. For car-hire firms at Marseille airport, see *www.mrsairport.com.* Shuttle buses run from Marseille Airport to Salon-de-Provence (in 1 hour for 3.70€) and Aix-en-Provence (in 30 minutes for 7.80€).

INSIDER TIP ›

A great short cut across the Vieux Port in Marseille is by ferry. This free service runs daily from 8am to 12:30pm and 1 to 5pm between Hôtel de Ville and Place aux Huiles.

WHAT TO SEE & DO

Children's Top 10 Attractions

❶ **Scoffing** almond-flavoured *calissons* in Aix (p. 146).

❷ **Exploring** the Calanques by boat or on foot (p. 149).

❸ **Walking**, if not talking, like the animals at Zoo La Barben (p. 151).

❹ **Learning** about Mediterranean trees and plants at the Forest Eco-museum (p. 152).

❺ **Camping** in a tepee at the OK Corral theme park (p. 155).

❻ **Finding** your inner artist at the Atelier Cézanne (p. 153).

❼ Making a clean getaway to the soap museum in Salon-de-Provence (p. 163).

❽ Visiting the Côte Bleue by train (p. 156).

❾ Swimming with exotic fish on an accompanied dive (p. 157).

❿ Feasting on sardines at the Fête de St.-Pierre in Cassis or Martigues (p. 146).

Child-friendly Events & Entertainment

Badaboum Théâtre
★★ **FIND** AGE 3 & UP

16 quai de Rive-Neuve, Marseille, ☎ *04 91 54 40 71, www.badaboum-theatre.com*

This little theatre on the Vieux Port puts on plays that are usually based on familiar stories such as *Little Red Riding Hood* or *Snow White*, so even if your children don't speak French, they might well get something out of the performance, which lasts an hour. They're often followed by workshops on costume, make-up, characters and improvisation (in French).

Open Daily 9am–midday and 1:30–6pm. Shows start 2:30pm **Adm** *Show 8€, workshop 8€.* **Credit** *Cash only.*

Les Rencontres du 9ème Art ALL AGES

Aix, ☎ *04 42 16 11 61, www.bd-aix.com*

The French love their comic strips, and this annual festival celebrates cartoons past and present in venues around town. There are free exhibitions by renowned BD (*bande dessinée*) artists, a competition, and workshops (in French) for children over 8.

Mar and Apr. **Adm** *Free.*

English-language Cinemas

For English-language films, look for 'VO' (version originale) indicated after film listings. For current listings, see the cinema's own website or go to *www.angloinfo.com*.

Cinéma 3 Casino, 11 cours Forbin, Gardanne ☎ *08 92 68 03 42*.

Espace Fernandel, Avenue Aristide Briand, Carry-le-Rouet ☎ *04 42 30 53 18/08 92 68 91 23*.

Le César, 4 place Castellane, Marseille ☎ *04 91 53 27 82*.

Le Mazarin, 6 rue Laroque, Aix ☎ *08 92 68 72 70, www.lescinemas aixois.com*.

Le Renoir, 24 cours Mirabeau, Aix ☎ *08 92 68 72 70, www.lescinemas aixois.com*.

Les Arcades, Place Gambetta, Salon-de-Provence ☎ *08 92 89 28 92*.

Variétés, 37 rue Vincent-Scotto, Marseille ☎ *08 92 89 28 92*.

Fête de St.-Pierre
★★ FIND ALL AGES

Cassis, 📞 *08 92 25 98 92, www. ot-cassis.com*

Martigues, 📞 *04 42 42 31 10, www. martigues-tourisme.com*

Every year in late **June**, fishing villages across the Mediterranean celebrate their patron, St. Peter, with a mass for the fishermen followed by a blessing of their boats. Then the partying begins: this usually involves boat-jousting, singing and a huge sardine barbecue.

Last weekend in June. **Adm** *Free.*

Cities, Towns & Resorts

Aix-en-Provence ★★★
Tourist office: 📞 *04 42 16 11 61, www.aixenprovencetourism.com*

Where Marseille is scruffy and earthy, Aix is shabby-chic and bourgeois. Founded by the Romans, this university town is best known as the birthplace and home of post-Impressionist artist **Paul Cézanne** (1839–1906), as well as for its café society and 17th-century mansions. It boasts 40 public fountains (yet few green spaces) and a futuristic arts centre, the **Fondation Vasarely**

(*www.fondationvasarely.fr*). Aix is an all-year destination so is perfect for Christmas breaks, when the Cours Mirabeau is lined with Christmas market stalls and a mini-fairground. Children love the almond-flavoured *calissons* sweets and the *santons* figurines from Fouques (p. 159), while mums and dads can enjoy some me-time in the **Thermes Sextius** (📞 *04 42 23 81 82, www.thermes-sextius.com*), a **hi-tech spa** built on the site of the ancient Roman baths. Day packages start at 90€.

INSIDER TIP ❯❯
Hôtel Aquabella (2 rue des Etuves, Aix-en-Provence, 📞 *04 42 99 15 00, www.aquabella.fr*) offers special spa packages at the neighbouring Thermes Sextius, as well as good accommodation deals for families.

Cassis ★★
Tourist office: 📞 *04 42 01 67 83, www.ot-cassis.fr*

The British, among them statesman Winston Churchill and writer Virginia Woolf, have long flocked to Cassis, and it's not difficult to see why: as well as offering excellent local white wine and freshly caught fish

Painters' Paradise—L'Estaque

Artists including Georges Braque, Raoul Dufy and Paul Cézanne flocked to the little fishing port of **L'Estaque** (*www.estaque.com*), a few kilometres west of Marseille, in the 19th century because of its unique light and landscape forms. Visit ideally after you've seen the originals in Marseille's **Musée Cantini** (p. 154); take paper and pens in case you or your children are inspired while walking the '**Circuit des** Peintres'.

AIX-EN-PROVENCE

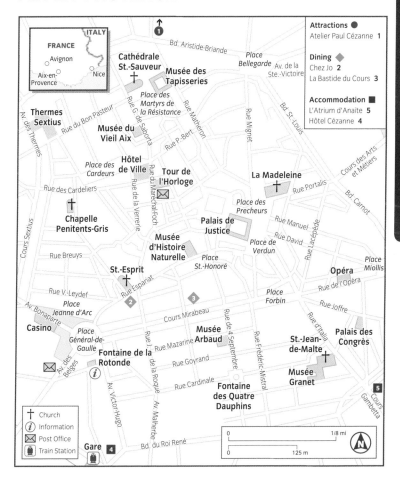

Attractions ●
Atelier Paul Cézanne 1

Dining ◆
Chez Jo 2
La Bastide du Cours 3

Accommodation ■
L'Atrium d'Anaïte 5
Hôtel Cézanne 4

† Church
ⓘ Information
✉ Post Office
🚆 Train Station

served up in the harbourside restaurants, it's on the doorstep of
the imposing *Calanques*
(p. 149). This small and family-
friendly resort is busy throughout the summer with events
such as the **Fête de St.-Pierre**
(p. 146) in June and the **wine
harvest festival** in September. A
walk around the protected old
town will give you plenty of
ideas for presents—the higgledy-
piggledy streets are lined with art

galleries, potters' workshops and
upmarket clothes shops. Other
draws are the daily **fish market**,
the views from **Cap Canaille** and
the boat trips along the coast.

INSIDER TIP ⟩⟩

If you're planning a day trip to Cassis in summer, it's best to catch
the bus here: parking is scarce and
the nearest train station is 3km
away. You can reach Cassis from
Aix within 1¼ hours and from
Marseille within 45 minutes.

Marseille ★★

Tourist office: ☎ *04 91 13 89 00,*
www.marseille-tourisme.com

Don't let Marseille's scary reputation put you off. France's second city buzzes with life, from its multicultural markets to the chanting blue sea of football fans following an inevitable home win by 'OM' (p. 150). You might not choose this city as the base for a family holiday, but it's certainly worth an overnight stay or a day trip—particularly to the pretty old port. You can take your pick from more than 20 museums, stroll around 100 sq km of parks and gardens, or relax along 57km of beach-dotted coastline.

Founded by the Greeks 2,600 years ago, France's oldest city has welcomed immigrants for centuries. This is most evident in the diversity of its restaurants and its rich cultural life. Kids can enjoy its thriving theatre scene at the **Badaboum Théâtre** (p. 145) or its artistic edge at the **Préau des Accoules** museum (p. 156). Best of all, it's constantly evolving: the current **Euroméditerranée** project (p. 142) is set to change this vibrant city's future for good.

INSIDER TIP 》

Hop onto Marseille's new tramway—a third line is planned for 2012. Tickets cost 1.50€ or you can buy a day city pass (valid for tram, metro and bus) for 20€ from the tourist office at 1 La Canebière (*www.marseille tourism.com*).

Salon-de-Provence ★★

Tourist office: ☎ *04 90 56 27 60,*
www.visitsalondeprovence.com

Halfway between the plain of La Crau and genteel Aix,

Marseille Harbour

MARSEILLE

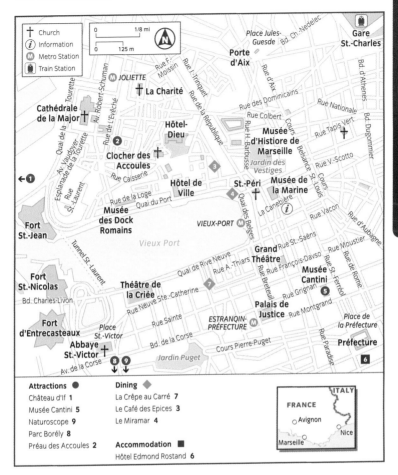

†	Church
ⓘ	Information
Ⓜ	Metro Station
🚉	Train Station

0 — 1/8 mi
0 — 125 m

Attractions ●
Château d'If **1**
Musée Cantini **5**
Naturoscope **9**
Parc Borély **8**
Préau des Accoules **2**

Dining ◆
La Crêpe au Carré **7**
Le Café des Epices **3**
Le Miramar **4**

Accommodation ■
Hôtel Edmond Rostand **6**

ITALY
FRANCE
Avignon
Nice
Marseille

Salon-de-Provence is a quiet Provençal town. Best known for being the home of soothsayer **Nostradamus** (p. 154) until his death in 1566, it's a convenient summertime stopover for families heading into the Vaucluse and beyond. Make sure you fit in a visit to the glorious castle and zoo **at Zoo La Barben** (p. 151). The Château de l'Empéri and the **Musée de l'Empéri**, its impressive military

museum (p. 155), and the **Musée du Savon Marius Fabre** (p. 155) are also worth a look.

Natural Wonders & Spectacular Views

Calanques ★★ ALL AGES

📞 *04 91 13 89 00, www.marseille-tourisme.com*

These striking Mediterranean fjords stretching along 20km of coastline between Marseille and

Droit au But (Straight for the Goal)

This is the slogan of Marseille's most famous export (apart from soap and *pastis*)—**Olympique de Marseille** football club or *l'OM* (*www.om.net*), as it is commonly known. One of France's most successful clubs, having won the French Ligue 1 and the Cup 10 times each, and the Champions League once, *l'OM* is evident everywhere you go in this passionate city. Famous past players include Eric Cantona and Fabien Barthez. The easiest place to buy tickets is from **FNAC** at 69 rue Paradis (*www.fnac.com*). You can take a tour of the club's home, the **Stade Vélodrome**, for 6€ (free for kids under 5; contact Marseille tourism, ☎ *04 91 13 89 03*, *www.marseille-tourism.com*), then head back to the Vieux Port for some sustenance at the surprisingly smart **Brasserie de l'OM** (☎ *04 91 33 80 33*).

Cassis soar up from the turquoise water, cutting into the limestone rocks to leave small beaches, many only accessible by sea. Although there is little soil here, there are more than 900 species of plants, including 15 that are protected. You might also spot a Bonelli's eagle, peregrine falcon or great horned owl. There are daily boat trips of varying duration from Marseille and Cassis (beware: the sea can be rough), or you can hike along the footpaths for bird's-eye views (paths are off-limits in July and August to reduce the risk of wildfires).

INSIDER TIP

If you don't fancy a boat trip, you can reach the Calanques by bus from Marseille; buses stop at nearby Callelongue, Morgiou and Sormiou.

Route Cézanne to the Montagne Ste.-Victoire
★★ ALL AGES

D17 from Aix-en-Provence to Le Tholonet and St.-Antonin, then on D56 to Peynier and Gardanne via D6, back onto D56 towards Meryreuil and then back to Aix, ☎ *04 42 16 11 61,* *www.aixenprovencetourism.com*

An Aix landmark and the inspiration for many of Paul Cézanne's

TIP For a Rainy Day

Make the most of a rainy day in Marseille with a trip to a bowling alley: Bowling de la Valentine (☎ *04 91 35 73 64*, *www.bowlingstar.fr*) at 12 route de la Sablière has 28 alleys including shorter ones for kids, billiards tables and bar. Meanwhile, kids over 9 years (or accompanied kids over 7 years) can have a go at **Lasergame Evolution** (☎ *04 91 26 79 75*, *www.lasergame-evolution.com*) at 280 boulevard Mireille Lauze.

TIP ▶ The Best Beaches ◀

Le Grand Large, Esplanade Charles de Gaulle, Cassis (☏ *04 42 01 81 00*, *www.cassis-grand-large.com*). This private sandy beach a stone's throw from Cassis harbour has loungers, parasols and a restaurant.

Plage du Verdon, La Couronne. This pretty Blue Flag beach is one of the best on the Côte Bleue for families, and has a car park.

Plages du Prado-Borély, Avenue Pierre Mendès-France, Marseille, near Parc Borély. This large stretch of reclaimed land offers plentiful beach activities including football, play areas and even a skate park.

---

post-Impressionist artworks, the 1,000m Montagne Ste.-Victoire is surrounded by historic sites and villages. On the drive around the mountain, your first stop should be **Le Tholonet**, with spectacular views of the peak and a Cézanne-immortalised château. From here carry on to **St.-Antonin**, where the little museum at the **Maison Ste.-Victoire** (☏ *04 42 66 84 40*) provides information about the area and offers guided walks. After the little village of Puyloubier, make your way south across the River Arc towards Peynier and then west towards the town of **Gardanne**, itself often painted by Cézanne. From there, head north towards famously

featured landscapes such as the Pont de Bayeux (near Meyreuil) and then Pont des Trois Sautets. Then return to Aix along the A8. It's best to allow at least half a day for this driving tour.

Animal Park

Zoo La Barben ★★★ ALL AGES

Route du Château, La Barben, 6km east of Salon-de-Provence on D572, ☏ 04 90 55 19 12, www.zoolabarben. com

With more than 600 animals from all five continents, there's something to interest all the family at this 33-hectare hill site. The zoo is active in international conservation programmes and

Young giraffe at Zoo La Barben

houses many animals rescued from laboratories. A 5-minute walk away is the **Château La Barben** (☎ 04 90 55 25 41, *www. chateaudelabarben.fr*), dubbed the 'princess castle' by my daughter, with its Le Nôtre-designed labyrinth where kids' workshops are held. I'd recommend a combined day trip to the zoo and château with lunch at **Le 7e Restaurant** (p. 163). In July and August, the zoo stays open until 8:30pm on Mondays to host children's entertainment.

***Open** Daily 9:30am–7pm July–Sept (until 8:30pm Mon July and Aug); daily 10am–6pm Oct–Nov and Feb–June; daily 10am–5:30pm Dec and Jan. **Adm** 14€, children 3–12 8€. Minitrain 1€. **Credit** MC, V. **Amenities** 🏞️ 🪑 🍴 ♿ 🛒*

Natural Reserves, Parks & Gardens

Ecomusée de la Fôret
★★ GREEN ALL AGES

Chemin de Roman, Gardanne, 15 minutes south of Aix-en-Provence on CD7, ☎ 04 42 51 41 00, www. institut-foret.com

At the Forest Eco-museum you can learn, among other fascinating facts, why some trees in Provence lean to one side. As well as the exhibition on Mediterranean flora and fauna, there's a 1km forest trail, with an accompanying booklet (available in English) containing a quiz about the plants and trees you come across. Watch out for the uneven ground. There are plenty of picnic spots but also a good courtyard restaurant that offers children's food on request.

***Open** Sun–Fri 9am–1pm and 1:30–6:45pm July–Aug; 9am–12:30pm and 1–5:45pm mid-Sept–June. **Adm** 5.50€, children 5–15 3.20€. **Credit** MC, V. **Amenities** 🏞️ 🛒*

Parc Borély ★ ALL AGES
Avenue du Parc Borély, Marseille

This pretty park complete with château covers 54 hectares near the Prado beach. It's the perfect place for young mums to push prams and for kids to paddle around the boating lake on pedalos. Garden enthusiasts will like the botanical and rose gardens, while horse lovers or wannabe tipsters can watch the races in the adjacent Hippodrome. From June to September, you can also visit the Plage Borély beach.

***Open** Daily 6am–9pm. **Adm** Free (botanical garden 2€), boat hire). **Amenities** ☕*

TIP ▶ **Look Skywards** ◀

A fun way for budding astrologists to pass a Wednesday or Saturday afternoon is at the **Planétarium Peiresc** (☎ 04 42 20 42 66, *www.aix-planetarium.fr*) in Aix-en-Provence's Parc St.-Mitre. After a short talk on the planetary system (some experts speak some English), you'll be taken into the darkened dome of the universe; my daughter Alexandra particularly liked the Milky Way.

Historic Buildings & Monuments

Atelier Paul Cézanne
★★ **ALL AGES**

9 avenue Paul Cézanne, Aix-en-Provence, 📞 *04 42 21 06 53, www.atelier-cezanne.com*

There's a lived-in feel to Cézanne's cottage-cum-studio; it's as if he's gone out for the afternoon to paint a view of the Montagne Ste.-Victoire (p. 150) and is due back any second. Many of his belongings (including some of the subjects of his multi-million-pound paintings, including a green jug and a rum bottle) are dotted around his high-ceilinged, brightly lit workroom. It's an ideal opportunity for children to see how the father of modern art worked, before heading to the **Musée Granet** (Place St. Jean de Malte, 📞 *04 42 52 88 32, www.museegranet-aixenprovence.fr*) to view some of his paintings. In July and August, bring a picnic and sit in the garden under the shady trees. If you visit late in the afternoon, you can enjoy a 30-minute guided tour in English.

Open *Daily 10am–6pm July–Aug; daily 10am–noon and 2–6pm Apr–June and Sept; Mon–Sat 10am–noon and 2–5pm Oct–Mar. 30-minute guided tour in English at 5pm (Apr–Sept) or 4pm (Oct–Mar).* **Adm** *5.50€, 13–25s 2€, under 13s free.* **Credit** *MC, V (min. 10€).*

Château d'If `OVERRATED` **ALL AGES**

Boats leave 1 quai de la Fraternité (formerly quai des Belges), Marseille, 📞 *04 91 46 54 65, www.monum.fr*

The best thing about this 16th-century fort made famous by Alexandre Dumas's novel, *The Count of Monte Cristo*, is the 20-minute boat journey to the small, bare island of If and the view of Marseille from the sea. Even so, children love pretending to be pirates and will also be

Atelier Paul Cézanne

Château d'If

intrigued when you tell them that a shipwrecked **rhinoceros** (a present for the then Pope) was kept here briefly in the 16th century. Boats also go to the other **Îles du Frioul**—bring your beach gear.

Open Daily 9:30am–6:15pm mid-May–mid-Sept; Tues–Sun 9:30am–5:30pm mid-Sept–mid-May. **Adm** 5€, under 25s free. **Amenities** ☕🛍

Top Museums

Musée Cantini
★★★ **FIND** **ALL AGES**

19 rue Grignan, Marseille, ☎ 04 91 54 77 75, **www.marseille-tourisme.com**

A great place to introduce children to 20th-century art. This is one of the best-displayed collections we've come across in Provence, housed on the ground floor of a white, light 17th-century building in the centre of town. Paul Signac's images of Marseille and Raoul Dufy's paintings of nearby **L'Estaque** (p. 146) show exactly why artists have flocked here for years—the light. Standing in front of a Shiraga (avant-garde artist who painted barefoot and hanging from a rope) or a Yoshihara (whose latter years were devoted to blacked-out circle paintings

Nostradamus

No trip to Salon-de-Provence (p. 148) is complete without learning a little about its most famous resident. Michel de Nostredame, aka Nostradamus (1503–66), is claimed by some to have predicted various world events. You may like to visit the **Musée Nostradamus** (☎ 04 90 56 64 31), in the house where he lived and wrote his famous Prophéties. And you'll certainly want to head around the corner to **Au Péché Mignon** in Place St.-Michel, to sample the chocolates named after him.

The Best Theme Parks

Aquacity (☎ *04 91 51 54 08*, *www.aquacity.fr*), off A51 between Marseille and Aix, near Plan de Campagne. This open-air water park has wave machines, slides, doughnuts and even a 'children's island'.

Magic Land (☎ *04 42 79 86 90*, *www.magic-park-land.com*), off the A55 near Carry-le-Rouet. Imagine your ideal theme park and double it—this place is very diverse.

OK Corral (☎ *04 42 73 80 05*, *www.okcorral.fr*), off the RN8 near Cuges-les-Pins. This is a Wild West theme park complete with a campsite where you can rent a fully equipped tepee for a week or two.

Village des Automates (☎ *04 42 57 30 30*, *www.villagedesauto mates.com*), off RN7 near St.-Cannat. Kids will love the giant dinosaurs and musical eggs at this theme park where fairytales and fables are brought to life.

reminiscent of *satori*, the enlightenment of zen) is a good time for a discussion on the nature of art.

Open *Tues–Sun 11am–6pm June–Sept; 10am–5pm Oct–May.* ***Adm*** *3€.*

Musée de l'Empéri ALL AGES

Château de l'Empéri, Montée du Puech, Salon-de-Provence, ☎ 04 90 56 22 36

Accumulated by two brothers and now owned by the state, this is said by experts to be the best collection of militaria in France outside of Les Invalides in Paris. Housed in the former residence of the archbishops of Arles, the museum takes you on a journey from the world of Louis XIV to World War I via hundreds of exhibits, including arms, uniforms and even Napoleon's bed from St. Helena. My son loves the life-size dummy horses. The museum sometimes closes without prior notice, so it's worth phoning in advance to check opening times.

Open *Mon and Wed–Sun 10am–noon and 2–6pm.* ***Adm*** *4.30€, under 25s 3€.* ***Credit*** *Cash only.*

Musée du Savon Marius Fabre ★ ALL AGES

148 avenue Paul Bourret, Salon-de-Provence, ☎ 04 90 53 24 77, www. marius-fabre.fr

Walk around any market in Provence and you'll see stalls selling mounds of scented soap stamped *savon de Marseille*—Marseille soap—made in the region since the medieval period. However, the 'real' Marseille soap we see today is manufactured according to rules laid down by Louis XIV in the 17th century. Marius Fabre started making his in 1900, and it's still 'cooked' in the traditional way in the original factory. You can see the soap-makers at work, read about the history of soap-making and admire the world's largest cube of Marseille soap.

Open Mon–Thurs 8:30am–noon and 1:30–5pm, Fri 8:30am–4pm; factory tour 10:30am Mon and Thurs. **Adm** 3.50€ for museum and soap factory, children under 15 free. **Credit** MC, V. **Amenities** 🛍

Arts & Crafts

Préau des Accoules
★★ **FIND** **AGE 4 & UP**

29 Montée des Accoules, Marseille, 📞 04 91 91 52 06

Situated in the heart of the old Panier district, this place is officially classed as a children's museum, but it's more of a space where young ones aged 4 and up can discover arts and crafts. There are two themed exhibitions a year (often associated with current exhibitions in other Marseille museums), and these include workshops where children can meet the artists, develop their understanding of themes through interactive exhibits, or create their own masterpieces.

Open Wed and Sat 1:30–5:30pm (daily in school holidays). **Adm** Free.

INSIDER TIP

If your kids enjoy cooking, you should try **Marc Heracle's Cooking School** (📞 04 42 61 87 47). We were welcomed at his beautiful bastide near Aix-en-Provence for a morning preparing traditional Provençal cuisine (from 85€ per person although he usually charges half-price for kids). While we waited for our three-course meal to cook, the kids had fun exploring the grounds and stroking the farm animals.

Child-friendly Tours

Côte Bleue by Train
★ **VALUE** **ALL AGES**

Marseille to Martigues, www.ter-sncf.com

A fun way to discover the Côte Bleue is to take the regional train from Marseille's St.-Charles station to Martigues. During the trip you can gaze down at the turquoise waters and little creeks, chug through tunnels (some embellished with original artwork) and roll over bridges and a viaduct. The journey takes about 40 minutes. Make sure you ask about the 'Découverte Enfant' reduction if you're travelling with at least one child under 12—this will cut 25% off the price of tickets for up to five members of your party. The top of Marseille's La Canebière and the Belsunce area is a little seedy and can feel uncomfortable to walk around: take the Métro or a taxi to St.-Charles station.

In the Steps of Cézanne **VALUE** **ALL AGES**

Start from tourist office, 2 place du Général de Gaulle, Aix-en-Provence, 📞 04 42 16 11 61, www.aixenprovencetourism.com

Rather than sign up for the expensive 'Sur les Pas de Cézanne' guided tour offered by the tourist office, pick up their free brochure on places of interest associated with their most famous former resident, such as the house where he was born and the cafés on Cours Mirabeau where he held court. The sites are marked by gold studs with a letter 'C' embedded in the pavements. Even if you're not particularly arty, it makes discovering the town more interesting.

Also worth a trip with children are the **Bibémus quarries** (just off the D10 before Vauvenargues), which are full of strange shapes that Cézanne loved to paint in the shadow of Montagne Ste.-Victoire—make sure you wear comfy walking shoes, and don't attempt it with a buggy.

Marseille—Le Grand Tour
★★ ALL AGES

Buses leave from Vieux Port. ☎ 04 91 91 05 82, www.marseillelegrand tour.com

As in many cities, open-top buses are a great way to explore Marseille when you haven't yet got your bearings. The 16 stops include **Parc Borély** (p. 152), **Notre-Dame de la Garde** church and the **Stade Vélodrome** (p. 150). If you don't have a car, it's also a good way to take a ride along the scenic Corniche, check out the sumptuous villas, decide which beach you

like the look of and take in the view over to **Château d'If** (p. 153). I find a game of *I Spy?* is a good way of getting our kids involved.

Combine the Grand Tour with a **City Pass** (☎ 04 91 13 89 00, *www.marseille-tourisme.com*), which gives you one (20€) or two (27€) days' access to many of Marseille's attractions.

*Open Daily 10am–7pm Apr–Oct; daily 10:45am–5:30pm Nov–Dec and Feb–Mar. **Adm** Adult 1-day pass 18€, children aged 4–11 8€, children under 4 free. **Credit** Cash only.*

Active Families

Côte Bleue Plongée
★★ AGE 8 & UP

Les Marins du Port, Sausset-les-Pins, ☎ 04 42 45 42 42, www.cote-bleue-plongee.com

Imagine floating weightlessly, surrounded by multi-coloured rocks and red coral, while shoals of exotic fish wiggle by you in slow motion. This diving school will make sure you have an unforgettable underwater experience (in English, should you wish) on the Côte Bleue,

Little Tourist Trains

Marseille has not one but two **Petits Trains Touristiques** (☎ 04 91 25 24 69, *www.petit-train-marseille.com*), both of which sport OM colours (p. 150) and offer year-round trips every 20 to 30 minutes (from 6€ for adults and 3€ for kids) from the Vieux Port to the Panier district or up to Notre-Dame de la Garde church. There are also tourist trains in Cassis (☎ 06 11 54 27 73, *www.cpts.fr*), departing from Cassis's tourist office on Esplanade du Général de Gaulle near the port, and in Aix (☎ 06 11 54 27 73, *www.cpts.fr*), leaving from Place de la Rotonde.

whether you're a novice or an old hand. Allow half a day for a first dive.

Open *Daily 8am–7pm mid-May–mid-Sept; daily 9:30am–noon and 4–7pm mid-Sept–mid-May.* **Adm** *First dive including equipment 55€, children aged 8–12 42€; advance booking required.* **Credit** *MC, V.*

Indian Forest Sud
★★ **AGE 5 & UP**

Les Petites Bastides, Bouc-Bel-Air, 📞 *04 42 94 03 19/06 13 01 19 86; Chemin de Figuerolle, Martigues,* 📞 *06 13 01 19 86,* **www.indian forest.fr**

Everyone from 5-year-olds to pensioners can test their nerve and skill on rope bridges along trails of varying height and difficulty at Indian Forest Sud. Each circuit takes about 2 hours and trails are allocated according to age and ability. Afterwards, you can enjoy a picnic in the meadow or a tasty bite in the on-site restaurant.

Open *Daily 9:30am–8pm July–Aug; Wed, Sat and Sun 10am–7pm*

Apr–June and Sept; Wed, Sat and Sun 10am–5:30pm Oct–Mar; closed Dec–Jan. **Adm** *17€, children 9–11 14€, children 5–8 11€.* **Credit** *MC, V.*

INSIDER TIP ≫

Cassis's diving school
(📞 *04 42 01 89 16,* **www.centre cassidaindeplongee.com**) organises 'first dives' in English for children over 12 for 63€, including equipment and insurance.

Naturoscope
★★★ **VALUE** **GREEN** **ALL AGES**

3 impasse du Meunier, Marseille, 📞 *06 23 87 75 30,* **www. naturoscope.fr**

If you speak French, this is a great way to explore Marseille's coastline—Naturoscope is an eco-friendly organisation that aims to introduce people to the local environment through guided walks and snorkelling tours. For a nominal fee per person you can spend the afternoon with an eco-guide on the **Îles du Frioul** (p. 154).

Léonard Parli, Aix-en-Provence

Fish Market, Marseille

Open Daily 9am–7pm. *Adm* 2€; advance booking required. *Credit* Cash only.

Shopping

Léonard Parli FIND

35 avenue Victor Hugo, Aix-en-Provence, 📞 04 42 26 05 71, *www.leonard-parli.com*

You won't go far in Provence without coming into contact with a calisson, an ellipse-shaped sweet made from ground almonds mixed with candied melon and fruit syrup, famous for being one of the 13 Christmas desserts (p. 165). Léonard Parli founded the first Calisson factory in this shop in Aix in 1874, and the business is still run by his family on the original premises. Sometimes visitors can see the sweets being made in the workshop downstairs (phone in advance).

Open Mon–Fri 8am–7pm, Sat 9am–12:30pm and 3–7pm. *Credit* MC, V.

Les Minots de Marseille ★★

26 place aux Huiles, Marseille, 📞 04 96 11 00 16, *www.lesminots.eu*

This little shop near the Vieux Port sells every kind of toy and game imaginable, from CDs of lullabies to baby's first drums and eco-friendly wooden toys.

Open Mon–Sat 10am–7pm. *Credit* MC, V.

Santons Fouque ★

65 cours Gambetta, Aix-en-Provence, 📞 04 42 26 33 38, *www.santons-fouque.com*

TIP **Read All About It**

Browse books over muffins at **Book in Bar** (Rue Joseph Cabassol, 📞 *04 42 26 60 07*, *www.bookinbar.com*). Just off the Cours Mirabeau in Aix, this English-language bookshop sells novels, travel guides, comics and children's books for all ages. There's a tearoom in the back.

Fish market: Quai des Belges, Old Port, Marseille, every morning.
Fruit & vegetable market: Cours Julien, Marseille, every morning (flowers and organic produce on Wed morning).
Food & fish market: Place Baragnon, Cassis, Wed and Fri mornings.
Local produce market: Place Richelme, Aix-en-Provence, every morning.

This is not just a shop, it's an experience. Since 1934, the Fouque family has been making *santons* in their boutique and workshop in a Provençal house surrounded by a perfume-laden Mediterranean garden. You can browse the little clay figures and cribs to the sound of traditional music, and sometimes even watch Mireille and her team at work. The shop is a 15-minute walk from the city centre. Call in advance for details of guided tours.

Open Mon–Sat 9am–noon and 2–6pm. **Credit** MC, V. **Amenities** ⚬

FAMILY-FRIENDLY DINING

Marseille & Around

The Vieux Port is lined with places to dine, including fish restaurants such as **Le Miramar** (p. 160) and steakhouses (from the well-established **Entrecôte**, ☏ 04 91 33 84 84, on Quai de Rive Neuve, to the family-friendly chain **Hippopotamus**, ☏ 04 91 59 91 40, on Quai des Belges). Nearby, you'll find everything from Provençal to Vietnamese in the **Place aux Huiles** linking onto Cours Honoré d'Estienne

d'Orves. Kids can run around these pedestrianised squares while you dine, before dragging you to the traditional toy shop **Les Minots de Marseille** (p. 159).

Among the tourist haunts, there are some reliable family-friendly restaurants such as La Crêpe au Carré (p. 161) and Fuxia l'Epicerie (☏ 04 55 91 02 63) on nearby Place Thiars, or grab self-service pasta at Pasta Basta. Meanwhile, two Marseillaise bastions of Provençal cuisine, Paule & Kopa (☏ 04 91 33 26 03) and Arceneaulx, (☏ 04 91 59 80 30) are best for a quiet evening without the kids.

EXPENSIVE

Le Miramar ★★

12 quai du Port, Marseille, ☏ 04 91 91 10 40, www.bouillabaisse.com

This restaurant in the Vieux Port is the very best place to taste *bouillabaisse*, the dish most associated with Marseille. It's smart, with DJ-wearing waiters, but offers simple fish and vegetables for children on request, although we've never actually seen any 'small people' here. If you prefer somewhere more child-friendly, walk a bit further down the quay to **Le Marseillois** (☏ 04 91 90 72 52), a sailing-ship-turned-restaurant offering a children's menu (without chips) as well as the prized local fishy feast.

Open *Tues–Sat noon–2pm and 7–10pm.* **Main courses** *35–60€. Bouillabaisse 55€.* **Credit** *AE, MC, V.*

MODERATE

Le Café des Epices ★★

4 rue du Lacydon, Marseille, ☎ *04 91 91 22 69,* ***www.cafedesepices.com***

Once you've tasted the food here, you won't want to go anywhere else. Aixois Chef **Arnaud de Grammont** is a culinary magician: even my 18-month-old son Charlie scoffed a grown-up portion of wild salmon cooked with blinis and caramelised onions. Green- and pink-painted tables are scattered around the pretty pedestrianised square beside the Hôtel de Ville, and the daily menu is written up on an oversized olive-tree pot. Sadly, there's no kids' menu.

Open *Tues–Sat 10:30am–3pm and 6–11pm.* **Menus** *two-course menu 21€, three-course menu 25€.* **Credit** *MC, V.*

Poissonnerie Laurent ★★★

5 quai Barthélemy, Cassis, ☎ *04 42 01 71 56*

What you'll immediately notice at this harbourside fish restaurant is the age range of the clientele, which extends from babies to grandmas. A family restaurant in every sense of the word, it's run by the latest generation of the fishing family who opened it about 150 years ago. Children will be fascinated by the fish counter. The owner, Eric, who has young ones of his own, is keen for children to eat well, and the *menu enfant* (8.60€) consists of fresh fish with vegetables. Sundays are especially busy, so book in advance or turn up early. Parents can enjoy a chilled glass of the renowned local white or rosé with their meal.

Open *Tues–Sun noon–2pm and 7:45–10pm June–Sept; daily noon–2pm Oct–Dec and Feb–May.* **Main courses** *from 13.90€. Children's menu 8.60€.* **Credit** *Cash only.*

INEXPENSIVE

La Crêpe au Carré ★

40 place aux Huiles, Marseille, ☎ *04 91 55 52 39,* ***www.lacrepeaucarre. com***

This stone-vaulted *crêperie* is built in a converted warehouse over the ancient canal that used

---

Aïoli

Aïoli is best described as garlic mayonnaise, but in Provence it can also refer to a complete dish consisting of boiled cod, potatoes, carrots, green beans and egg, topped with the sauce. For an authentic recipe, see ***www.aixenprovencetourism.com/uk/aix-aioli.htm*** (snails are optional).

The Best Local Ice Cream

Fam...

...t ice cream in Aix is sold at **Philippe Segond** (☎ *04 42 38 19 69*), ...Mirabeau, which as well as making yummy ices, offers *tarte Aixoise—* ...shaped like, and tasting of, a *calisson* (p. 159). In Marseille, top-dog is the **Brasserie Beau Rivage** (☎ *04 91 54 97 28*), 13 quai de Rive-Neuve, where flavours include white chocolate, pineapple and (not very French, admittedly) Snickers. In **Cassis**, head for **Snack des Calanques** (☎ *04 42 01 73 13*), 1 rue Victor Hugo, just off the harbour.

to bring oil to Marseille's soap factories. Nowadays, a multitude of savoury *sarrasin galettes*, sweet pancakes and salads are on offer. My daughter Alexandra likes the caramelised apple crepe with whipped cream. Tables spill out onto the pedestrianised square where kids can run around, while parents relax with sports matches playing on the wide-screen TV.

Open *Sat and Sun noon–midnight, Mon–Fri noon–3pm and 6:30pm–midnight.* **Menu** *two-course menu 10.90€.* **Credit** *MC, V.*

Aix-en-Provence

The **Cours Mirabeau** is perfect for people-watching over coffee in Belle Epoque café-bars such as **Le Grillon** (☎ *04 42 27 58 81*), but varying quality and tourist-priced menus mean that better restaurants can be found in the myriad pedestrianised back-streets.

Parents seeking fine French dining will enjoy the stone-vaulted cellars of foodie mecca **Le Formal** (☎ *04 42 27 08 31*) on Rue Espariat. Mini-gourmets are also well catered for at market-fresh **Tomate Verte** (☎ *04 42 60 04 58*) on Rue des Tanneurs,

where kids choose any main course and dessert for 9€.

You can take your pick of places for a cheap family snack in the pretty pedestrianised Place Richelme. Gorge on sandwiches and herb-seasoned chips at **L'Authentique** (☎ *04 42 63 10 33*) or *tartines* (open sandwiches), eggy breakfasts and seasonal specialities such as wintertime raclette at **Le Pain Quotidien** (☎ *04 42 23 48 57*), with its huge oak tables for communal dining.

EXPENSIVE

La Bastide du Cours

43–47 cours Mirabeau, Aix-en-Provence, ☎ *04 42 26 10 06,* **www. bastideducours.com**

On Aix's answer to the Boulevard St.-Germain in Paris, this smartly decorated local hangout makes up for its elevated prices with a relaxed atmosphere and beautifully presented Provençal and international dishes garnished with local herbs. However, it's the desserts that really take the biscuit—try the *dessert provençal* (*calisson* and melon sorbet served with thyme-flavoured liqueur). Children get their own two-course burger-and-chips menu.

TIP ▶ ## Picnic with a View ◀

Situated on the eastern side of the entrance to Marseille's Vieux Port, the **Parc du Pharo** has an impressive château and gardens and an unimpeded view of the Château d'If and Îles du Frioul (p. 154). It's perfect for picnics.

Afternoon-long opening hours make it practical for parents juggling kids' meal times.

Open Daily noon–midnight. **Main courses** 16€–28€. **Amenities** 草 **Credit** MC, V.

INEXPENSIVE

Chez Jo ★★

59 rue Espariat, Aix-en-Provence, ℓ 04 42 26 12 47, www.pizzeria chezjo.com

Locals and celebrities alike flock to Chez Jo, overlooking the fountain in Rue Espariat. Run for the last 30 years by Aixoise Jo and now by her son Alexandre, this long-established pizzeria is famed for its tasty anchovy pizzas and lasagne straight from the wood-fired oven.

Open Daily noon–3pm and 7pm–1am. **Main courses** from 11.50€. **Credit** MC, V.

Salon-de-Provence

Salon-de-Provence isn't known for its fine dining. However, there are two notable exceptions for an expensive romantic meal without the kids: the **Abbaye de Ste.-Crox** (p. 166), with its panoramic terrace and menus from 71€, and **La Salle à Manger** (ℓ 04 90 56 28 01) on Rue du Maréchal Joffre, with its

flamboyant interiors (expect a bill of 30€ to 50€ per person). My favourite family-friendly place is **Le 7e Restaurant** (ℓ 04 90 55 24 05, www.le7e.fr) near Barben Zoo. It has vaulted stone interiors and an outdoor terrace, and offers homely French cuisine plus a 10€ kids' menu. In central Salon, a convenient place for a family snack is the **Crêperie de Salon** (ℓ 04 90 55 93 43) on pedestrianised Rue de l'Horloge.

FAMILY-FRIENDLY ACCOMMODATION

Marseille & Around

Accommodation in Marseille is a curious mix of the good, the bad and the ugly. One such curate's egg is the **Hôtel Le Corbusier** (ℓ 04 91 16 78 00, www.hotelle corbusier.com, family studios from 94€), whose stark architecture both wows and horrifies families in equal measure. Walking around the dimly lit corridors is like being in an episode of *Dr Who*—you expect to bump into a platoon of Judoon at any moment. An alternative way to see this architectural milestone with older kids is to go for a gastronomic lunch at 24€.

A safer bet in the city is the swish **Sofitel Vieux Port** (📞 *04 91 15 59 00, www.sofitel.com*). Situated at the water's edge overlooking the Vieux Port, the hotel has a pool, spa and connecting rooms for families. It's worth upgrading to a superior room to make the most of the wonderful harbour views. On the other side of the port, looking up towards Notre-Dame de la Garde, the **Résidence du Vieux Port** (📞 *04 91 91 91 22, www.hotelmarseille. com,* two-room family apartments at 260€) is a well-priced alternative. View-seekers will also love **La Suite Cassis** (📞 *06 22 31 63 57, www.lasuitecassis. com*). It has three rooms (from 125€) and a swimming pool overlooking the Cap Canaille; this diminutive B&B is our favourite place in Cassis.

INEXPENSIVE

Auberge de Jeunesse La Fontasse GREEN

La Fontasse, Cassis, 📞 *04 42 01 02 72, www.fuaj.org*

This is the 'wild' card in every sense of the word, and definitely the place to come if you want to get back to nature. Situated in the middle of Calanques country, Cassis's youth hostel operates entirely on eco-principles, using solar- and wind-powered electricity, a rainwater cistern and no hot water or showers. It's a great base for walking, climbing and swimming. Accommodation is in standard dormitories of 10 beds, and only children over the age of 7 are allowed. Although it's a bit of a hike to get there, you'll be rewarded with panoramic views over the Calanques cliffs and the turquoise sea.

Closed Jan–mid-Mar Berths 50. Rates from 12€pp. Credit Cash only. Amenities 🅿 ⊠ ✿ ⋀

Camping Lou Souleï ★★ FIND

Carry-le-Rouet, 📞 *04 42 44 75 75, www.lousoulei.com*

The ideal spot for a budget family holiday right on the Côte Bleue, this four-star campsite has tent or caravan pitches plus chalet-style mobile homes sleeping four adults plus two children under 6. It's well equipped, with three swimming pools, a large supermarket and a programme of summertime activities for all the family; the rest of the year it's handy for exploring the Calanques, Martigues and Marseille. About 1½km from the campsite, Carry-le-Rouet is renowned for its February sea urchin festival and for being the final home of singer Nina Simone.

FUN FACT ❯❯ **Little Saint**

The word *santon* comes from the Provençal word *santoun*, which means 'little saint'.

Christmas in Provence

The festive period in Provence begins on December 4th, when families begin to assemble their *santon*-filled Nativity scene. These figurines represent local villagers from the 19th century, when the crib scene is set. December sees *santon* fairs across the region, notably in Marseille, along with eye-catching craft and food markets. Christmas dinner, comprising seven meatless dishes, is traditionally eaten on Christmas Eve before the family heads off to midnight Mass. In some villages, the Mass includes a nativity play sung and spoken in Provençal. The family returns home to finish the festivities with 13 desserts, representing the diners at the Last Supper.

Berths *700.* **Price** *Mobile home rental July and Aug from 82€ per day, rest of year from 432€ per week.* **Credit** *MC, V.* **Amenities** 🖼️ 🖼️ 🛏️ 🛍️ 🍴 🍽️ 📷

Hôtel Edmond Rostand ★★ VALUE

31 rue Dragon, Marseille, 📞 *04 91 37 74 95, www.hoteledmondrostand.com*

A well-priced place for a short stay in the centre of Marseille. Though it's only a 5-minute walk from the Vieux Port, it's on a quiet street in the antiques quarter. Philippe, the friendly owner, has renovated the hotel extensively since he took over in 2007, furnishing its contemporary bedrooms with wooden floors and flatscreen TVs. In an adjacent building there are comfortable family studios with fully equipped kitchens. As a native of Cassis, Philippe can give you plenty of advice on sightseeing.

Rooms *15.* **Rates** *65€–99€. Breakfast 8.50€. Cot free.* **Credit** *AE, MC, V.* **Amenities** 🛗 💻 🍴 **In room** A/C 🗄️

Aix-en-Provence

MODERATE

Hôtel Cézanne ★★★ FIND

(formerly Mercure Paul Cézanne) 40 avenue Victor Hugo, Aix-en-Provence, 📞 *04 42 91 11 11, http://cezanne.hotelaix.com*

This former Mercure hotel in central Aix has been transformed under the imaginative guidance of ex-Parisian journalist Catherine Spieth-Ducret. She ensures all the right details are in place: free minibar, plush bed linen, free Wi-Fi, free secure car parking and a sumptuous champagne breakfast complete with truffle omelette. The contemporary bedrooms have been signed off by Charles Montemarco, one of the designers of Aix's ultra-luxury Villa Gallici. Meanwhile, Cézanne himself no doubt would have approved of artist Zidan's fire-inspired paintings that decorate the reception area. Connecting rooms 310 and 311 are perfect for families. There's no restaurant, but you can order take-away pasta for 18€ with a choice of 10 sauces and 9 different pastas.

Rooms 55. **Rates** from 159€. Breakfast 19€ + 3€ in room, children under 12 free. **Credit** AE, MC, V. **Amenities** ▭ **In room** A/C @ □

L'Atrium d'Anaïte

15 cours Gambetta, Espace Forbin, Aix-en-Provence, ☎ 04 42 99 16 00, **www.residence-atrium-aix-en-provence.federal-hotel.com**

This modern *hôtel-résidence* welcomes families with its self-catering, brightly coloured two-room apartments for up to four people—one room has a double bed, the other a sofa-bed. Conveniently located near Aix's historic Mazarin district, it has a private car park—a boon given that parking spaces are scarce in this city. The friendly receptionists are happy to advise on sightseeing. If you don't want to make your own breakfast, you can eat it in the café downstairs.

Rooms 140. **Rates** from 89€, four-person studios from 117€. Cot free. Breakfast 12€, children under 12 6€. **Credit** AE, MC, V. **Amenities** ▣ ☑ **In room** A/C ☒ □

Salon-de-Provence

The **Abbaye de Ste.-Croix** (☎ 04 90 56 24 55, **www.hotels-provence.com**) makes a luxurious stopover for families heading on to explore inland Provence. It's a quiet place to lie by the pool, explore the extensive grounds and enjoy the sweeping views from its two-room family suites (from 475€). It's worth fitting in a visit to the glorious Barben Château and Zoo nearby. North of Salon-de-Provence, holiday village **Pierres et Vacances Pont-Royal** (☎ 08 92 70 01 30, **www.pierreetvacances.com**) rents cottages and apartments (family studios 290€ to 1,360€) per week), in a pretty park complete with kids' club, pools, playground, farm, golf and tennis.

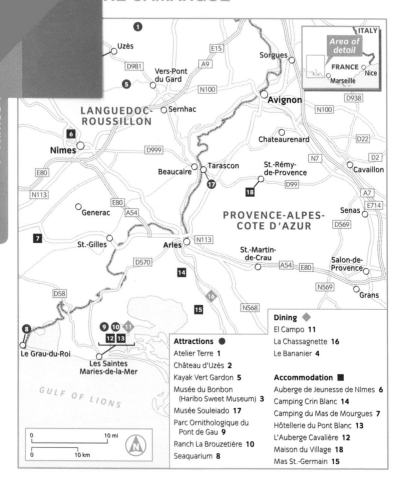

Uzès

E15

Sorgues

D981   Vers-Pont
du Gard

A9

N100

Avignon

D938

LANGUEDOC-   Sernhac
ROUSSILLON

N100

Chateaurenard

D22

Nîmes

D999

St.-Rémy-
de-Provence

N7

D2

Beaucaire   Tarascon

Cavaillon

E80

D99

A7

N113

Musée Souleiado

D99

E714

Generac

E80

A54

PROVENCE-ALPES-
COTE D'AZUR

Senas

D569

St.-Gilles

Arles   N113

St.-Martin-
de-Crau

A54   E80

Salon-de-
Provence

D570

D58

N569

Grans

Le Grau-du-Roi

N568

Les Saintes
Maries-de-la-Mer

GULF OF LIONS

Dining
El Campo 11
La Chassagnette 16
Le Bananier 4

Attractions
Atelier Terre 1
Château d'Uzès 2
Kayak Vert Gardon 5
Musée du Bonbon (Haribo Sweet Museum) 3
Musée Souleiado 17
Parc Ornithologique du Pont de Gau 9
Ranch La Brouzetière 10
Seaquarium 8

Accommodation
Auberge de Jeunesse de Nîmes 6
Camping Crin Blanc 14
Camping du Mas de Mourgues 7
Hôtellerie du Pont Blanc 13
L'Auberge Cavalière 12
Maison du Village 18
Mas St.-Germain 15

0   10 mi

0   10 km

From the rolling, lavender-scented landscapes of the Gard to the rice fields of the Camargue, you've just arrived in one of France's wildest and weirdest regions. Flamingoes and half-wild black bulls inhabit the wetlands and lagoons where the mighty Rhône meets the Mediterranean, in a region that is still patrolled by colourfully garbed *gardians* mounted on their famous white horses. Join them to ride across the marshes, or build sandcastles on the longest and least crowded beaches in Provence, or explore well-preserved Roman amphitheatres in Arles and Nîmes. Ancient and modern architecture lie cheek-by-jowl, from Uzès's fairytale castle to Norman Foster's **Carré d'Art** and Philippe Starck's Abribus bus stop.

Although the mosquitoes that gather in summer months might bug you, this otherwise unspoilt region has plenty to entertain children from tots to teens. Depending on their age, they'll love to watch falcons performing at Beaucaire castle, dressing up like a cowboy in Nîmes, canoeing on the **river Gardon** or heading off the beaten track to the windswept expanse of **L'Espiguette**. Above all, don't miss colourful festivals that prove how the Spanish, Italian and Gypsy cultures have shaped local life over the centuries.

VISITOR INFORMATION

Nîmes, Uzès, Pont du Gard and **Aigues-Mortes** are all in the Gard *département*, covered by *www.gard-tourisme.com*. For information on **Arles** and the **Camargue**, both in the Bouches du Rhône, see *www.camargue.fr* or *www.visitprovence.com*.

Getting There

By Air The most convenient airport for this area is Nîmes-Garons (*www.nimes-aeroport.fr*), about 10km outside the city; a shuttle bus (5€, 📞 *04 66 29 27 29*) will take you into the city centre in about 40 minutes. **Ryanair** (*www.ryanair.com*) operates flights to **Nîmes** from London Luton and Liverpool.

By Train You can get from London to Nîmes by train in about 6 hours, taking the **Eurostar** from London St. Pancras to either Lille or Paris, then the **TGV**. For timetable information and bookings contact **Rail Europe** (p. 32).

By Car See p. 34.

Orientation

The **N86** takes you north from **Nîmes** to **Remoulins**, where it turns into the **D981**, which passes the entrance to the **Pont du Gard** and carries on to **Uzès**. **Arles** is connected to **Nîmes** by the **N113** and to the **Camargue** by the **D570**, which ends at Stes-Maries-de-la-Mer. Alternatively, take the **D36** from **Arles** along the eastern side of the Étang de Vaccarès for **Le Sambuc** and **Salin de Giraud**. To reach **Aigues-Mortes**, take the **N113** south from **Nîmes** to Gallargues and then the **D979**, which ends in Le Grau-du-Roi. From **Arles**, take the **N572** west towards Aimargues, where it joins the **D979**.

Getting Around

If you're exploring the area using public transport, it's easiest to base yourself in **Nîmes** or **Arles**, both well connected to surrounding towns and villages by bus or train. See *www.lepilote. com* for **Cartreize** buses serving Arles, Stes-Maries-de-la-Mer and Tarascon (in French only). The 'Entre Ter et Mer' rail service connects Nîmes with Vauvert, Aigues-Mortes and the seaside resort of Le Grau-du-Roi for a flat fare of 6€: it's a great way of

Fast Facts: Nîmes & the Camargue

Banks: Banque de France (☎ *08 11 90 18 01*) is at 2 square du 11 Novembre 1918, Nîmes, next to Les Arenes. In Arles, Credit Agricole (☎ *04 90 18 30 30*) is at 12 boulevard des Lices and 45 avenue Stalingrad.

Hospitals: Centre Hospitalier Universitaire de Nîmes (☎ *04 66 23 97 16*, *www.chu-nimes.fr*), Place du Regis Debre. In Arles, **Centre Hospitalier d'Arles Joseph Imbert** (☎ *04 90 49 29 29*) at Quartier Fourchon.

Internet Cafés: Cyber Saladelle (☎ *04 90 93 13 56*), 17 rue de la République, Arles.

Pharmacies: Grande Pharmacie de la Croix Bleu (☎ *09 60 01 97 52*), 2 place de la Salamandre, Nîmes, is open 7:30am to 9:30pm Monday to Saturday. In Arles, **Pharmacie de la Mairie** (☎ *04 90 96 01*), 46 rue de l'Hôtel de Ville, is the most central.

Post Offices: Nîmes's most central post office is at 6 rue du Verdun (☎ *04 66 67 21 51*); open 8:30am to 6pm Monday to Friday and 9am to 12:30pm Saturday. In Arles, La Poste (☎ *08 00 00 90 42*) is at 5 boulevard des Lices.

Shopping: See p. 184 and, for markets, p. 185.

---

avoiding the traffic jams that plague the coast in summer and can reduce children (and, indeed, mums and dads) to impatient tears. For more information on regional trains, visit *www.ter-sncf.com* (in English).

Check out *www.travelsupermarket.com* for a price comparison of car-hire companies in the region. Rental firms at Nîmes airport are listed on the airport website *www.nimesairport.com*.

WHAT TO SEE & DO

Children's Top 10 Attractions

❶ **Pretending** to be a gladiator in Nîmes's Roman amphitheatre (p. 173).

❷ **Following** in the brushstrokes of Van Gogh in Arles (p. 173).

❸ **Horse-riding** in the Camargue (p. 183).

❹ **Imagining** yourself as a medieval knight on a walk around Aigues-Mortes's ramparts (p. 172).

❺ **Experiencing** the sights and smells of the Saturday-morning market in Uzès (p. 175).

❻ **Gasping** in awe at the birds of prey in Beaucaire (p. 177).

❼ **Sampling** sweets at the Musée du Bonbon in Uzès (p. 180).

❽ **Discovering** where your jeans come from in the Musée du Vieux Nîmes (p. 181).

9 Learning about flamingoes at Pont de Gau ornithology park (p. 176).

10 Canoeing under the Pont du Gard Roman aqueduct (p. 179).

Child-friendly Events & Entertainment

Féria de Nîmes ★ ★ AGE 10 & UP

Around Nîmes, ☎ 04 66 58 38 00, www.ot-nimes.fr

You probably won't want to attend the bullfights in this Roman arena, but you'll have fun wandering around soaking up the atmosphere (not to mention the fumes from *pastis* and sangria) at Nîmes's 5-day Whitsun festival. Both locals and tourists get decked out in Camargue or flamenco-style finery; try Les Indiennes de Nîmes (p. 185), if you want to join them. Be warned that accommodation in central Nîmes gets booked up years in advance of this annual event.

*May. **Adm** Free.*

Fêtes de la Tarasque
★ ALL AGES

Tarascon, ☎ 04 90 91 03 52, www.tarascon.org

In days of old the citizens of Tarascon lived in mortal fear of a **man-eating monster** with a lion's head and a dragon's tail, named the *tarasque*, that had its lair on the banks of the Rhône. Thankfully, St. Martha subdued the beast with holy water long enough for the locals to stone it to death. These days the event is commemorated by a colourful replica of the monster paraded through the streets of the town, charging into the crowd and snapping at spectators.

*June. **Adm** Free.*

La Tarasque

FUN FACT >> ## Read & Learn <<

Camille and the Sunflowers by Laurence Anholt (Frances Lincoln), an illustrated story of a little boy who befriends Van Gogh, provides kids with a good introduction to the great Dutch artist's work.

Festival du Cheval

★ ★ ★ **AGE 10 & UP**

Stes-Maries-de-la-Mer and around, ☎ *04 90 97 85 86, www.festivaldu cheval.camargue.fr*

The Camargue is the perfect setting for 3 days of horsey heaven, with dozens of events (some free) in Stes-Maries-de-la-Mer and at the nearby Domaine Paul Ricard Méjanes, giving you an insight into the role of horses in this bull-dominated region. Children will love watching the horses and bulls run through the streets (*abrivado*) from a safe distance, observing a *course camarguaise* (a game where men called *razeteurs* try to snatch a rosette from between a young bull's horns), and seeing a horse show set to flamenco music.

July. **Adm** *Tickets for the climactic Grand Spectacle Equestre cost 12€ for under 12s, 30€ adults. Make sure you get numbered (numerotées) seats—they cost a little more, but it's worth it.*

INSIDER TIP >>

Remember to pack some powerful repellent against the mosquitoes that often plague the Camargue, and which seem undeterred by 'natural' repellents containing citronella oil. To keep them off, use any of the versions containing DEET (diethyl toluamide) available from all UK and most French pharmacies.

Cities, Towns & Resorts

Aigues-Mortes

Tourist office: ☎ *04 66 53 73 00, www.ot-aiguesmortes.fr*

'Dead Waters' is hardly an enticing name, but Aigues-Mortes's fortified walls certainly look impressive when you approach. Once a thriving port, this 13th-century town with its criss-cross streets now houses dozens of restaurants and a number of both smart and more bo-ho shops selling clothes, home decor and art. Children love to tour the

St.-Laurent d'Aigouze

St.-Laurent d'Aigouze is the only place in Europe to have its church attached to a bullring, and among its 3,000 inhabitants is the Chilean woman who invented Botox. This Camargue town is worth a visit on your way to or from Aigues-Mortes, especially during the *fête votive* in August, when Camargue traditions are brought to life. The village's tourist office (☎ *04 66 88 17 00*) is on Boulevard Gambetta.

The fortified walls of Aigues-Mortes

ramparts, then visit the shop beneath them for all things medieval, including princess and page outfits and castles to make out of card. If you arrive in town in the morning, you might spy fishermen unloading their catch on Quai Colbert. Don't miss the nearby seaside resort of Le Grau-du-Roi, with its **Seaquarium** (p. 177).

Arles ★★★

Tourist office: 📞 *04 90 18 41 20,* ***www.tourisme.ville-arles.fr***

The warmth, the colours and, above all, the sunlight that give Arles its unique glow have inspired more than a few painters. Smaller than Nîmes, the town comes into its own on a mellow summer evening, when you see the setting sun turning the stone orange and hear the animated buzz of cafégoers. Visit the famous Roman arena or walk around the narrow streets in the *vieille ville* (old town) to get a feel of what it was like

when Vincent **Van Gogh** and Paul **Gauguin** were here. Arles still has a thriving artistic life that includes the world-famous photography festival, **Les Rencontres d'Arles**, from July to September every summer.

Be warned that the old town is not pedestrianised, and cars tend to hurtle through the narrow streets at top speed.

Nîmes ★★

Tourist office: 📞 *04 66 58 38 00,* ***www.ot-nimes.fr***

The first thing that strikes you about Nîmes is how comfortably the ancient and the modern sit side-by-side here. The focal point of the town is the Place de la Maison Carrée, where **Maison Carrée**, a Roman temple, lies opposite the **Carré d'Art**, a 1993 contemporary art museum and library designed by British architect Lord (Norman) Foster. Nîmes was founded by Roman soldiers who were awarded the land after successfully defeating

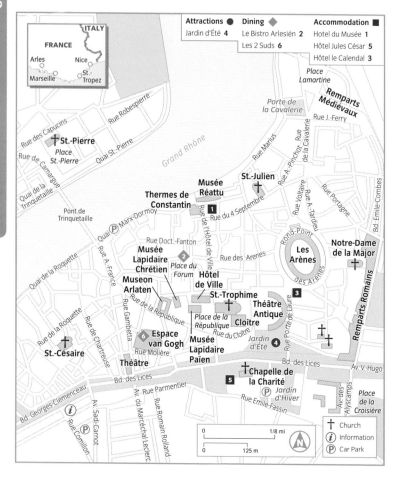

Attractions ●	Dining ◆	Accommodation ■
Jardin d'Été 4	Le Bistro Arlesién 2	Hotel du Musée 1
	Les 2 Suds 6	Hôtel Jules César 5
		Hôtel le Calendal 3

the Egyptians—2,000 years later, you and your children can enjoy spotting the image of a crocodile and a palm tree (celebrating this military triumph) all over town. It's the city's emblem and the

FUN FACT 》 **Spot the Croc** 《

Nîmes's city emblem of the crocodile can be glimpsed everywhere, including in the fountain in the Place du Marché. If you visit the Hôtel de Ville (town hall), and turn left when you're through the entrance, you'll see four of them, suspended from the ceiling at the top of the staircase. How many more can you spy throughout the city?

NIMES

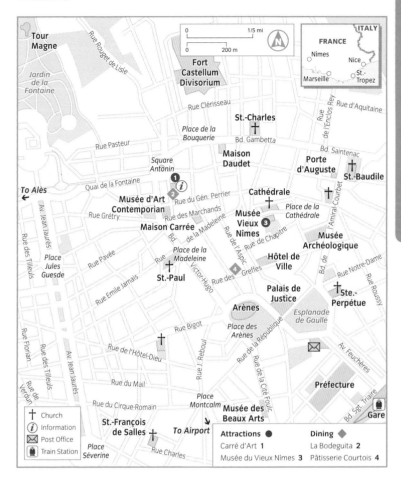

St.-François
de Salles

Attractions ●	Dining ◆
Carré d'Art 1	La Bodeguita 2
Musée du Vieux Nîmes 3	Pâtisserie Courtois 4

✝ Church	
ⓘ Information	
✉ Post Office	
🚆 Train Station	

nickname of the local football team, 'Les Crocos'.

Uzès ★★

Tourist office: 📞 *04 66 22 68 88,*
www.uzes-tourisme.com

Uzès is a duchy and the whole town is built around the fairytale castle, **Château d'Uzès** (p. 179), with a real live Duke (who, naturally, lives mainly in Paris). The best time to visit the town is on a Saturday morning when the market in the Place aux Herbes is in full swing: the smells, colours and sounds will give you an insight into everyday life in a Provençal town. Other family attractions are the **Haribo sweet museum** (p. 180) and **Haras d'Uzès** National Stud (p. 177). Uzès is also a good base for exploring the surrounding area, the highlights of which are the **Pont du Gard** (p. 179) and canoeing on the **river Gardon**

(p. 184). There are plenty of events throughout the year too, such as a **truffle festival** in January and a **donkey festival** in September.

Natural Wonders & Spectacular Views

La Crau ★

Between Arles and Salon-de-Provence; head from Arles to Salon-de-Provence on the N113 then go south along N568 towards Fos-sur-Mer before turning north on N569 to rejoin N113.

The last **steppe-like plain** in France, made from fused pebbles deposited by the Durance river in the Ice Age, this rocky outcrop originally covered 40,000 hectares from the southern Alpilles to the sea. Sheep such as the Arles merino have been farmed on the green part of it since ancient times, and *transhumance* (when sheep and goats go to the mountains for summer) still takes place every June. There is also an impressive bird population, including France's only colony of pin-tailed sandgrouse, and it is only one of two sites in the country where the lesser kestrel nests. To find out

Maison Carrée, Nîmes

more, visit the **Eco-Museum** in St.-Martin de Crau (📞 *04 90 47 02 01* or *www.espaces-naturels-provence.com/ecomuse.htm*), which includes exhibitions on farming and transhumance, plus a Provençal crèche at Christmas.

Aquaria & Animal Parks

Parc Ornithologique du Pont de Gau ★ ★ ★ FIND

4km from Stes-Maries-de-la-Mer on D570, 📞 *04 90 97 82 62, www.parcornithologique.com*

TIP ❯❯ **The Camargue's Best Beaches** ❮

L'Espiguette, Le Grau-du-Roi. An 18km Blue Flag beach best suited to families with older children; there are no facilities.

Plage des Amphores, Stes-Maries-de-la-Mer. A family-oriented beach in front of the village; busy in high season.

Plage Sud, Le Grau-du-Roi. A good option for younger families; situated in front of the Marina.

La Garrigue

You'll probably smell the so-called garrigue scrubland before you see it—the perfume of thyme, lavender, rosemary and other bushy plants that cover the region permeates the air whenever you leave a town.

Fred, the English-speaking guide, refers to this nature reserve as a 'bird hotel', and that's just what it is. He and his family manage a 60-hectare site that facilitates the stay of migrating birds, including thousands of flamingoes and egrets. They also look after injured birds and take part in breeding programmes. Children of all ages enjoy walking the paths around the lakes and spotting bulls; the info boards are in French but an English-language book is available at reception. The best time to visit is either first thing in the morning or after 5pm, when it's quieter; you could spend anything from an hour to a day here, depending on your ornithological interests.

There are plenty of picnic spots on-site, plus a café-bar, while the neighbouring **Hostellerie du Pont de Gau** (℡ *04 90 97 81 53, www.hotelpontdegau.com*) has one of the finest restaurants in the Camargue.

Open Daily 9am–sunset Apr–Sept; 10am–sunset Oct–Mar. Adm 6.50€, children 4–10 4€. Credit AE, MC, V.

Seaquarium ★★

Avenue du Palais de la Mer, Le Grau-du-Roi, ℡ 04 66 51 57 57, www. seaquarium.fr

Down on the Farm

Young children love **Le Vieux Mas** (Route de Fourques D15, Beaucaire, ℡ *04 66 59 60 13, www.vieux-mas.com*), a reproduction of a working farm as it was in 1900, with goats, lambs and piglets to feed and cuddle. It's open daily 10am to 6pm April to June and September; 10am to 7pm July and August; 1:30 to 6pm October to March. Admission is 7€ for adults, 5.50€ for children 4 to 16, free for under-4s.

The **Haras d'Uzès** (Mas des Tailles, Uzès, ℡ *04 66 22 98 59; www. haras-nationaux.fr*), a National Stud Farm, is dedicated to the breeding and conservation of horses from Languedoc-Roussillon, Provence-Alpes Côte d'Azur, and Corsica. Guided visits to the stables, forge and tack room take place from mid-March to 1 July, daily 2 to 5pm, and there are guided tours every Monday and Thursday at 3pm from July to mid-September, taking around 90 minutes. Performances by the famous 'dancing horses' take place every Wednesday in July and August. Admission for the guided visits is 8€ adults, 4€ under 12s; shows cost 15€ for adults and children.

Even mums and dads will enjoy a couple of hours in the Palais de la Mer, where marine life from around the world is on view in large tanks. The highlight is a walk through the shark tunnel followed by a 20-minute film about the predators, although it's possible to spend ages watching the sea-lions basking or swimming—look out for Simba, who's the size of a walrus. Older children will be interested in the sea museum, which focuses on the fishing history of Le Grau-du-Roi; little ones will love playing on the wooden sea-lions in the garden. The interactive exhibits are in English as well as French. There's a lift to all floors, a café and a souvenir shop. The **Babyland** theme park is next door.

Open Daily Apr–May and June–Sept 9:30am–7:30pm; July–Aug 9:30am–11:30pm; Oct–Mar 9:30pm–6:30pm. **Adm** 11:30€, children 5–15 8:30€, family ticket for two adults and two children 35€. **Amenities** Café. Shop. Baby-change. **Credit** MC, V.

Natural Reserves, Parks & Gardens

Jardin d'Été

Arles

Wedged between the Théâtre Antique and the Boulevard des Lices, this little park is an ideal spot for a picnic or to bring young children, with a playground offering activities

Snapshot of the Camargue

In 1953, a film about a boy and his horse won the Best Short Film category at the Cannes Film Festival. *Crin Blanc* ('White Mane') was filmed entirely on location in the Camargue (at the Hôtel de Cacharel, **www.hotel-cacharel.com**) and sparked an ongoing fascination with this wild and water-locked part of France, a national park and nature reserve.

On an average day you'll spot local men and women going about their business in Provençal-patterned shirts and moleskin trousers—these are the *gardians* (cowboys). But though the traditional way of life—raising **horses** and **bulls** and growing **rice**—continues, many *manadiers* (ranchers) have turned their *mas* (farmhouses) into hotels. Around the **Étang de Launes** and elsewhere, you'll notice small white houses with rounded walls and thatched roofs: traditional *cabanes de gardians*, many now providing self-catering holiday accommodation (contact the tourist office in Stes-Maries-de-la-Mer for details: ☎ 04 90 97 82 55).

If you're short on time and want to learn more about the area, its animals and culture, visit the **Domaine Paul Ricard Méjanes** (☎ 04 90 97 10 10, **www.mejanes.camargue.fr**), where you can explore a microcosm of the Camargue by train, bike, horse or on foot.

Roman Around

They came, they saw, and they certainly left their mark. In fact, the region got its name because it was a 'province' of the Roman Empire. The highlight of the area's Roman remains is the **Pont du Gard** ★★★ (☎ *08 20 90 33 30*; *www.pontdugard.fr*), part of a 50km aqueduct that was built in 1st century AD to transport water to Nîmes. A family day-ticket (up to five people) costs 10€.

In Nîmes itself, children love a visit to the **Roman arena** ★★ (☎ *04 66 21 82 56*, *www.arenes-nimes.com*), the best-preserved amphitheatre of the era, where they can visit rooms dedicated to gladiators and bullfighting. Follow this with a trip across town to the **Maison Carrée** for a 30-minute 3D film, *Heroes of Nîmes*. Admission is 7.80€ for adults, 5.90€ for under-12s.

No visit to Arles is complete without checking out the **Musée de l'Arles et de la Provence Antiques** ★★ (☎ *04 90 18 89 88*, *www. arles-antique.cg13.fr*); admission is 7.50€ adults, 5.50€ under-12s. It is built on the site of the Roman *circus* (chariot racetrack) and displays major finds from the area. If you're passing through St.-Rémy-de-Provence, stop off at **Glanum** ★ (☎ *04 90 92 23 79*, *www.glanum. monuments-nationaux.fr*), a well-preserved Greek and Roman town. Admission is 7€ for adults; accompanied under-18s enter free.

colour-coded according to age. Look out for the sculpture commemorating former Arles resident Vincent Van Gogh (1853–90), and come to hear live music on summer evenings. **Open** Daily dawn–dusk. **Adm** Free.

Historic Buildings & Monuments

Château d'Uzès ★★

Place du Duché, Uzès, ☎ 04 66 22 18 96, www.duche-uzes.fr

If Hollywood ever needs the perfect fairytale castle for a film, this is it. Yet what strikes you most about this building, belonging to the oldest dukedom in France, is that it is alive and lived in, albeit sporadically, by the 17th duke, Jacques de Crussol d'Uzès, and his wife and son. Guided tours (available in English) take place every day: you'll see the living areas, wine cellar and little chapel, all still in use. Younger children will love the display of *santons* (figurines).

FUN FACT ➤ **Which bull is which?** ◄

Question: How do you to tell a Camargue bull from a Spanish bull?
Answer: The horns of a Camargue bull are shaped like a lyre.

Nimes Amphitheatre

Note that buggies aren't allowed, and that the 135 steps up to the vista point may be overwhelming for younger children.

Open *Daily 10am–12:30pm and 2–6:30pm July and Aug; 10am–noon and 2–6pm Sept–June.* **Adm** *16€, children 12–16 12€, children 7–11 5€.* **Credit** *Cash only.*

Top Museums

Carré d'Art ★★★

Place de la Maison Carrée, Nîmes, ☏ 04 66 76 35 35 (museum), ☏ 04 66 76 35 03 (library)

Designed by Lord (Norman) Foster and opened in 1993, this architectural gem is the cultural hub of Nîmes. As well as housing the city's Contemporary Art Museum, with more than 250 European works dating from the 1960s onwards, it is also the base of the main library and has an excellent top-floor restaurant with panoramic views. Children are well catered for (although they'll need to speak French): they have their own library with more than 30,000 volumes, regular film screenings, and courses in computer art in the multimedia area, and there are weekly workshops (for families and children on their own) relating to current exhibitions, art and language.

Museum: *open 10am–6pm Tues–Sun.* **Library:** *open 10:30am–7pm Tues, Thurs and 10:30am–6pm Wed, Fri, Sat.* **Adm** *Permanent collection free. Museum free to under-25s. Exhibition prices vary.* **Credit** *Cash only.* **Amenities** ☕

⭐ Musée du Bonbon (Haribo Sweet Museum) ★★

Pont des Charrettes, Uzès, ☏ 04 66 22 74 39, www.haribo.com

It's not quite as exciting as Willy Wonka's place, but the interactive exhibition here (with English translations) challenges little ones to work out ingredients by smell, and rewards their efforts with a packet of liquorice. They won't believe their eyes when they clock the 1-kilogram bags of rainbow-coloured sweets in the shop on the way out. If you're here in August, come first thing in the morning because the place gets very busy. A visit lasts about an hour. Next door are go-karts, a trampoline and an inflatable for energetic sorts.

If you're hungry after your visit, hop across the road to the **Auberge d'Uzès** (📞 *04 66 22 16 15, www.auberge-uzes.fr*), which makes great Provençal food for all the family. Expect to pay 10€ to 15€ for the fixed-price menu.

Open *Tues–Sun 10am–7pm July and Aug; 10am–1pm and 2–6pm last week Jan–June and Sept–Dec.* **Adm** *6€, children 5–15 3€.* **Credit** *MC, V (over 12€).*

Musée du Vieux Nîmes ★

Place aux Herbes, Nîmes, 📞 *04 66 76 73 70, www.ville-nimes.fr*

You might even be wearing Nîmes's most famous export when you visit… the word 'denim' allegedly originated from cloth manufactured here called *serge de Nîmes,* one of the most popular materials made by the city's thriving Protestant textile industry. It was originally exported to the US (via Genoa in Italy, from where we get the word 'jeans') for use as wagon cover, before Mr Levi Strauss had the idea to turn it into a pair of trousers. This little museum, housed in the 17th-century bishop's palace, explores life in Nîmes from the Middle Ages, giving an insight into how both the textile industry and religion shaped the city. There is a fine display of *serge* including some 18th-century aprons as well as examples of local furniture, pottery, silk shawls and objects from

Carré d'Art

daily life including a 19th-century silkworm incubator.

Open *10am–6pm Tues–Sun.* **Adm** *Free.*

Arts & Crafts

Atelier Terre

Office Culturel, 15 rue du Docteur Blanchard, St.-Quentin la Poterie, ☏ 04 66 22 74 38, www.office culturel.com

The land around Uzès has long been renowned for the quality of its clay, and this little village is *the* centre for pottery making. As well as the opportunity to buy from one of 20 or so ceramicists, adults and children can try to make their own masterpieces in one of the workshops.

For some ideas before you start, see how the art has developed through the ages in the **Musée de la Poterie Mediterranéenne** (☏ *04 66 03 65 86, www.musee-poterie-mediterranee. com*), 14 rue de la Fontaine. It's open daily in July and August from 10am to 1pm and 3 to 7pm; and Wednesday to Sunday from February to May and October 2 to 6pm, in June 10am to 1pm and 3 to 7pm, and in September from 10am to noon and 2 to 6pm. Admission is 3€ for adults, under-12s free.

Musée Souleiado

39 rue Proudhon, Tarascon, ☏ 04 90 91 50 11, www.souleiado.com

Wherever you go in Provence you'll see bright patterns on pottery, clothes and household linen. These designs are part of the region's identity—and it's all thanks to Louis XIV, the Sun King, whose passion for Indian painted fabrics inspired a textile manufacturing industry in France. Based in the historic Souleiado textile factory, this museum charts the history of print-making and design from its 17th-century origins, ending with a 15-minute film (also in English). French-speakers should ask about the regular workshops for all ages, including designing, printing and sewing.

Open *10am–6pm daily May–Sept, 10am–5pm Tues–Sat Oct–Apr.* **Adm** *6.10€, children under 12 free.* **Credit** *Cash only.* **Amenities** 🛍

Little Tourist Trains

Nîmes: the **Train Touristique de Nîmes** leaves from the Esplanade (April through October).

Aigues-Mortes: the **Petit Train d'Aigues-Mortes** departs from the town's main entrance, Porte de la Gardette (April through September).

Arles: the little train leaves from outside the tourist office on Boulevard Gambetta (Easter through October). All commentaries are available in English and tours take about 45 minutes. Adults pay 4€, children 2.50€; *www.trainstouristiquesdefrance.com.*

English-language Cinemas

For English-language films, look for the 'VO' (version originale) symbol. For current listings, see the cinema's own website or visit **www.angloinfo.com**.
Le Capitole, 11 rue Xavier-Sigalon, Uzès, 📞 *08 92 89 28 92*.
Le Sémaphore, 20 rue Porte de France, Nîmes, 📞 *04 66 67 83 11*, **www.semaphore.free.fr**.

Child-friendly Tours

Arles Walking Tours
★★★ VALUE

Start from Arles tourist office (p. 173)

For the nominal cost of a booklet, you and your family can explore Arles at leisure: itineraries include 'Arles Antique', taking in the Roman remains; 'Arles Medieval', including the 12th-century **St.-Trophime church** with its impressive doorway; 'Arles Renaissance and Classical', culminating in the **Arlaten** museum of Provençal culture; and 'Arles and Vincent Van Gogh', featuring sites depicted in the artist's paintings, such as the Langlois bridge. The self-guided walks take between 1 and 3 hours and are signposted with colour-coded markers embedded in the pavements.

Open *Daily 9am–6:45pm Apr–Oct (times vary rest of year).* **Adm** *booklet 1€.* **Credit** *Cash only.*

Camargue Safari ★★

Mas Lou Rayas, Stes-Maries-de-la-Mer, 📞 *04 90 97 52 52, www.manade-arnaud.camargue.fr*

You'll see plenty of adverts for 'Camargue Safari' tours in a 4WD or *calèche* (cart), but the best way to do it is with an authentic *manadier* (or rancher). Gilbert Arnaud has been giving guided tours of his property for 23 years, so he knows his stuff better than most, and a 2-hour visit will allow you an extended glimpse into the life of a Camargue rancher and his animals. You'll need some understanding of French.

Open *Daily; advance booking required.* **Adm** *30€, children 4–11 15€.* **Credit** *Cash only.*

For Active Families

Horse-riding in the Camargue ★★★

There's only one real way to experience the Camargue, and that's from the back of one of its inhabitants—the Camargue horse. However, drive into Stes-Maries-de-la-Mer and you'll be put off by the roads lined with sorry-looking horses tethered up waiting for the next client. Instead, head to the **Ranch La Brouzetière** (📞 *04 90 97 82 40*, **www.labrouzetiere.camargue.fr**), where owner Magali will take you from marsh to beach past bulls and flamingos on hour-long to day-long treks (16€ to 70€).

Little ones are not left out: there are 30-minute pony rides (10€). For a real adventure, overnight bivouac trips leave at 4:30pm for a campfire supper and a night under the stars, returning at 11:30am the next day.

Kayak Vert Gardon

★ ★ **AGE 7 & UP**

Berges du Gardon, Collias, ☎ *04 66 22 80 76, www.canoe-france.com/ gardon*

What better way to spend a hot summer's day than messing about on the river? Specifically the Gardon, which runs 133km from the Cévennes to Beaucaire, where it enters the Rhône. Kayak Vert Gardon offers 2-hour to 2-day descents (8 to 30km) of the river for adults and children over 6 (all participants have to be able to swim a distance of 25m). You can paddle under the Pont du Gard aqueduct (p. 179) and the 12th-century St.-Nicolas bridge, stop for a picnic on the riverbank, then bathe in the cool, clear water accompanied by the sound of *cigales* (cicadas) and the smell of the *garrigue* (p. 177).

Open *Daily 9am–7pm Mar–Oct.* **Adm** *from 19€, children under 12 from 9.50€.*

Shopping

Au Bois de Mon Cœur

8 place Aux Herbes, Uzès, ☎ *04 66 22 14 16*

Although it's small, this is one of the best toy shops in the region, spoiling children for choice with its stock that ranges from gladiator outfits, wooden swords and medieval costumes to traditional wooden toys, games and well-made plastic animal figurines.

Open *9am–7pm Tues–Sun.* **Credit** *MC, V.*

La Cure Gourmande ★ ★

23 Grand Rue Jean Jaurès, Aigues-Mortes, www.la-cure-gourmande. com

It can be sweet agony indeed making your selection from the hundreds of sweets, biscuits and chocolates on display at this branch of the chain with several shops in the South (see the website for others). It only sells products made by artisans from

---

TIP ≫ **The Best Waterparks** ≪

Aquatropic, 39 chemin de l'Hostellerie, Nîmes, (☎ *04 66 38 31 00, www.vert-marine.com*). This has indoor and outdoor pools with slides and wave machines; open weekends only. Admission for adults and over-8s is 5.25€, under 8s 1.40€.

La Bouscarasse (☎ *04 66 22 50 25, www.bouscarasse.fr*), 8km from Uzès on the D981. This waterpark has several pools featuring waterfalls, fountains and inflatables, plus a picnic area and restaurant. Family rates are available. Open Monday to Friday 10am to 7pm, Saturday and Sunday 10am to 8pm, from the end of May to the end of August. Admission for adults is 13€, ages 5 to 11 11€, under-5s free.

Arles Market

old recipes (my favourites include *glacé* fruits and fig or orange caramels), but grab a freebie from a passing sales assistant.

Open Daily 9am–7pm. **Credit** MC, V.

Les Caprices de Marine
★ FIND

21 rue des Suisses, Arles, ☎ *04 90 91 21 08, www.lescapricesdemarine.fr*

This is the kind of sweet-shop you always hope you might find in France—beautiful to look at and full of unusual, old-style confectionery. Proprietor Marie-Ange buys from local artisans, and will help you choose from

such delights as Arles nougat, small squares of caramel flavoured with Camargue salt, cherry biscuits and the ubiquitous *olives de Provence* (small chocolates that look like olives).

Open 9:30am–12:30pm and 2:30pm–7pm Tues–Fri, 9:30am–7pm Sat. **Credit** MC, V.

Les Indiennes de Nîmes

2 boulevard des Arènes, Nîmes, ☎ *04 66 21 69 57; Place de la République, Arles,* ☎ *04 90 18 21 52, www.indiennesdenimes.fr*

You might not want to don the full *gardian* get-up (moleskin trousers, velvet jacket and black

TIP ≫ The Best Local Markets ≪

Food & flower market: Boulevard des Lices, Arles, Sat morning.
Food & flower market: Place aux Herbes, Uzès, Sat morning.
Covered market: Les Halles, Rue Général Perrier, Nîmes, every morning.

felt sombrero) but a shirt or a skirt in a vivid Provençal fabric may be the perfect souvenir of your stay in the land of the Camargue cowboy. Founded in Nîmes in 1935, and still in the same family, this firm sells children's versions (ages 2 and up) of the garments. Local children wear the traditional outfits, as do adults, during festivals and for special occasions such as marriages.

Open *Mon 3–7pm, Tues–Sat 10am–noon and 2–7pm.* **Credit** *MC, V.*

Nature et Senteurs—Savonnerie du Duché Chantois
★★ FIND

7 rue Salin, Place du Duché, Uzès, ☎ *04 66 03 25 37, www.lesavon bioduzes.com*

Opened in 2007, this shop sells the owner Martine's hand-made perfumed soaps, including an organic range, a skincare range and seasonally themed versions. Children will love the animal-shaped or name-inscribed soaps. If you're here at the right time, you can all watch Martine at work.

Open *Daily 9am–8pm.* **Credit** *MC, V.*

FAMILY-FRIENDLY DINING

Nîmes offers the usual southern French mix of solid regional restaurants dedicated to lunching locals; an ever-growing selection of bland snack-restaurants, creperies and pizzerias (most of which offer comfortingly

familiar menu choices for younger diners); and a sprinkling of truly excellent splash-out options for gastronomes, such as Michelin-starred chef Michel Kayser's **Alexandre** (☎ *04 66 70 08 99*), about 8km from town en route to the airport—not a good choice with tots or toddlers, but a gourmet experience to be remembered. In town, **Le Magister** (☎ *04 66 76 11 00*) is hung with paintings by local artists, has been serving fine local food for more than 30 years, and offers a child-friendly menu. Down in the Camargue, you're deep into steak and pizza country—the famed **Camargue beef** is on every menu. Aigues-Mortes has more than its share of pizzerias, and Stes-Maries-de-la-Mer has a promenade dotted with *gelateries* as well as some rather decent seafood restaurants.

Nîmes & Around

Families will find the usual array of fast-food joints, cafés and pizzerias in and around Nîmes, serving up a familiar array of salads, burgers, pizzas and pasta. More exciting dining options are, sadly, a bit thin on the ground in this part of the world.

MODERATE

La Bodeguita ★★ VALUE TAPAS

3 boulevard Alphonse Daudet, Nîmes, ☎ *04 66 58 28 29, www. royalhotel-nimes.com*

This authentic and lively slice of Iberian-influenced Nîmes is a hive of activity all year, and particularly during the May Féria (p. 171), when you'll find yourself rubbing shoulders with bullfighting glitterati. It's also fun to share tapas (olives, ham, shrimps, different kinds of cheese and sausage, to mention just a few) with all the family and listen to the flamenco singers at the weekend. After they've eaten, children can run among the shallow fountains on the adjoining Place d'Assas, built to pay homage to Nemausa, the spring around which the city grew up. The restaurant is part of the three-star **Royal Hôtel**, which has been well refurbished and has a fashionable new look (original features, stone floors and white walls) but is noisy at the weekend.

Open *Mon–Sat 7–11pm.* **Tapas** *from 5€ per dish.* **Credit** *MC, V.*

Le Bananier
★ ★ VALUE FAST FOOD

16 place aux Herbes, Uzès, ☎ *04 66 22 50 68*

Even the fussiest eaters will find something to whet their appetite in this little café serving 25 salads, 36 pizzas, several types of quiche and 25 ice creams at the last count. Pizzas (also available to take away) are bigger than the plates and easily feed two or three children, depending on

their age/size/appetite. There is also a *menu enfant* (burger or sausage and chips followed by ice cream for about 10€). It's quiet during the week and very busy on Saturdays, when the Place aux Herbes's must-see market (p. 185) takes place (although there's plenty of room for children to run around when it packs up at about 1pm).

Open *9am–late daily.* **Main courses** *9€–20€, children's menu about 10€.* **Credit** *MC, V.*

Pâtisserie Courtois
★ ★ ★ FIND PATISSERIE

8 place du Marché, Nîmes, ☎ *04 66 67 20 09*

Everything is made on the premises at this celebrated Nîmes patisserie dating from 1892 and retaining its original interior. As well as take-away cakes, quiches and ice cream, it offers sit-down meals, indoors or on the terrace. Try a traditional *salade nîmoise*, a *pâté nîmois* (a beef and mutton pie resembling a small pork pie) and a dollop of *brandade* (mashed cod and potato; see below) followed by a *nélusko* (a flat, round chocolate cake filled with biscuit and praline, invented by the original owner). If none of that tempts children, they can enjoy a hamburger and

---

FUN FACT **Brandade de Morue**

This child-friendly Nîmes speciality combining cod, potatoes, garlic, milk, olive oil, mixed herbs and lemon is very simple to make: see ***www. languedocsun.com*** and click on 'recipes'. Alternatively, buy the real deal from Brandade Raymond, 34 rue National, Nîmes (☎ *04 66 27 11 98*, ***www. brandadedenimes.com***).

>> **Picnic With a View** <<

If you are in Uzès for the Saturday market in the Place aux Herbes, a lovely picnic idea is to buy a whole spit-roast chicken with potatoes from a stallholder and sit in the shade on the **Promenade des Marronniers,** admiring the countryside in the hazy sunlight while the children can play hide-and-seek behind the chestnut trees.

---

frites plus an ice cream from the two-course children's menu (about 7€). Inside it's a bit cramped for energetic youngsters or parents with buggies, but there's plenty of room outside on the pedestrianised square.

Open Daily 8am–7pm (to 11pm July and Aug). **Main courses** 7€–15€, children's menu 7€. **Credit** MC, V. **Amenities** 🎏

Arles

MODERATE

Le Bistro Arlesién PROVENCAL

12 place du Forum, Arles, ☏ 04 90 96 07 22

You can eat well in all the restaurants on Place du Forum; this place stands out for its spacious terrace, handy for those with buggies, and its long opening hours. The menu features the usual locally inspired salads and Camargue beef but you're really coming here for the sense of history—this square was the original **Roman forum**, and you can still see one of its columns in the wall of the plush **Hôtel Nord Pinus.**

A few doors down is the inspiration for Van Gogh's **Café de la Nuit;** nearby shops sell postcards of the painting, which

children can compare with the still-very-yellow original.

Open Daily 7:30am–12:30am. **Main courses** 8€–14€. **Credit** MC, V.

INEXPENSIVE

Les 2 Suds ★ FIND CREPERIE

Espace Van Gogh, Arles, ☏ 04 90 93 34 56

Among the tasty *galettes* served at this crêperie in the Espace Van Gogh, I especially love the *provençale* with aubergine, tomato and goats' cheese. Children can munch a ham and cheese *galette* followed by a sweet *crepe* for about 8€ before running around the flower-filled garden. They also serve salads, teas and cakes.

Open Mon–Sat 8am–7pm. **Main courses** 5€–11€; children's menu 8€. **Credit** MC, V.

The Camargue

EXPENSIVE

La Chassagnette ★★★ GREEN

Domaine de l'Armellière, Route du Sambuc, 12km south of Arles on D36, ☏ 04 90 97 26 96, **www. chassagnette.fr**

This fashionable organic restaurant in the heart of Camargue country is presided over by Armand Arnal, a protégé of Alain

Soleileis Ice-Cream Parlour, Arles

El Campo ★ ★ FIND

13 rue Victor Hugo, Stes-Maries-de-la-Mer, ☏ *04 90 97 84 11, www.elcampo.camargue.fr*

This is the best place to come to hear authentic Gypsy flamenco (call for details of days and times) and eat traditional Camargue food. Our meal of bull steak and *frites* followed by creamy, cocoa-rich chocolate ice cream was far better (and cheaper) than the equivalent we ate in a 'top' restaurant just up the road.

Open *Daily 8am–12:30am (except Wed in June).* **Main courses** *10€–16€, children's menu 12€.* **Credit** *MC, V.* **Amenities** 🍴

FAMILY-FRIENDLY ACCOMMODATION

Nîmes and Arles have their complement of good-quality hotels, but neither town is an ideal base for a longer family hotel as kids will find hotels in city streets a bit too confining for comfort. For a week or more, you might want to consider seeking out a self-catering *gîte* with a pool in

Ducasse, who completed his apprenticeship in New York and Japan. This is reflected in his dishes, which are simple, fresh and cooked to perfection. Food is sourced locally, and all vegetables and herbs are grown in the garden. Children's food is available on request—and you can guarantee it won't be burger and chips. You can also just pop in for a cup of tea, pick your own herbs, wander around the garden or browse the library full of books on gastronomy, the Camargue and art.

Open *Thurs–Tues noon–2pm and 8–10pm.* **Main courses** *20€–35€.* **Credit** *MC, V.* **Amenities** 🍴

TIP ≫ **The Best Ice Cream Stop**

The very best ice cream shop in this region is Arles's Soleileis (9 rue Docteur Fanton), where flavours include fig, plum and chocolate. If you have time (and room), sit outside and enjoy a delectable *Trio de Georges*—spicy bread with ginger, cinnamon and vanilla ice cream topped with a raspberry coulis.

In Nîmes, head for **Patisserie Courtois** (p. 187), and in Aigues-Mortes for **Bella Vista** or **Palais de la Glace,** both just inside the main gate on Rue Jean Jaurès.

the surrounding countryside (try *www.gites-de-france.fr*) or a small country hotel (try *www.logis hotels.com*). Down in the Camargue, there are plentiful seaside places to stay, and well-appointed camping sites and mobile home parks (many with big swimming pools) offer another excellent alternative.

Nîmes & Around

MODERATE

Auberge de Jeunesse de Nîmes ⋆

257 chemin de l'Auberge de Jeunesse, about 4km from Nîmes, ☎ 04 66 68 03 20, www.hinimes.com

To celebrate its recent 70th birthday, this family-friendly youth hostel was renovated and now offers a block of four-bed 'family' rooms with ensuite shower and WC. There is also room for six tents. Children can have fun playing on the climbing frame or identifying the regional aromatic plants in the little botanical garden. You can hire bikes to explore the area, and the friendly staff will offer plenty of ideas for sightseeing and regularly organise activities such as treasure hunts for guests. You need to belong to Hostelling International to stay here but membership can be purchased on arrival. There is car parking and a regular bus service from the centre of town.

Rooms 20. *Rates* 49€ for four-bed room. Breakfast 3.60€. *Credit* MC, V. *Amenities* 🅿 ☒ ☀ @ 📱 ❚❙

Maison du Village ⋆

10 rue du 8 May 1945, St.-Remy, ☎ 04 32 60 68 20, www.lamaison duvillage.com

This very stylish retreat is superb value for money, and its portfolio of suites are great for families, though perhaps a little too beautifully decorated for comfort if you have boisterous toddlers in tow. Breakfast, lunch and afternoon tea are served in summer in a pretty courtyard (or indoors in less clement seasons). You'll have to go out for dinner, but there are lots of great restaurants within toddling distance in the surrounding village, as well as a fab ice cream parlour next door.

Rooms 5 suites *Rates* from 150€ double, extra bed from 30€. *Credit* MC, V. *Amenities* 🐾 ☀ 🖼 *In room* 🄰/🄲 ✏ ⬜

Arles

EXPENSIVE

Hôtel Jules César

9 boulevard des Lices, Arles, ☎ 04 90 52 52 52, www.hotel-julescesar.fr

Of several good upmarket hotels in this region, this four-star hotel occupying a converted 17th-century convent is the best for families, with its relaxed atmosphere and friendly staff. Although it's situated on a busy street in the centre of Arles, all rooms face the Mediterranean garden with its heated pool—making it a surprisingly tranquil oasis in the city. It even has a listed chapel and, more practically, a renowned restaurant, Lou Marques, which offers children's menus at 13.50€.

If it's full, another good option in the area is the **Mas de Peint** in Le Sambuc (☎ *04 90 97 20 62, www.masdepeint.com*), which has rooms sleeping up to four people.

Rooms 60. *Rates* 160€–385€. Breakfast 20€. Extra bed 50€, cot free. *Credit* MC, V. *Amenities* 🅿 ☼ 🖼 🍴 *In room* A/C 🗂

With its excellent views over Arles's Roman remains, the inexpensive **Hôtel le Calendal** (☎ *04 90 96 11 89, www.le calendal.com*) is a good family-friendly alternative to the Jules César. Although it doesn't have a pool, children are kept entertained with toys, books and English-language DVDs. Doubles from 109€, family quad rooms from 129€.

INEXPENSIVE

Hotel du Musée ★★ FIND

11 rue du Grand Prieuré, Arles, ☎ 04 90 93 88 88, www.hoteldumusee. com

This 16th-century former home of the lords of Someyre is a convenient place to lay your head in central Arles, with several rooms sleeping three and four. It's situated between the Musée Réattu, with its Picasso collection, and the Roman baths, and is a stone's throw from the banks of the Rhône, which is good for an early evening stroll. Breakfast is taken on a pretty patio and there is also

an art gallery. There's no lift, but the stairs are wide and there are just two floors. The main entrance opens directly onto a road, so you'll have to watch little ones.

Rooms 28. *Rates* Doubles 55€–60€, rooms for three 70€–80€, rooms for four 85€–95€. Cot free. *Credit* MC, V. *In room* A/C 🖥 🗂

The Camargue

MODERATE

L'Auberge Cavalière
★★★ FIND

Route d'Arles (D570), Stes-Maries-de-la-Mer, ☎ 04 90 97 88 88, www. aubergecavaliere.com

For an authentic Camargue experience in comfortable surroundings, this is the place to come. It's a four-star hotel offering accommodation in individual *cabanes de gardian* (smaller versions of traditional Camargue homes) comprising a double bed on the ground floor and one or two beds on a mezzanine. These are only suitable for older children, however, as the staircase is steep— families with younger children should opt for a different style of room. You should also note that the hotel is not fenced off from the water that surrounds it.

The restaurant is well regarded, and owner Delphine, who has three children of her own, will discuss with children what they would like to eat or try. Best of all,

Horses Change Colour ◀

Camargue horses are born black and turn white as they grow older.

the hotel has its own riding stables (☏ 06 09 54 24 40, **www.ecuries-cavaliere.camargue.fr**)—the only one in the area with state-qualified instructors who insist that everyone wears hard hats.

Rooms 44. **Rates** 140€–195€. Breakfast 14€. Cots free. Triples 180€–240€. **Credit** MC, V. **Amenities** 🅿️ 🖼️ 🍴 **In room** A/C 📺 🛏️ ☐

INSIDER TIP ▸

For a similar but cheaper experience in two-star style, also with a pool, you can't go wrong with the nearby **Hôtellerie du Pont Blanc** (☏ 04 90 97 89 11, **www.pont-blanc.camargue.fr**). Rates from 58€.

INEXPENSIVE

Camping Crin Blanc
★ ★ ★ VALUE

CD 37 Hameau de Saliers, Albaron, ☏ 04 66 87 48 78, **www.camping-crin-blanc.com**

In the heart of the Camargue, this campsite is great for families on a budget, with accommodation in mobile homes or chalets, most sleeping up to six people (cots and highchairs are available on request). Children enjoy splashing around in the two heated pools (one specifically for children), playing tennis and ping-pong, running riot in the playground or making new *amis* in the miniclub (hosting activities for 3- to 10-year-olds in July and August). The friendly proprietors will also organise horse-riding, diving lessons, carriage trips and visits to local places of interest.

Places 150. **Rates** from 35€ per day for two adults, two children aged

7–15, tent pitch and car; see website for special offers. **Credit** MC, V. **Amenities** 🍷 🖼️ 👶 📷 🖼️ 📷 🔒 📷 📷 **In room** ☐ ✖️ 🪑

INSIDER TIP ▸

If you prefer to bring your own camping equipment, or prefer things a little less 'organised' and more rustic, head for **Camping du Mas de Mourgues**, a few kilometres away in Vauvert (☏ 04 66 73 30 88, **www.masdemourgues.com**). Run by a friendly English couple, it has 70 pitches, and two resident donkeys.

Mas St.-Germain

Villeneuve-Camargue, ☏ 04 90 97 00 60, **www.massaintgermain.fr**

Stay at this *mas* (farm) if you want to find out what being a *manadier* (rancher) is all about: raising horses, bulls and Arles merino sheep, along with growing rice and cereals. It has four self-catering, TV-free *gîtes*, one of which sleeps up to seven, and also offers B&B. Owner Pierre's family have farmed here for more than 300 years, and he will proudly show you around the property, situated on the banks of the Étang de Vaccarès, in his 4WD (you'll need to understand some French) or on horseback. Come in April to see the new-born foals frolicking in the fields.

Although this place is quite remote, there are some good restaurants in the area: try **L'Estrambord** (7 route de l'Abrivado, Le Sambuc, ☏ 04 90 97 20 10).

Rates Gîte 480€–500€ per week. End-of-stay cleaning 25€. **Credit** Cash or bank transfer only. **Amenities** 🚲 **In room** ✖️

8 Avignon & the Vaucluse

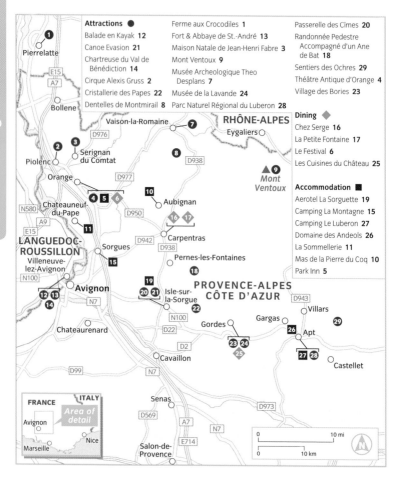

Attractions ●
Balade en Kayak **12**
Canoe Evasion **21**
Chartreuse du Val de
  Bénédiction **14**
Cirque Alexis Gruss **2**
Cristallerie des Papes **22**
Dentelles de Montmirail **8**

Ferme aux Crocodiles **1**
Fort & Abbaye de St.-André **13**
Maison Natale de Jean-Henri Fabre **3**
Mont Ventoux **9**
Musée Archeologique Theo
  Desplans **7**
Musée de la Lavande **24**
Parc Naturel Régional du Luberon **28**

Passerelle des Cîmes **20**
Randonnée Pedestre
  Accompagné d'un Ane
  de Bat **18**
Sentiers des Ochres **29**
Théâtre Antique d'Orange **4**
Village des Bories **23**

Dining ◆
Chez Serge **16**
La Petite Fontaine **17**
Le Festival **6**
Les Cuisines du Château **25**

Accommodation ■
Aerotel La Sorguette **19**
Camping La Montagne **15**
Camping Le Luberon **27**
Domaine des Andeols **26**
La Sommellerie **11**
Mas de la Pierre du Coq **10**
Park Inn **5**

With its western borders marked by the wide wet ribbon of the Rhône and its eastern by the fertile fields and vineyards of the Luberon, the Vaucluse is the very heart of Provence. Here, you can climb rocky hillsides, with a donkey to carry your picnic, visit colourful Provençal markets and watch cargo barges chugging up the Rhône, with cars, bikes and even gardens loaded on their decks. Families will enjoy the leisurely pace in this beautiful part of southern France that—despite the best efforts of travel writers and the tourist industry—remains tranquil. But it's not all about lazing about: wrinkled by steep mountains, river valleys and timeless hill villages, this land-locked region has much to offer active families. You can imagine yourself taking part in the Tour de France as you cycle up the killer slopes of Mont Ventoux, spend an afternoon kayaking down the Durance or bash across the Vaucluse hinterland in a Mad Max-style buggy. And then sit back and draw breath, just as the Romans did here before conquering the rest of Gaul

VISITOR INFORMATION

The **Vaucluse Regional Tourism Committee** runs the website *www.provenceguide.com*, with listings of attractions and events, a practical guide and links to accommodation providers. Even more useful for families is *www.provence-enfamille.com*, also resourced by the VRTC.

Where there isn't a tourist office in evidence, seek out the mairie (town hall) or local syndicat d'initiative for information—even the smallest towns usually have one or both.

Getting There

By Air Flybe (p. 29) flies from Southampton, Exeter, Birmingham and Manchester to Avignon in about 2 hours. **Jet2** (p. 29) connects with Leeds. The airport is around 6km east of the city centre at 141 allée de la Chartreuse (☎ *04 90 81 51 51, www.avignon.aeroport.fr*). Annoyingly, there are no shuttle buses into town, but taxis await each flight on a rank right outside the Arrivals hall. **Ryanair** (p. 29) flies from London Stansted to Nîmes, about 40 minutes' drive from Avignon.

By Train Eurostar (p. 32) has direct services to Avignon from London St. Pancras International, taking between 6 and 7 hours, July to September, once weekly. **TGVs** (*www.sncf.com*) also connect Avignon with Marseille, where you can link with **TER** regional trains (*www.ter-sncf.com*) to destinations east and north of Marseille.

Avignon's TGV station is about 3km from the old-town centre—a taxi should cost about 10€.

By Car See p. 30.

Orientation

The A7 ('Autoroute du Soleil') follows the Rhône valley past Orange, then passes southeast of Avignon as it heads toward Salon-de-Provence and Marseille. If you don't like *autoroutes*, the slower (and toll-free) N7 *route nationale* runs more or less parallel to the A7, passing through Orange and Avignon.

From these main routes, two smaller *routes nationales* cut east into the heartland of the Vaucluse—the D94/D994, which leaves the Rhône north of Orange and passes through Nyons and Serres on its way to Gap; and the N100, which runs east from Avignon through Apt

Fast Facts: Avignon & the Vaucluse

Banks: Société Générale (📞 *04 90 14 51 50*) is at 9 rue de la République, Avignon.

Hospitals: Centre Hospitalier Général (📞 *04 32 75 33 33*, ***www. ch-avignon.fr***), 305 rue Raoul Follereau, Avignon. In Orange, Centre Hospitalier Louis Giorgi (📞 *04 90 11 22 22*), Avenue de Lavoisier.

Internet Cafés: Le Site, 25 rue Carnot (📞 *04 90 27 12 00*), Avignon, open noon to midnight.

Pharmacies: Pharmacie de l'Universite, 10 route Lyon (📞 *04 90 82 01 82*), Avignon. In Orange, Pharmacie du Centre (📞 *03 82 58 51 22*), 160 Grand Rue, is the most central, but there are plenty in other parts of town.

Post Offices: The most central Avignon post office is at 4 cours du Président Kennedy (📞 *04 90 27 54 10*), open 8:30am to 6pm Monday to Friday and 9am to 12:30pm Saturday. In Orange, La Poste (📞 *04 90 11 11 00*) is at 679 boulevard Edouard Daladier.

Shopping: See p. 212 and, for markets, p. 212.

---

to connect with the A51 *autoroute* west of Digne-les-Bains.

A web of smaller and more picturesque (but often serpentine) roads connects smaller communities in the hinterland with these main thoroughfares. Signposting—to attractions and hotels as well as towns and villages—is generally excellent.

INSIDER TIP ▶

Although the Vaucluse shares a Mediterranean climate with the Riviera, temperatures in this inland region often drop below 0°C in winter, and when the wind blows down the Rhône valley from the north it can get chilly very quickly. So pack fleeces, gloves and woolly hats if you're planning to visit any time between December and the end of March.

Getting Around

TGV trains link Orange and Avignon with Marseille and points east, and also take you south to Montpellier, but there are no other passenger rail services in the hinterland, and bus services are limited, so independent families who want to explore really need a car.

Car hire in Avignon (at the airport and in the city centre) is available via Avis, Hertz, Budget, Europcar, Sixt, Ada and National/Citer (p. 36). Local tourist offices can provide details of local bus services, taxis and bike-hire firms (though away from the level fields of the Rhône valley, cycling can be tough on both little legs and unfit mums and dads).

Children's Top 10 Attractions

❶ **Wandering** along country lanes with a docile donkey to carry your lunch, water and kit (p. 210).

❷ **Watching** scaly giants at the Ferme aux Crocodiles (p. 203).

❸ **Joining** the circus for a day at the Château du Cirque in Piolenc (p. 203).

❹ **Messing** about in boats on the Rhône (p. 209) or the Sorgue (p. 209).

❺ **Seeing** the world from tree-top height at the Passerelle des Cîmes (p. 210).

❻ **Walking** to the end of the famous Pont St.-Bénezet, symbol of Avignon (p. 206).

❼ **Dreaming** of a vanished empire at the Roman theatre in Orange (p. 206).

❽ **Time-travelling** back to the Stone Age at the Village des Bories (p. 207).

❾ **Exploring** tiny beasts at Jean-Henri Fabre's Jardin des Insectes (p. 204).

❿ **Looking** down from Mont Ventoux, the giant of the Vaucluse (p. 202).

Child-friendly Events & Entertainment

Forteresse de Mornas Visites Animées ★★ ALL AGES

Mornas, ☎ *04 90 37 01 26, www. forteresse-de-mornas.com*

All summer long you can take your family back to the 13th century at the castle of Mornas in the Haute Vaucluse. Older children, boys especially, will enjoy the demonstrations of swordplay and quarterstaff combat by actors in historical attire. The storytelling is in French, but the tales are still amusing even if you don't understand everything.

Apr–Sept (10am–5pm Apr–June Sat, Sun and public holidays; July–Sept daily); five performances daily. **Adm** *7€ adults, 5€ under-12s.*

Marché Médievale ★★
ALL AGES

Mornas, ☎ *04 90 37 01 26, www. mornas.fr/marche-medieval.htm*

They're clearly fond of time-travel in Mornas when, at the beginning of July, knights in armour, troubadours, jugglers and elegantly dressed ladies and their retinue take over the town for a day, transforming it into a medieval market. The flower-adorned streets are lined with stalls and pavilions selling food and drink (not all medieval in flavour).

First Sun in July. **Adm** *Free.*

Festival de la Sorgue ★★
ALL AGES

Isle-sur-la-Sorgue and around, ☎ *04 90 38 04 78, www.oti-delasorgue.fr*

Each summer the villages along the Sorgue, including Isle-sur-la-Sorgue, La Thor and Fontaine de Vaucluse, celebrate their history and heritage at this fun (and mostly free) event during which you can learn how to catch river-fish the old-fashioned way, watch a night-time nautical parade and a 'battle of flowers' on the river, and visit a traditional floating market. There's also usually at least one open-air *foire de brocante* where children can squander their holiday pocket money on bric-a-brac of all kinds.

1–31 July. **Adm** *Free (most events).*

Festival d'Avignon ⋆
AGE 10 & UP

Various venues, Avignon, ☎ *04 90 14 14 14, www.festival-avignon.com*

Some of the more pompous performances at Provence's biggest arts festival will go over the heads of British children, but the fringe festival, **Avignon Public Off**, is more likely to entertain, with more than 500 acts at 100-plus venues, many of them outdoors. But best of all, the festival attracts droves of mime artists, puppeteers, fire-eaters, jugglers, stilt-walkers and street musicians, all of whom are guaranteed to liven up your day in Avignon. The best place to watch them for free is Place d'Horloge, which has lots of outdoor café tables.

Middle 2 weeks in July. **Adm** *Street performances free; entrance charge for some events.*

Font'Arts ⋆ ⋆ ⋆　**ALL AGES**

Various venues, Pernes-les-Fontaines, ☎ *04 90 61 31, www.ville-pernes-les-fontaines.fr*

This well-known summer festival of street music and theatre is perfect for children, especially given that it's free. Circus performers, marionette theatres, dancers, acrobats and musicians from more than 30 companies take over the square and courtyards of the old village centre.

Mid-Aug. **Adm** *Free.*

Cities & Towns

Apt ⋆

Tourist office: ☎ *04 90 74 03 18, www.ot-apt.fr*

Apt can't make up its mind whether it's a small town or a big village. Its **Saturday market** is one of the best places in the area to stock up for a picnic or for a week's self-catering; stalls are crammed with such local delicacies as candied cherries and truffles, as well as lavender oil. Apt is also the main gateway to the **Parc Naturel Régional du Luberon** (Luberon Regional National Park; p. 204), and the

English-language Cinemas

For English-language films, look for the 'VO' (version originale) symbol. For current listings, you can also consult *www.angloinfo.com*.
Cinéma César I & II, 12 rue Scudéry, Apt, ☎ *04 90 74 16 46.*
Le Femina, 58 cours Gambetta, Cavaillon, ☎ *08 92 89 28 92.*
Utopia la Manutention, 4 rue des Escaliers Ste-Anne, Avignon, ☎ *04 90 82 65 36.*

AVIGNON

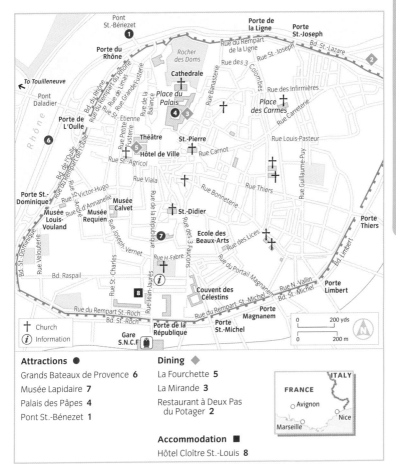

Attractions ●
Grands Bateaux de Provence **6**
Musée Lapidaire **7**
Palais des Pâpes **4**
Pont St.-Bénezet **1**

Dining ◆
La Fourchette **5**
La Mirande **3**
Restaurant à Deux Pas
  du Potager **2**

Accommodation ■
Hôtel Cloître St.-Louis **8**

† Church
ⓘ Information

dramatic ochre landscapes of the **Colorado de Rustrel** are close at hand too.

Avignon ★★★

Tourist office: 📞 *04 32 74 32 74,*
www.avignon-tourisme.com

Its famous bridge aside, Avignon is one of the most charming cities in France, with excellent restaurants, plenty of pavement cafés and just enough sightseeing to fill a few days without

wearing out too much shoe leather. It's really two cities for the price of one—the medieval city, on the east bank of the wide Rhône, and the slightly newer (600-year-old) **Villeneuve lez Avignon** on the opposite bank, with a beautifully preserved 14th-century Benedictine *chartreuse* (charterhouse; p. 205) and a hilltop castle, **Fort St.-André** (p. 204). A stroll out to the end of the famous

King Philip the Fair

Philip the Fair (1268–1314)—so-called because of his good looks—made enemies of the Pope, the English and the Knights Templar, but patriotic Scots remember him as the founder of the 'Auld Alliance' between Scotland and France. This secret treaty was signed in 1294 when Scotland, led by Robert the Bruce, was battling for independence. Philip fortified Villeneuve lez Avignon to symbolise French defiance of the power of the Pope and the Holy Roman Empire. In 1307, he set about destroying the power of the Knights Templar (of *Da Vinci Code* fame) and in 1313 he had the Grand Master of the Templars, Jacques de Molay, burned at the stake. With his dying breath, de Molay cursed the King—a year later Philip was gored by a wild boar while out hunting, and later died.

Pont St.-Bénezet (p. 206) is mandatory—this 900-year-old bridge no longer crosses the river, but the view of the **Palais des Pâpes** (p. 206) looming over the old town will take your breath away.

INSIDER TIP

For a stunning view of Avignon and the Rhône, climb more than 100 steep stairs to the top of the 13th-century **Tour Philippe le Bel** (04 32 70 08 57) in Villeneuve lez Avignon, built by King Philip the Fair. Admission is 1.60€ for adults, 0.90€ for 12–17s, under 12s free.

Carpentras ☆

Tourist office: 04 90 63 00 78, **www.carpentras-ventoux.com**

The charm of Carpentras lies in its very absence of must-see attractions—the historic centre does have its share of old buildings, including a medieval synagogue (the oldest still in use in France) and a singularly unimpressive Roman arch, but don't feel guilty about bypassing these in favour of an amble around its attractively sleepy streets and a browse at the **Friday-morning market** in the Cour de l'Hôtel Dieu, one of the liveliest in the

Avignon from the Rhone river

Vaucluse. Of most interest to children is the fact that Carpentras is the Vaucluse's *ville sucrée* ('city of sweets'), known for its tooth-rotting delicacies for centuries. The town's most famous sugary speciality is the *berlingot*, an old-fashioned, pyramid-shaped, hard sugar sweet in any of six flavours—mint, coffee, lemon, aniseed, melon and strawberry.

INSIDER TIP »

The **Carpentras Berlingot card** (free from the tourist office for anyone staying one night or more in the area) gives families a range of discounts at shops and restaurants and for leisure activities in and around town. Additionally, at 11am every Monday in July and August the tourist office offers card-holders a free glass of wine (or non-alcoholic *sirop*), a tasting of local products and a goodie bag for children.

INSIDER TIP »

Young children will love **Le Jarditrain** (☎ *04 90 40 45 18, www.lejarditrain.com*) in St. Didier, 6km southeast of Carpentras on RD4/RD39, where 25 miniature trains putter through a garden of scale-model landscapes complete with stations, roads and villages. It's open Monday to Friday, April to June and September, 2:30pm to 6pm; July and August from Monday to Friday 10:30am to midday and 3pm to 6:30pm. Admission for adults is 6€, for 3–12s 4€.

Orange ★★

Tourist office: ☎ *04 90 34 70 88,* **www.otorange.fr**

The small town of Orange is literally overshadowed by the grandeur of its past; the huge **Roman theatre** (p. 206) is the best-preserved in Europe, and the grandiose **Arc de Triomphe** (p. 207) the third-largest on the continent.

Although you may well get the feeling that not a lot has happened in Orange since the Romans left, it's pleasant to stroll past the triumphal arch, then up the **Colline d'Eutrope** for a swim, a picnic and a free view of the theatre from above. Don't miss the lively **market** on Place Georges Clemenceau (in front of the cathedral) on Thursday mornings, where, as well as all the olives, cheeses, fresh fruit and vegetables that you could possibly want, you'll find newly hatched chicks, ducklings and baby rabbits.

Vaison-la-Romaine ★★★
ALL AGES

Tourist office: ☎ *04 90 36 02 11,* **www.vaison-la-romaine.com**

You don't need to be hooked on history to be impressed by the ancient **Roman theatre**, with its rows of stone benches and towering stone columns, at Vaison-la-Romaine—definitely the most family-friendly heritage site in the Vaucluse. The old quarter, with its chic 17th-century town houses and flower-filled courtyards, is traffic free, so good for a wander, while the more

Hidden by Mud

Vaison's story will appeal to Indiana Jones fans. The Roman city was abandoned after the Empire collapsed in the 5th century AD and gradually vanished beneath mud carried by the Ouvèze, only to be rediscovered by archaeologists as recently as 1907. The statues that you see around the ancient theatre are copies of the originals found on the site, which are now in the museum nearby.

modern part has heaps of lively pavement cafés. Make sure you fit in a visit to the 2,000-year-old *pont romain* (Roman bridge) crossing the Ouvèze river and the dramatic 12th-century **castle**.

Natural Wonders & Spectacular Views

Dentelles de Montmirail ★★
www.web-provence.com
These 'little teeth' form a miniature mountain range in which tiny hill villages cling like swallows' nests to chalk cliffs. The Dentelles are in the foothills of the Mont Ventoux massif, roughly midway between Carpentras and Vaison-la-Romaine.

To get there, turn west off the D938 at Malaucene, and be prepared for some serpentine country roads. By local standards, they hardly qualify as mountains—the highest point is only 730m (2,400 ft) above sea level—and there are some easy but softly adventurous walks (suitable for children about 11 and up) with plenty of café or picnic stops.

Mont Ventoux ★★★
30km northeast of Carpentras on D974, ***www.ventoux-en-provence.com***

At 1,909m (6,236 ft), Mont Ventoux dominates and defines the Vaucluse like a white-headed giant—in winter it's usually

Mont Ventoux

Pretty Roussillon

With its old stone houses painted in a dozen shades of mellow yellow, red and orange dug from the ochre quarries nearby, **Roussillon** (tourist office: 📞 *04 90 05 60 25*, *www.roussillon-provence.com*) is the prettiest village in the Vaucluse, bar none. Perched on a hilltop, it has steep streets that can challenge little legs and buggy-pushers. It's very much a tourist town these days, and every other building, it seems, is a boutique or a smart restaurant. Nearby, the colourful hilltop village of **Gordes** is home to one of the most impressive castles in the Vaucluse.

snow-capped, while in summer the bare limestone peak glows white. You can drive to the top, and the lower slopes are a hotbed of outdoor activities in summer and winter.

Mont Ventoux is also notorious as the toughest stage finish of the world's toughest cycle race, the **Tour de France**, and has defeated some of the world's best cyclists (including British racer Tom Simpson, who collapsed and died on the mountain in 1967).

Animal Parks

Cirque Alexis Gruss ★ ★ ★
ALL AGES

Château du Cirque, N7, Piolenc, 6km northwest of Orange, 📞 *04 90 29 49 49, www.alexis-gruss.com*

You can meet elephants, watch splendid stallions being put through their paces and ride in a horse-drawn carriage at the headquarters of one of the world's oldest circuses. Children can also learn the basics of juggling, tightrope walking and trapeze in a circus-arts workshop,

or join a theatrical makeup workshop in a 2-hour session (2 to 4pm) as part of a full-day visit. Older children who really want to learn the tricks of the circus can even sign up for a 1-week residential course.

Open mid-May–Sept, Tues–Sun 10am–5pm. **Adm** *18€, children 3–12 16€ (25€/20€ at weekends).* **Amenities** 🅿 🍽 ♥

Ferme aux Crocodiles ★ ★ ★
ALL AGES

Les Blachettes, Pierrelatte, north of Orange via RN7 or A7 (leave autoroute at Bollène exit), 📞 *04 75 04 33 73, www.lafermeauxcrocodiles.com*

Listen to your children as they 'ooh' and 'aah' at the little crocs that hatch out in the incubators. The Crocodile Farm is a huge tropical greenhouse that is home to more than 400 rare crocodilians, ranging from newly hatched 6-inchers fresh from the park's incubators to 2m (6 ft) monsters, as well as a group of giant tortoises from the Seychelles and flocks of tropical birds. All staff speak English, and all the information is multilingual. Since it's mostly indoors, it's an excellent fall-back for families if you hit a rare rainy day—there are enough little monsters here to keep your own interested for a whole morning or afternoon.

Open Daily 9:30am–7pm Mar–Sept, 9:30am–5pm Oct–Feb. **Adm** 12.50€, children 3–12 8€. **Amenities** 🖼 🛒 ☕ 🅿

Maison Natale de Jean-Henri Fabre ★ ★ ★ ALL AGES

St.-Leons, Route d'Orange, Serignan du Comtat, 📞 04 90 30 57 62, **www. musee-jeanhenrifabre.com**

This is one of our family favourites. The birthplace and home of Provence's 'insect man', Jean-Henri Fabre, is lovingly preserved. With its fireplace, simple wooden furniture, copper pans and other household tools and utensils, it offers a glimpse back into 19th-century Provence. However, the real fun is outside, in the insect garden, with a guided safari into the micro-world of the *petites bêtes* that Fabre loved so much: crickets, locusts, ants, mason bees, dragonflies and more. Provence is crowded with creepie-crawlies, so you might as well learn about them.

Open Feb–May and Oct–Dec 11am–12:30pm and 1:30pm–5pm; June–Sept daily 10am–7pm. **Adm** 3.50€, children 5–14 3€, under-5s free. **Credit** Cash only. **Amenities** 🅿

Natural Reserves, Parks & Gardens

Fort & Abbaye de St.-André

Villeneuve lez Avignon, 📞 04 90 25 45 35, **www.gard-provençal.com**

Toddlers can romp and chase the troop of resident kittens inside the walls of the medieval Fort Saint-André, which contains beautifully laid out Italianate abbey gardens. There's a fantastic view of Avignon, the river and the surrounding countryside from the garden terrace or the castle battlements.

Open 10am–12:30pm and 2–6pm Apr–Sept, 10am–noon and 2–5pm Oct–Mar. **Adm** 6.50€, children under 6 free. **Credit** MC, V.

Parc Naturel Régional du Luberon ★ AGE 5 & UP

Maison du Parc du Luberon (park HQ), Place Jean-Jaurès, Apt, 📞 04 90 04 42 00, **www.parcduluberon.fr**

This regional natural park in the southeast corner of the Vaucluse comprises almost 1,120 sq km of woodland, pasture and cedar-cloaked limestone valleys on the southern slopes of the Luberon hills, overlooked by the 1,125m (3,690 ft) peak of **Mourre Nègre**. It's home to an array of rare species of eagle, owl and many other birds, butterflies, flowers, reptiles and mammals. Depending on how old, tough and active your family is, you can explore the park on a choice of hiking trails; the most family-friendly is the **cedar forest trail** starting in Bonnieux and

FUN FACT ▶▶ This Way Up ◀◀

Look out for strange symbols cut into the cornerstones of the Chartreuse's walls. When the monastery was being built, none of the builders knew how to read, so Ikea-style instructions were cut into the stone to show them where to put each block. Hence, an arrow-like mark might mean 'this way up, stupid'.

meandering for 6km through shady woods with plenty of good picnic spots. For more challenging trails, call at the Maison du Parc du Luberon in an 18th-century manor in Apt, which has maps, guides, exhibitions and a video room.

Open *Maison du Parc (park HQ) Apr–Sept 8:30am–noon and 1:30– 6pm Mon–Sat.* **Adm** *Free.* **Amenities**

Historic Buildings & Monuments

Chartreuse du Val de Bénédiction ★★ ALL AGES

Villeneuve lez Avignon, 📞 *04 90 27 50 00,* **www.chartreuse.org**

The vast echoing cloisters of this 14th-century monastery make for a cool refuge from the heat of the day and the crowded summer streets of Avignon. Around the cells where the monks lived are shady courtyards and herb gardens where they grew medicinal herbs (still cultivated, and sold in the gift shop), and where you and your children are free to wander. During the French Revolution, the monks were turfed out and revolutionary soldiers (and their horses) occupied the Chartreuse—you can still see the occasional bullet hole in the ceilings. There's a family-friendly open-air restaurant.

Palais des Pâpes

Open *Daily 9am–6:30pm Apr–Sept;
9:30am–5:30pm Oct–Mar.* **Adm**
6.50€, children under 6 free. **Credit**
MC, V. **Amenities** ☕🍴🛍

Palais des Pâpes ★ ★ ★
ALL AGES

Place du Palais, Avignon, ☎ *04 90 27
50 00,* **www.palais-des-papes.com**

Even children without a massive
interest in history will be wowed
by the sheer scale of this, the
biggest Gothic palace in the
world, with huge, echoing halls
and chapels. Built in the 14th
century, when the papacy fled
Rome and set up home in Avignon, it was stripped of its treasures during the French
Revolution, but there are still
colourful wall-paintings to
admire in the Great Audience
Room. The ticket price includes
a room-by-room audio-guide
(available in English).

Open *Daily 1–14 Mar 9am–6:30pm;
15 Mar–30 June 9am–4pm; July and
1–15 Sept 9am–8pm; Aug 9am–9pm;
16 Sept–1 Nov 9am–7pm; 2 Nov–Feb
9:30am–5:45pm.* **Adm** *10.50€, children under 18 8.50€.* **Credit** *MC, V.*
Amenities ☕🛍

Pont St.-Bénezet ★ ★ ★
ALL AGES

Avignon, ☎ *04 32 74 32 74*

This is the bridge that the song's
about: '*Sur le pont d'Avignon, on y*

danse tout en rond' ('On the
bridge at Avignon, there they
dance, all in a circle')—or, as our
family sings it, '*...on y danse* Two
Ton Ron' (we like the idea of a
rotund bloke in a stripy T-shirt
dancing all by himself at the end
of the ruined bridge). Avignon's
famous bridge juts out into the
Rhône but doesn't make it all the
way to the other side—floods
caused it to collapse several times,
and in 1688 they gave up repairing it. Only four of the original
22 arches still stand. About halfway along the bridge is the little
Chapelle St.-Nicolas, named for
the patron saint of river boatmen,
built in the 16th century.

Open *Daily 9:30am–5:45pm.* **Adm**
4.50€, children 8–14 3.50€. **Credit**
MC, V.

Théâtre Antique d'Orange
★ ★ ★ **AGE 4 & UP**

Place des Frères Mounet, Orange,
☎ *04 90 51 17 60,* **www.theatre-
antique.com**

Orange's ancient **Roman theatre**, the most impressive heritage
site in the Vaucluse, will fascinate
older children with an interest in
the ancient empire; younger ones
will simply enjoy scrambling over
the multiple tiers of stone seats.
The theatre was built about 25
BC, in the reign of the Emperor
Augustus, and a 3½m statue of

FUN FACT ▶ **Under the Bridge** ◀

The original lyrics of 'Sur le pont d'Avignon' weren't sur le pont
(on the bridge) but *sous le pont* (under the bridge)—the locals danced on the
sands of the riverbank under the shelter of the arches.

the emperor dominates the scene. With its flights of wooden steps, however, it is impossible to explore with a buggy.

Another Roman monument worth a look is the **Arc de Triomphe** on Avenue de l'Arc de Triomphe, built about the same time as the ancient theatre to commemorate Roman victories over the Gauls. The carved sea-monsters and mythical beings on this triumphal arch will entertain curious children for a while, and it's free.

Open *Daily Easter–Sept 8am–6:45pm, Sept–Easter 9am–noon and 2–5pm.* **Adm** *8€, children 7–17 6€; second child accompanying two adults free.* **Credit** *MC, V.*

Village des Bories ★★★
ALL AGES

Route de Cavaillon, 4km west of Gordes, ☎ *04 90 72 03 48*

All over the Vaucluse you'll see little stone houses—*bories*—that look like beehives (or maybe holiday homes for hobbits or gnomes), standing in pastures and on hillsides. Made of stone slabs, they are built to a design dating back more than 5,000 years, and were still used as tool sheds and shelters for farm workers and their animals until the 20th century. Most of them, sadly, are beginning to collapse into heaps of stones, but at the Village des Bories near Gordes you can walk inside some of 20 *bories* that have been carefully rebuilt. Children, especially, find them more exciting than the great cathedrals and castles, and you can only marvel together at the skill of the masons who made them.

Open *Daily 9am–sunset.* **Adm** *5.50€, children 10–17 3€.* **Credit** *Cash only.*

INSIDER TIP »

If you need to while away a couple of hours in Vaison-la-Romaine (p. 201), pay a visit to the **Musée Archeologique Theo Desplans** (☎ *04 90 36 50 48*, *www.vaison-la-romaine. com*). Among the ancient Roman statuary you'll be treated to the extraordinary sight of a shared, six-seater ancient latrine—clearly, the Romans were not concerned about privacy.

Roman Theatre, Orange

Top Museums

Musée de la Lavande ★★

ALL AGES

Route de Gordes, D2, Coustellet, midway between Gordes and Cavaillon, 📞 *04 90 76 91 23, www.musee delalavande.com*

Lavender is the best-known symbol of the Vaucluse, and it's worth visiting this museum just to see the vast tracts of purple lavender fields that surround it from June to August, and to breathe the heady perfume of the flowers. Inside, you learn how lavender oil has for centuries been distilled from the blossoms using copper alembics, and can buy pure lavender essence, oils, soaps, candles and dried blooms to take home. Audio-guides in English are available, but hardly needed.

Open *Daily May–Sept 9am–7pm, Feb–Mar and Nov–Dec 9am–12:15pm and 2–6pm, April and Oct 9am–1pm and 2–6pm.* **Credit** *Cash only.* **Amenities** 🅿 🛍

Musée Lapidaire ★★ AGE 5 & UP

27 rue de la République, Avignon, 📞 *04 90 86 33 84, www.musee-lapidaire.org*

This museum will appeal to your family's ghoulish side—the high point is the scary medieval sculpture depicting the man-eating monster of Tarascon, the *tarasque* (p. 171), but you'll also find ancient sarcophagi from Roman times, a morbid collection of Venetian death-masks and a superb statue of the Greek god Apollo slaying another mythical monster, the Python.

Tiny tots may find it all a bit nightmare-inducing.

Open *Wed–Mon 10am–1pm and 2–6pm June–Sept, Wed–Mon 9:30am–1pm and 2–5:30pm Oct–May.* **Adm** *6€, children 12–18 3€.* **Credit** *Cash only.*

Arts & Crafts

Cristallerie des Papes

Fontaine de Vaucluse, about 20km south of Carpentras, 📞 *04 90 20 32 52*

During a visit to this glassworks shop you can watch as local glass-blowers turn red-hot molten blobs into delicate crystal lamps, ornaments and vases.

Open *Mon–Fri 9am–noon and 2–5pm, Sat 9am–noon.* **Adm** *Free.* **Credit** *MC, V (in shop).*

INSIDER TIP

No trip to Carpentras would be complete without a visit to one of the town's famous sweetie factories (tourist office: 📞 *04 90 63 00 78, www.carpentras-ventoux. com*) to see how its signature sweets—*berlingot* and nougat—are made.

Child-friendly Tours

Grands Bateaux de Provence ALL AGES

Allées de l'Oulle, Avignon, 📞 *04 90 85 62 25, www.avignon-et-provence.com/mireio*

This company offers a choice of five different cruises up and down the Rhône on its restaurant-ships *Le Mireio*, *La Saone* and *St. Nicolas*. All these just chug up and down the Rhône for durations of 1 to 5 hours (up-river to

Little Tourist Trains

Vaison-la-Romaine's steep streets can be a challenge for anyone, especially toddlers and buggy-pushers on a hot summer day, so the town's *petit train* (📞 *04 90 36 02 11*, *www.vaison-en-provence.com*) is a welcome alternative to foot-slogging. Starting at the tourist office, it loops round all the main sights of the town, including the Roman remains and the medieval chapel of St.-Quenin, and crosses the famous Roman bridge en route. There are daily departures from 1 April to 30 September, on the hour from 10am to 4pm, leaving from the tourist office, and the whole trip takes about 30 minutes. Adults cost 4.50€, teens from 12 to 17 pay 2.50€, while children 11 and under go for free.

Avignon's tourist train (📞 *06 11 16 38 99*), with its multilingual commentary, provides a great introduction to the city's chequered past, from the 12th century (when the legendary bridge was built) to the 18th century, the town's golden age. It's perfect on very hot days, or if you have tots with easily tired legs. There are daily departures every 30 minutes, Easter to October, from Place du Palais des Pâpes. Tickets cost 7€ for adults and older children and 4€ for children aged 8 and under.

Châteauneuf-du-Pâpe and downriver as far as Arles). Only the shorter cruises can really be recommended for families, as some children will quickly get bored on board. There's a choice of five set menus, including a '*menu mousse*' for under 12s, which offers quiche, chicken and chips, and a dessert. Reservations are advisable.

Open *Daily May–Oct; contact for times.* **Adm** *from 52€, children 5–14 29€.* **Credit** *MC, V.* **Amenities** 🍷 🍴

Active Families

Balade en Kayak AGE 6 & UP

Chemin de Halage, Ile de la Barthelasse, Avignon, 📞 *04 90 03 17 25.* *www.kayak-avignon.fr*

These gentlest of kayak trips (in one- or two-seater kayaks) take you over the backwaters of the Rhône, around the Île de la

Barthelasse on the right bank of the river; they're open to all ages but we don't think they're suitable for anyone much under the age of 6. After meeting at the west end of the Pont Daladier, you're given basic instruction by a qualified guide before setting off in a flotilla of kayaks, accompanied by your guides. Lifejackets and safety helmets are provided.

Open *Daily 9 July–19 Aug 2–6:30pm.* **Adm** *15€ for 1 hour, including insurance and equipment; children under 9 free.*

Canoe Evasion ★ ★ ALL AGES

Isle-sur-la-Sorgue, 📞 *04 90 38 26 22,* *www.canoe-evasion.net*

This firm runs easygoing guided family canoe adventures down the Sorgue, from Fontaine de Vaucluse to Isle-sur-la-Sorgue. The 8km trip takes about 2 hours and you don't need any special skills; staff say it's accessible to all, but we'd think twice about taking children aged under 3. Buoyancy jackets and helmets are included; you should also wear shorts and footwear that doesn't mind water, and have towels and dry clothes in your car. Falling in is optional, but a certain amount of splashing is inevitable so don't bring expensive cameras. At the end of the float, a minibus awaits to carry you back to your start point.

Open *Daily (departures 10am, 11am, 2pm, 3pm and 4pm); advance booking required. Seasonal variations.* **Adm** *From 17€, children 7–14 11€.* **Credit** *MC, V.* **Amenities** 🅿

Passerelle des Cîmes ★★★
AGE 6 & UP

Allée Jean Giono, Batiment D, No 23, Isle-sur-la-Sorgue, 📞 *04 90 38 56 87,* **www.parcours-aerien.fr**

You need a certain head for heights to enjoy clambering around the treetops on this network of rope bridges and walkways, swings and nets, where children aged 6 and over can discover what it's like to be a tree-dwelling chimpanzee. There are 11 levels of treetop acrobatics, from easy-peasy to slightly scary; safety equipment is provided. This is a great confidence-builder for any children who are slightly hesitant about outdoor action and adventure.

Open *Daily 9am–5pm July and Aug, Sat and Sun 9am–4pm Mar–June and Sept–Nov.* **Adm** *18€, children 9–16 15€, children 6–9 12€.* **Credit** *MC, V.* **Amenities** ☕ 🅿

Randonnée Pedestre Accompagné d'un Ane de Bat ★★★
AGE 6 & UP

L'Asinerie, Le Fraischamp, Le Beaucet, 15km north of Carpentras, 📞 *04 90 66 14 53,* **www.asidudevens.free.fr**

This walking trip with **donkeys** is our favourite family trip in the Vaucluse. Load up your gentle donkey with picnic supplies and head off along the winding paths around **Le Beaucet**, a pretty hilltop village surrounded by vineyards and olive groves, for a day in the countryside. You can rent a donkey for a half-day or for up to 2 days (B&B accommodation or camping can be arranged). Owner Catherine (who speaks English) provides good maps and advice to help you find your way. All-terrain bikes are also available.

Open *Daily 9am–5pm; advance booking required.* **Adm** *25€ per half-day.*

Sentiers des Ochres ★
AGE 5 & UP

From Rustrel tourist office, Place de la République, 📞 *04 90 04 96 07*

Welcome to cowboy country; the 16km Colorado Provençal would make a perfect set for a Western. This expanse of red and orange, carved and sculpted cliffs and rock pinnacles was shaped by 2 centuries of quarrying the rich ochre rock to make the deep orange and yellow dyes and paints still so typical of Provence. Short (self-guided) ochre walking trails (30 to 90 minutes) lead through the

Biking & Buggies

Découverte du Terroir en Buggy, Les Vignerons du Mont Ventoux, Quartier la Salle, Bédoin (📞 *04 90 65 95 72*, *www.bedoin.com*). Children from 10 years can explore the vineyards of Mont Ventoux in a convoy of two-person, stripped-down mountain buggies, with an English-speaking guide. Starting from Bédoin on the lower slopes, you vroom to vineyards up to 500m above sea level, offering dizzy views of the whole of the Vaucluse spread out below. The whole trip takes 2½ hours; once back in town, parents can taste wines from the *terroirs* you've just visited. A family of four will need two buggies (with one adult and one child in each). All ages are welcome, but though older children will have great fun riding shotgun, we can't recommend this for little ones.

Devalkart, Station du Mont Serein, Beaumont du Ventoux (📞 *04 90 63 42 02*, *www.stationdumontserein.com*). Dads (or grandads) who remember building downhill go-karts from old pram wheels and bits of scrap timber will love introducing their offspring to these hi-tech descendants of the old-fashioned 'soap-box' kart. Powered only by gravity, these non-motorised vehicles go as fast or as gently as you like over pistes used for snow sports in winter. You just hook your kart to the ski-lift to be towed back to the top for another ride. Little ones (over 4-years old) can potter around in mini-electric karts at the foot of the slopes while their older siblings (over 12) hurtle down the slopes.

Fun Parc Aventure, Chemin du Bois, Richerenches (📞 *06 08 90 12 13*, *www.funparcaventure.com*), around 30km northwest of Vaison-la-Romaine. There's more than a whiff of testosterone in the air at this adventure site in the Haut Vaucluse, with laser-gun range and quad-bike and moto-cross circuits (quads and bikes are available for 6-year-olds and over).

Holiday Bikes, 20 boulevard St. Roch. Avignon (📞 *04 32 76 25 88, www.holiday-bikes.com*). This is part of a France-wide network offering bicycle hire for all ages, plus scooters, quads and—most popular among teens and sub-teens—mini-motorbikes. Parents may have qualms about risking their offspring, but helmets are provided and mini-bikes can only be ridden off-road or on designated trails. Ordinary push-bikes are a cheaper and less noisy way to explore the outskirts of Avignon and the banks of the Rhône; helmets are provided.

Quad Location, Le Cours, Crillon-le-Brave (📞 *06 19 06 05 92*, *www.ventoux-quad.com*), 18km northeast of Carpentras. Here you can rent all-terrain quads from mini to monster size for off-road outings.

Ochre

Ochre is a kind of hard clay rich in iron oxide, which gives it a deep rust-orange colour. People have been using it as a pigment for 30,000 years—including the cave-painters who left their drawings of mammoths and other animals on grottoes in France and Spain, and the ancient Greeks and Romans who coloured their pottery with it. In 1780 one Jean-Etienne Astier from Roussillon found a way of making ochre into a washproof dye, and the Luberon ochre rush began—40,000 tons of the stuff were dug out of these hills every year until the 1930s, when cheaper artificial dyes were invented, ochre became unprofitable and the quarries were abandoned.

quarries, starting from Rustrel village; they're open to all ages, but under-6s may find it tough going and they're definitely not buggy-friendly. To avoid the heat, we'd recommend going first thing in the morning, and don't forget to take hats, sunscreen and plenty of cold drinks.

Open Mon–Sat 9:30am–7:30pm, Apr–Sept. **Adm** 3.50€, children 6–10 1.75€. **Credit** MC, V.

Shopping

Bébé 9

89 place du Général de Gaulle, Carpentras, 📞 *04 90 63 13 40 www.bebe-9.com*

This Carpentras toy-shop sells toys, games and amusements for all ages, from dolls and teddies to ray-guns and cowboy outfits. It's not exactly educational, but it will attract young family members with holiday money burning holes in their pockets. There's another branch in nearby Cavaillon.

Open Mon and Wed–Sat noon–2pm and 7–9:30pm.

Le Chat Botté ★ ★

62 impasse de la République, Isle-sur-la-Sorgue

The hand-made wooden toys here make a change from the humdrum plastic tat that has taken over so many French shopping streets—we were recently very taken with the

TIP ➤ The Best Local Markets ◀

Covered food market: Les Halles, Place Pie, Avignon, Tues–Sun mornings.
Flower market: Place des Carmes, Avignon, Sat morning.
Food market: Place Georges Clemenceau, Orange, Thurs morning.
Provençal market: Cour de l'Hôtel Dieu, central Carpentras, Fri morning.
Provençal market: Isle-sur-la-Sorgue, Sun morning.
Provençal market: central Apt, Sat morning.

wooden Pinocchio doll with two detachable noses, a long one for when he is telling fibs and a shorter nose for when he is telling the truth. The shop also sells rocking horses, teddy bears and even pull-along xylophone cars. For older children, there are skipping ropes and wooden skittles.

Open *Mon–Sat 9:30am–12:30pm and 3–7pm, Sun 10am–7pm.*

Santons et Tissus de Provence ★★

Place du Château, Gordes, 📞 *04 90 72 09 83*

Collectors from all over the globe return here again and again to look for new *santons* to add to their collection of these Provençal clay figures. 'They are all made and signed by Provençal artists, and none of them are made in China!' boasts Christine. The smallest *santons* cost 13€, but there are also smaller clay animals for 6€. You will also find brightly patterned dresses, skirts, blouses and shirts for girls and boys aged 2 to 14, starting at around 10€, and babywear.

Open *Daily 10am–5pm.* **Credit** *MC, V.*

FAMILY-FRIENDLY DINING

Avignon & Orange

In the summer months Avignon's **Place de L'Horloge** is a mass of café and brasserie tables from noon till midnight. Like other traffic-free squares dotted around Provence, it lends itself to alfresco dining and is handy for letting your children potter around after lunch, while you enjoy a post-prandial coffee. But, restaurant-wise, the city is one big tourist trap.

Piglet, Carpentras Market

TIP ⟩⟩ **Wine Time—Châteauneuf-du-Pâpe** ⟨⟨

Châteauneuf-du-Pâpe—'the Pope's new castle'—isn't as new as the name implies: it was built in the 14th century as a holiday home for the French popes of Avignon. It's now a ruin, on a hilltop that overlooks vast vineyards producing one of the Rhône region's famous red wines. Although there's not much to attract children, parents might enjoy attending a wine-tasting at one of the town's two winemakers' co-ops. Call the tourist office (📞 *04 90 83 71 08*) for details. Your best bet is probably **Prestige et Tradition,** 3 rue de la République (📞 *04 90 83 74 01*; Monday to Friday 8am to noon and 2 to 6pm), which stocks wine from around a dozen individually owned local vineyards.

Our gourmet tip for a romantic dinner is **La Mirande** (📞 *04 90 14 20 20*, *www.la-mirande.fr*) in Place Mirande, with a terrifyingly smart dining salon within a jasmine- and orange-tree-scented garden. Mind-bogglingly expensive (see the website for à la carte menus and wine list), but worth every penny.

EXPENSIVE

Restaurant à Deux Pas du Potager ★ FRENCH CLASSIC

45 rue Edmond Delteil, Avignon, 📞 *04 90 85 46 41, www.a2pasdupotager.fr*

'The restaurant two steps from the kitchen garden' is so named because it used to be the *potager* (kitchen garden) for the Halles d'Avignon market; today its garden supplies the fruit and vegetables that appear on your plate. A sunny, south-facing terrace is perfect for outdoor lunches, but there's also an indoor, air-conditioned dining room for days when it's too hot (or chilly) to sit outside. The menu is very French, with a southern emphasis, naturally, on garden-fresh ingredients. There's off-street

parking; if you ask nicely when booking a table for lunch, they'll let you park a couple of hours earlier to go sightseeing.

Open *Daily noon–3pm and 7–10pm.*
Main courses *Set menu 30€ (lunch), 35€ (dinner). Children's menu 25€.*
Credit *MC, V.* **Amenities** 🅿 🍽

MODERATE

La Fourchette ★ ★ PROVENCAL

7 rue Racine, Avignon, 📞 *04 90 86 17 07*

Like many French restaurants, La Fourchette assumes that children are small grown-ups, which means it offers them the same old-style southern French cooking as their parents rather than a children's menu. The monkfish stew with endive and the *daube* (stew) of beef with macaroni gratin may be a bit too challenging for smaller appetites, but the fresh sardines, simply grilled, should please everyone and are a revelation to British children who have only previously encountered the tinned variety. We rate it as one of the few affordable spots in Avignon that doesn't pander to (or rip off) the tourist hordes—it's mostly filled with local families enjoying a weekend lunch or dinner. In keeping with its name ('The Fork'), the walls are eccentrically decorated with collections of antique cutlery, as well as old-fashioned postcards and depictions of that most Provençal of insects, the *cigale* (p. 114). Booking is essential.

Open Daily 12:15–1:45pm and 7:15–9:45pm except weekends 4–26 Aug and 9–16 Mar. **Main courses** Set menu 31€. À la carte mains 15€–20€. **Credit** MC, V. **Amenities** ⚐

Le Festival ★ FRENCH

5 place de la République, Orange, ☏ *04 90 34 65 58*

This is the classiest-looking of the half-dozen restaurants and cafés on Orange's cobbled, traffic-free main square, a couple of minutes' walk from the Théâtre Antique (p. 206). Its tables, shaded by trees and umbrellas, are well spaced out, so there's room for families to manoeuvre. Main courses are reasonably priced and service is prompt. The *menu enfant* gives a choice of chips, fish with rice or *steak*

haché, plus dessert. If under-6s grow restless, they can play on the mini merry-go-round a few steps away across the square.

Open Daily noon–2:30pm and 7–11pm. **Main courses** 12€–20€, children's menu 7.50€. **Credit** AE, MC, V.

East of Avignon

Chez Serge ★ FRENCH

90 rue Cottier, Carpentras, ☏ *04 90 63 21 24, www.chez-serge.com*

This restaurant on a courtyard surrounded by ancient arches is usually full of local families. Easy to find, and open later than most, it's a godsend if you arrive in Carpentras late in the evening in high summer, although reservations are recommended, especially at night. The menu is full of straightforward, unpretentious French cooking, including perfectly prepared cuts of lamb and beef; the children's menu features *steak haché* with chips or vegetables, or ham and cheese pizza, followed by vanilla or chocolate ice cream. Most of the friendly, efficient staff speak English.

TIP **The Best Ice Cream Stops**

Glacier Gelatoshow in Orange (at the corner of Place de la République opposite Le Festival) sells *granita* in more colours than the rainbow; flavours include lemon, green apple, mango and orange, or there's a bright-blue version simply called *azzurro*. If you worry about chemical colourings, there are 22 flavours of ice cream too.

In Gordes, east of Avignon, **La Canelle**, 2 rue Baptistan Picca, a few steps from the castle and the main square, has a handful of tables and chairs outside and a dozen flavours of ice cream, as well as sorbets and ice lollies. It also serves pizzas, salads and cold drinks.

Café by Palais des Pâpes, Avignon

Open *Daily noon–2pm and 7–11:30pm July and Aug; noon–2pm Sept–June.* **Main courses** *12.50€–28€; children's menu 12€.* **Credit** *AE, MC, V.*

La Petite Fontaine

13–17 place du Colonel Mouret, Carpentras, 📞 *04 90 60 77 83*

Just around the corner from the Place de la Cathédrale, this small restaurant is a welcome escape from the crowds that pack the square and surrounding streets on market days. It's easy to find, so it makes a good family rendez-vous point too. There are tables outside beside a small fountain, and although this narrow street isn't pedestrianised, there's very little traffic. Tables inside are crammed close together, so are tricky to navigate with a buggy. The children's menu at 9.50€ offers the usual choice of *steak haché* or pizza.

Open *Mon and Wed–Sat noon–2pm and 7–9:30pm.* **Main courses** *from 15€. À la carte menu 27€. Children's menu 11.50€.*

TIP ▶ Down on the Farm ◀

Feed the animals and enjoy trying fresh organic produce on a visit to **La Ferme de l'Oiselet** (Oiselet Farm; 📞 *04 90 65 57 57*, *www.oiselet.com*) in Sarrians. Families can stay in tent-like Mongolian yurts, while kids from 6 to 12 can take part in themed workshops. It's open Monday to Friday 9am to midday and 2 to 5pm, and on Saturday afternoons from 2 to 5pm.

TIP >> **Picnic with a View**

Looking down on Orange's ancient Roman theatre (p. 206) and with views all the way east to the Dentelles de Montmirail (p. 202), the land-scaped **St.-Eutrope hill** on Rue Portoules is in a good spot for a post-sight-seeing picnic, with plenty of shade under the trees, children's play areas and the **Piscine des Cedres**, an open-air swimming pool (with lifeguards) very popular with local families in summer. If you don't bring a picnic, there's also a café-restaurant.

Meanwhile, the formal gardens of the **Rocher des Doms** stand on the site of the earliest known settlement in Avignon, behind the cathedral of Notre-Dame-des-Doms. Boasting statues, flower beds, shade trees, topiary and a pond, they offer sweeping views of the town and across the river to Villeneuve.

Les Cuisines du Château ☆

5 place Genty Pantaly, Gordes, 📞 *04 90 72 01 31*

We like this place for its loca-tion, right under the white stone walls and turrets of the medieval castle, beside a gurgling foun-tain, shaded by plane trees and away from most of the traffic. There is no children's menu but plenty of things to appeal to smaller appetites, including good Greek salads with feta, tomato and mozzarella, or *salade niçoise*. The puddings—profiteroles, tiramisu and chocolate brownies (all 9€)—are outstanding.

Open Daily midday–3pm and 7–10:30pm. Main courses 10€–15€. Credit AE, MC, V.

FAMILY-FRIENDLY ACCOMMODATION

Avignon, Orange and Châ-teauneuf-du-Pâpe are essentially medieval towns that have grown beyond their original

boundaries. Within the historic core of each, there are plenty of hotels, some of which are very luxurious, while many more are small and comfortable. It has to be said, however, that very few are truly family-friendly. Rooms—even in luxury hotels— are on the small side, and few if any town-centre hotels have spaces for children to romp and relax. If you're planning to stay in the area for more than a few nights, look for a base in a *gîte*, a hotel or a campsite on the out-skirts of town rather than in the crowded historic centre.

Avignon, Orange & Châteauneuf-du-Pâpe

MODERATE

Hôtel Cloître St. Louis
★ ★ VALUE

20 rue du Portail Boquier, Avignon, 📞 *04 90 27 55 55, www.cloitre-saint-louis.com*

In a city with a dearth of genu-inely child-friendly places to stay, this hotel just inside Avignon's old walls is the best base for a **short family stay**, as well as one of the only hotels in the old town with a swimming pool (a rooftop one with terrace where you can hang out in the heat of the afternoon).   Everything is within walking distance, and above all it is easy to find.

The 16th-century main building surrounds an enclosed courtyard where smaller children can play safely. Bedrooms are coolly modern, unusually for France, and well fitted out. Bathrooms have baths as well as showers and bidets, and the TV pulls in MTV and the Cartoon Channel to help keep children amused. Breakfast is a lavish affair and well worth the 16€ extra (no reduction for children), with a big buffet of fresh fruit, rolls and fresh bread, cheese, ham and sausage and a variety of conserves—certainly enough to set the family up for a morning's exploring.

Rooms 80. **Rates** Standard 175€–210€, Superior 250€–300€, Suites 300€–360€. Extra bed 26€ but one child up to 16 shares parent's room free and 50% discount for under-16s in separate room; cot free. **Credit** AE, MC, V. **Amenities** ▼ £ 🖼 ¶¶ **In room** A/C ▼ 🛏

La Sommellerie ★★★

Route de Roquemaure, Châteauneuf-du-Pâpe, ☏ 04 90 83 50 00, www.la-sommellerie.fr

Master-chef Pierre Paumel's La Sommellerie is a converted 17th-century farmhouse set in its own peaceful gardens and surrounded by vineyards—in summer the

cicadas are the loudest noise you'll hear. This is a small, intimate hotel that would suit a family with smaller children for a night or a week. Two of the rooms are comfortable family suites with double beds and sofa beds suitable for families with one or two small children, but more rumbustious sub-teens may find it restrictive after a night or two.

Unsurprisingly, the restaurant has an excellent local wine list to accompany meals, which are served on a shaded terrace overlooking the swimming pool—handy for parents who want to take their time over lunch but have trouble luring their children away from the water. In cooler weather there's an indoor dining room and a cosy lounge with log fire. Breakfast is an array of yoghurt, fruit, conserves, cheeses, ham and salami.

Rooms 14 plus 2 suites. **Rates** Standard doubles 74€–109€, family suites 99€–151€. **Amenities** ▼ ₽ 🖼 ¶¶ **In room** A/C 🛏

INEXPENSIVE

Aerotel La Sorguette ★ FIND

871 route d'Apt, Isle-sur-la-Sorgue, ☏ 04 90 38 07 51, www.camping-sorguette.com

What fun! For something a little different, why not stay in cosy Mongolian-style yurts or Native American tipis on the banks of the Sorgue, just outside a pretty village famous for its antiques and broquante shops and street markets (even if you don't buy anything, kids will enjoy rummaging through piles of bric-a-brac in search of treasures). For those who prefer accommodation that's a little less exotic, there are ensuite wooden chalets and mobile homes.

Rooms 40 tipis, lodges, yurts and mobile homes. **Rates** 280€–497€ for four. **Credit** MC, V. **Amenities** 🔒 📶 **In room** ✕ ✈

Park Inn ☆ VALUE

Route de Caderousse, Orange, 📞 *04 90 34 24 10, www.orange.parkinn.fr*

This chain hotel on the outskirts of Orange is an excellent place for a stopover—it's easy to find, just off the *autoroute* and only 1½km from the centre, and offers free secure parking and, among the many amenities you'd expect in a four- or five-star hotel, a full-sized outdoor pool and a toddler's pool. Family rooms sleep up to four people in a double bed and sofa bed. The restaurant is adequate for a family dinner after a long day's drive.

Rooms 99. **Rates** Double 90€–100€. Extra bed 20€, cots 10€. **Credit** AE, MC, V. **Amenities** 🍸 🆓 📶 🖼 🍴 **In room** A/C 📶 🍸 📺

East of Avignon

VERY EXPENSIVE

Domaine des Andeols ☆ ☆ ☆

Les Andeols, St. Saturnin-les-Apt, 📞 *04 90 75 50 63, www.domaine-des-andeols.com*

Alain Ducasse's fourth venture is a collection of gorgeous houses set in tranquil gardens on the outskirts of picturesque Gordes. Each house is individual; decor ranges from quirkily modern

and eclectic to classical and serene. It's all absolutely fabulous, though one feels that children may need to be on their best behaviour in the public areas. On the other hand, you could quarantine them in splendid isolation by staying in the Maison des Voyageurs or the Maison des Cascades, each of which has a private pool and its own garden. The restaurant, of course, is superb.

Rooms 9 houses, 7 with 2 bedrooms and 1 with 3 bedrooms. **Rates** From 1,400€ for 2 nights (minimum stay 2 nights). **Credit** AE, MC, V. **Amenities** 🅿 ☀ 🖼 🍴 **In room** ✏ 📹 📺

MODERATE

Mas de la Pierre du Coq
★★★

Chemin de Loriol, Aubignan, 📞 *04 90 67 31 64, www.masdelapierreducoq.com*

This restored 17th-century farmhouse is one of our family favourites in the Vaucluse, combining the cosiness of your own *gîte* with hotel-style service. The latter includes a tasty breakfast (included) of fresh fruit, freshly squeezed juices, croissants, yoghurt, ham and cheese, plus an excellent dinner on request for 28€ (no reduction for children). It's a diminutive place with just one family suite (double bed, single bed and sofa bed) along with four double/twin rooms, and is surrounded by flower-packed gardens that are safe for toddlers and younger children, though you need to keep an eye on little ones around the pool.

Hosts Martine and Stéphane will treat you like old friends. A network of walking and cycling trails starts on the doorstep; Stéphane will lend you bicycles and recommend routes. Avignon, Orange and Mont Ventoux are all within an hour's drive.

Rooms 4. **Rates** Double 120€, family suite 180€. Baby cot available by arrangement, free. **Credit** MC, V. **Amenities** 🚲 🅿 ☀ 🖼 In room 🚿

Camping La Montagne ★

944 chemin de la Montagne, Sorgues, 📞 04 90 83 36 66, www.campinglamontagne.com

If you're on a budget but want a family base within shouting distance of Avignon, this reasonably priced campsite offers the best of several worlds. First, it's only 10 minutes from the city. Second, you don't have to sleep under canvas, as there are chalets and mobile homes sleeping four to six with well-equipped kitchenettes. Third, but not least, there's a big open-air pool and a children's play area with a crew of child-minding *animateurs* to keep them amused and give parents a welcome breather. You'll also be able to play volleyball, pétanque, table tennis and billiards. You may not fancy the weekly calendar of karaoke evenings and fancy-dress nights, but nobody's forcing you to join in.

Chalets and mobile homes 50. **Rates** Chalet/mobile home 45€–70€ per night, 175€–650€ per week. Cot 25€ week. **Credit** MC, V. **Amenities** 🅿 🖼 🎿 🖼 🍴 🔒 ♀ In room ❌

Camping Le Luberon

Route de Saignon, D48, Apt, 📞 04 90 04 85 40, www.camping-le-luberon.com

Set on a 5-hectare site 1½km from the shops and restaurants of Apt, this campsite has plenty of space for those with their own tents. If you have a bigger budget and the desire for more comfort, self-contained stone houses (with kitchens) sleep five or six people in two bedrooms and on sofa-beds; and there are dinky wooden chalets with two bedrooms, a sheltered outdoor deck and a kitchen. These are all set away from the main and busiest camping area, which is focused around two swimming pools (heated in spring and autumn) and a toddlers' pool.

In summer, the Luberon is a veritable United States of Europe, with families from Germany, the Netherlands, Belgium and Italy, as well as France and the UK. The **Parc Naturel Régional du Luberon** (Luberon Regional National Park; p. 204) and facilities for other activities (including tennis, riding, climbing and mountain-biking) are nearby.

Places 80 tent pitches, 31 chalets and mobile homes. **Rates** Tent pitches 16.90€–18.90€ for two adults, tent and car, then additional person over 6 6.20€, under 6 4.60€; wooden chalet 350€–780€ per week; mobile homes 330€–750€ week (minimum stay 2 nights). **Amenities** 🖼 🖼 ♀ In room ❌

9 Alpes de Haute-Provence

ALPES DE HAUTE-PROVENCE

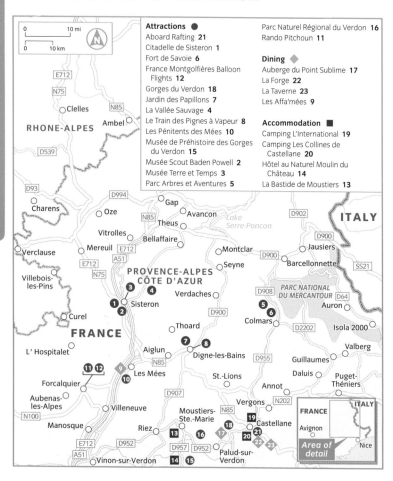

Attractions ●
Aboard Rafting **21**
Citadelle de Sisteron **1**
Fort de Savoie **6**
France Montgolfières Balloon Flights **12**
Gorges du Verdon **18**
Jardin des Papillons **7**
La Vallée Sauvage **4**
Le Train des Pignes à Vapeur **8**
Les Pénitents des Mées **10**
Musée de Préhistoire des Gorges du Verdon **15**
Musée Scout Baden Powell **2**
Musée Terre et Temps **3**
Parc Arbres et Aventures **5**

Parc Naturel Régional du Verdon **16**
Rando Pitchoun **11**

Dining ◆
Auberge du Point Sublime **17**
La Forge **22**
La Taverne **23**
Les Affa'mées **9**

Accommodation ■
Camping L'International **19**
Camping Les Collines de Castellane **20**
Hôtel au Naturel Moulin du Château **14**
La Bastide de Moustiers **13**

Bordered by plateaux and limestone ravines, Provence's sparsely populated Alpine hinterland rises up to 3,000m (9,850 ft). From Hannibal with his Carthaginian war elephants to Napoleon, it's a mountainous area that has often been caught between warring empires. These days you can wander through car-free, cobblestoned villages, fly in a hot-air balloon over lavender fields and olive groves, and marvel at the impregnable citadels that stand above every mountain pass and river crossing.

Accessible only via the fertile valley of the Durance, Provence's least-discovered region appeals to adventurous families, who can paddle around its deep-blue mountain lakes on pedalos or plunge giddily down deep limestone ravines in the Verdon gorges. In fact, this is one of the top adventure-sports destinations in the whole of France, with everything on offer from white-water kayaking and canyoning to par-ascending, abseiling and free-climbing.

VISITOR INFORMATION

The **Alpes de Haute-Provence Tourist Development Agency (ADT)** has an English-language website, *www.alpes-haute-provence.com*, listing activities, attractions, festivals and other events. It also has links to help you find accommodation and navigate your way around, and lists of all the local tourist offices in towns and larger villages.

Getting There

By Air There are no airports within this area itself, but several within easy reach. Nice airport (p. 58) is about 80 to 90km by road from the region's southern or eastern boundaries; Marseille airport (p. 117) is about 120km away; Nîmes airport (p. 170) is about 130km away; and Avignon airport (p. 194) is about 100km away.

Outside Provence, Grenoble airport (*www.grenoble-airport.com*), about 140km north of Gap, is served by Ryanair (p. 29) from Dublin all year, and by easyJet (p. 29), although many of these only operate from airports across the UK during the winter ski season.

By Train For Eurostar services to Avignon, see p. 194. TGVs connect Avignon with Marseille, from which there are links on TER regional trains (*www.ter-sncf.com*) to points north of Marseille along the Durance valley, to Gap and beyond (see 'Getting Around', p. 224). Alternatively, you can take the TGV from Paris to Valence and connect with Gap from the north. There's also the privately run *Train des Pignes* (*www.train provence.com*; p. 231) daily from Nice to Digne-les-Bains and the Haut-Verdon valley.

By Bus SNCF (p. 224) operates coach services (bookable on its website) from Gap, Avignon and Aix-en-Provence to many towns and villages in the Alpes de Haute-Provence.

By Car See p. 224.

Orientation

The A51 *autoroute* runs along the Durance valley, linking Sisteron, Manosque and other towns and villages with Aix-en-Provence, and the coast with Gap. The N85 Route Napoleon, named in honour of the emperor's advance in 1815, branches off the A51 at Château-Arnoux and winds its way through Digne-les-Bains and Castellane to Grasse and Cannes on the Riviera. The N202 connects the heart of Haute-Provence with Nice. Winding, scenic *routes départementales* link these main roads with the more remote villages.

Getting Around

TER trains (p. 58) connect Sisteron and other towns and villages along the Durance valley (Vif, Cielles-Men, Lus-la-Croix-Haute, Veynes-Dévoluy, Serres, Laragne, Château-Arnoux-St-Auban, Manosque–Gréoux-les-Bains and Meyrargues) with Aix-en-Provence and Marseille to the south and Gap and Grenoble to the north. There are no passenger rail services in the hinterland—SNCF operates quite a comprehensive bus service connecting with its main stations, but if you want to explore you really need a car. For car-hire firms at Avignon, Marseille, Nice and Nîmes airports see p. 196, 144, 58 and 170.

There are plenty of local cycle-hire firms, but unless you're in top shape those steep valleys may be a bit of a challenge. Local tourist offices can give you details of these, and of local taxi operators.

> **INSIDER TIP** ≫
>
> **Alpes de Haute-Provence**
> (aka Haute-Provence) has a scattering of winter sports stations, most around the flanks of Mont Pelat or above the valley of the Ubaye, where Haute-Provence meets the Hautes-Alpes. They offer good facilities and adequate but not outstanding skiing. They are probably not worth the effort of reaching them from the UK. There are better ski resorts within easier reach.

WHAT TO SEE & DO

Children's Top 10 Attractions

❶ **Swimming**, sailing and splashing around at the **Lac de Ste. Croix** (p. 229).

❷ **Chugging** through the hills aboard the **Train des Pignes** (p. 231).

❸ **Learning** the French for woggle at the **Musée Scout Baden Powell** (p. 231).

❹ **Coming** face-to-face with cave people at the **Musée de Préhistoire des Gorge du Verdon** (p. 230).

❺ **Counting** dozens of different butterflies in Digne's **Jardin des Papillons** (p. 228).

❻ **Encountering** furry marmots and fierce wild boar in the **Vallée Sauvage** (p. 229).

❼ **Floating** high above lavender fields aboard a **hot-air balloon** (p. 233).

❽ **Swinging** Tarzan-style from tree to tree at **Parc Arbres et Aventure** (p. 233).

❾ **Imagining** you're a gallant musketeer fending off your enemies at the **Fort de Savoie** (p. 230).

❿ **Peering** down into the dizzying **Grand Canyon du Verdon** (p. 228).

Fast Facts: Castellane

Banks: **Crédit Agricole** (📞 *04 92 83 63 65*), Place Marcel Sauvaine.

Hospitals: **Hôpital Locale** (📞 *04 92 83 98 00*), Boulevard St -Michel.

Pharmacies: **Pharmacie Léocard** (📞 *04 92 75 00 03*), 18 rue Nationale.

Post Offices: the Castellane post office is at Place Marcel Sauvaire (📞 *04 92 83 99 80*); it's open 8:30am to 6pm Monday to Friday and 9am to 12:30pm Saturday.

Shopping: See p. 234 and, for markets, p. 236.

Child-friendly Events & Entertainment

Les Folklories de Pernes

Jardins de la Mairie, Pernes-les Fontaines, 📞 *06 71 49 75 21, E: vfgennet@wanadoo.fr*

Older children and parents will enjoy these days of open-air music and traditional dance in the village gardens, with a cast of performers from all over the world. All the action starts at 9pm, however, so this isn't an event for babies and younger toddlers.

16–18 July. **Adm** *2€.*

Rues en Fête

Sisteron, 📞 *04 92 62 67 71, www. sisteron.stationverte.com or www. sisteron.fr*

Sisteron plays host to a mixed-bag of evening entertainment for about 3 weeks in high summer, with mime artists, jugglers, conjurers, dancers and singers performing in streets around the old-town centre. Most events start about 9pm.

18 July–8 Aug. **Adm** *Free.*

Corso de la Lavande ★★

Digne-les-Bains, 📞 *04 92 36 62 62, www.ot-digneslesbains.fr.*

Digne comes over all purple for 4 days in August, during the lavender harvest. The best bit for children is the final day, when flower-covered floats and costumed dancers parade down the town's main street and the whole place is sprayed with lavender-scented water.

1st week in Aug. **Adm** *Free.*

Towns & Villages

Castellane ★★★

Tourist office: 📞 *04 92 83 61 14, www.castellane.org*

High up in the Verdon valley, Castellane is the top spot for active families—it's the best base for exploring the **Parc Naturel Régional du Verdon** (Verdon Regional Natural Park; p. 229), and its streets are crammed with shops selling outdoor kit and equipment, from kayaks to inflatable rafts, including **L'Échoppe** (p. 234). It's a cheerful, cosmopolitan place in summer, and

English-language Cinemas

For English-language films, look for the 'VO' (version originale) symbol. For current listings, see **www.angloinfo.com**.
Le Cinématographe, Centre Culturel Simone-Signoret, Château-Arnoux, ☎ *08 92 68 01 28.*
Le Félibrige, Place des Airs, Gréoux-les-Bains, ☎ *08 92 89 28 92.*

there are lots of pleasant camp-sites nearby, most of them with lakeside or riverside locations.

Colmars ★★★

Tourist office: ☎ *04 92 83 41 92,*
www.colmars-les-alpes.fr

Reeking of medieval romance, Colmars is Haute-Provence's most impressive fortress village, set in the upper reaches of the Verdon valley and overlooked by the region's highest peak, the 3,050m (10,007 ft) **Mont Pelat**. Although it takes a bit of getting to, it makes a good base for adventures into Mercantour National Park. Its ancient walls and towers are still intact, and you can walk (keeping a firm grip on little ones) around the para-pets where bowmen once stood to let fly at enemies below. The maze of narrow, cobbled streets has a handful of cafés and a 19th-century fountain in the main square. Outside the walls, mean-while, younger children will enjoy the park and playground with swings, slides and seesaws, as well as a child-sized treadmill where they can find out what it feels like to be a human hamster.

Digne-les-Bains ★★

Tourist office: ☎ *04 92 36 62 62,*
www.ot-digneslesbains.fr

Your children may have read about natural hot springs or seen them on TV, but the reality will surprise them. Digne has seven, admired since Roman times for their supposed health-giving properties. This is a peaceful and pretty spot, and although many visitors are on the elderly side, families can enjoy the modern sculptures dotted all over the centre and the walled **Jardin Botanique des Cordeliers** in the grounds of a former convent, full of medicinal plants and herbs used in traditional cures.

Forcalquier ★

Tourist office: ☎ *04 92 75 10 02,*
www.forcalquier.com

Set in the hills west of the Durance valley, Forcalquier is a magical little town in a low-key way. Although it has a rich his-tory, and was once the set of medieval barons and the capital of the region, there are no big 'sights'. Still, it's a pleasant place to spend a morning, with a bus-tling Saturday market where you can shop for local lavender and honey as well as more run-of-the-mill fruit and vegetables. It also claims to have the clearest air in France, which is why the **Obser-vatoire de Haute-Provence** (*www.obs-hp.fr/www/visites/visites.html*) was built here during the 1930s. The old-town centre is partly pedestrianised, though cobbles and occasional steep slopes make buggy-pushing difficult, and finding a place to park anywhere near the centre is murder: leave your car in one of the car parks outside the centre.

Lurs ★★

Tourist office: ☏ *04 92 75 10 02, www.forcalquier.com*

In the hills on the west bank of the Durance, Lurs feels a bit artificial, but children usually enjoy it. Entering the walled village through the centuries-old **Porte d'Horloge** feels like the beginning of an adventure, and the ruined castle of the prince-bishops (who ruled here a thousand years ago) adds atmosphere. Abandoned in the late 19th century, the village came back to life in the 1950s when a trickle of artists and craft workers began moving back into the dinky houses inside the ramparts. The best part is the

Promenade des Évêques (Promenade of the Bishops), a 300m, reasonably buggy-friendly walk lined with medieval chapels and affording views out over the orchards, olives and flower fields of the Durance valley.

Moustiers-Ste.-Marie

Tourist office: ☏ *04 92 74 67 84, www.moustiers.fr*

High above the Lac de Ste. Croix (p. 229), Moustiers is one of the prettiest villages in Haute-Provence, with a babbling brook running through its centre and views from the clifftop church of **Notre Dame**. Unfortunately, it's very far from being a secret—in summer its cafés and restaurants are packed, and there's often a long tailback of cars in both directions in and out of the village.

Sisteron ★★★

Tourist office: ☏ *04 92 61 36 50, www.sisteron.com*

Sitting on the west bank of the Durance, Sisteron is one of the gateways to Haute-Provence. Its

Near Moustiers Ste.-Marie

red-roofed houses look like mini-skyscrapers, rising from the banks of the jade-green river. Above the town, an intimidating medieval citadel on a grim limestone crag (**Citadelle de Sisteron** p. 229) affords far-reaching views from its ramparts (smaller children may need a helping hand on these, and they are beyond the reach of buggies). The fortress' inner keep and dungeons inspire sword-and-sorcery fantasies in children (and adults) who have overdosed on *Harry Potter* or *The Lord of the Rings*. This is also the venue for the annual highbrow **Nuits de la Citadelle** festival of classical music and dance (*www.nuitsdela citadelle.fr*) held in Sisteron in late July and early August.

Natural Wonders & Spectacular Views

Gorges du Verdon ★★★

Between Castellane and Lac de Ste. Croix

No trip to Haute-Provence would be complete without a trip to this spectacular limestone ravine that plunges to depths of up to 700m. The best views of it are from the **Corniche Sublime**, a giddy road that's certainly not for nervous drivers or passengers, and from Point Sublime, where many stop to stretch their legs. The even giddier **Route des Crêtes** ends up at the small village of **Palud-sur-Verdon**, where you can stop for ice cream and drinks before pushing on to the turquoise expanse of the **Lac de Ste. Croix** (p. 229), an inland sea that was created by damming the Verdon river in 1974.

Open *Always.* **Adm** *Free.* **Amenities**

Les Pénitents des Mées ★★

Les Mées, 27km west of Digne-les-Bains

The best view of this bizarre cavalcade of natural limestone pinnacles stretching more than 2km is from the church of **St.-Roch**, above the little village of Les Mées in the Durance valley. Legend says the rocks are the petrified remains of monks who, in the 6th century, fell for the charms of a gaggle of Moorish slave-girls—a cave-dwelling hermit, St. Donat, turned them into stone for abandoning their vows of celibacy. Some of the columns are more than 100m tall… they must have been very big monks.

Open *Always.* **Adm** *Free.*

Animal Parks

Jardin des Papillons ★★★

Digne-les-Bains, 📞 *04 92 31 83 34,* *www.proserpine.org*

Tots can hunt wriggly caterpillars on the lush food-plants in this butterfly garden; older children who like to know the names of everything are in seventh heaven—of the 250 or so kinds of butterfly in France, more than half have been spotted in this 1-hectare garden planted with the flowers and shrubs that the creatures love. A stroll through the Jardin des Papillons with an enthusiastic guide is a good way to put names to the many butterflies you'll see in the wild around Haute-Provence.

Open *Guided visits daily July 11am, 2:30pm, 4pm; Aug 10am, 11:30am, 2:30pm, 4pm; Apr, May and Sept by request Mon–Fri; June by request daily.* **Adm** *5€, under-12s 3€.* **Credit** *MC, V.* **Amenities** 🛍

La Vallée Sauvage ★★

Ferme du Vieux Moulin, St. Geniez, ☎ 04 92 61 52 85, www.lavallee sauvage.com

The 'wild valley' isn't very wild at all: this paradise of furry critters in 15 hectares of meadows, woodland, ponds and streams is designed with buggy-pushing parents and toddlers in mind. Everyone loves the place, and especially the marmots (probably the cutest of all— you will have to resist pleas to take one home), the dabbling ducks, deer, chamois and *mouflon* (wild sheep). There are also wild boar, which aren't cuddly at all, and a whole menagerie of farmyard animals from bunnies to bantams. Most of the staff speak good English.

Open *Daily 10am–7pm Apr, July, Aug and Nov; Wed, Sat, Sun and public holidays 10am–7pm May, June, Sept and Oct.* **Adm** *9.80€, children 3–16 7.90€.* **Credit** *MC, V.* **Amenities** 🏞 🅿 🪧 🛍 🍴

Natural Reserves, Parks & Gardens

Parc Naturel Régional du Verdon ★★★

Domaine de Valx (park HQ), Moustiers-Ste.-Marie, ☎ 04 92 74 68 00, www.parcduverdon.fr

Created in 1997, and thus one of France's newest nature reserves, the Verdon Regional Natural Park has more than 700km of walking trails and bridle paths, accessible on foot, on horseback or by mountain bike. In the wilder reaches of the park, above the tree-line, the limestone peaks are home to chamois, wild goats, marmots and spectacular bird-life, including golden eagles and lammergeyer vultures. These wilder regions may be *too* wild for tots and toddlers; you'll find gentler country with tidy patch-works of green and purple lavender fields on the sunny Valensole plateau, and sheep pastures and green oak woods surrounding Artuby. At the other extreme, the deep chasms of the Gorges du Verdon (p. 228) are terrifyingly grand.

The park is also home to the **Lac de Ste. Croix**, an inland sea that you can paddle around in pedalos, dinghies and canoes. You can lie around on its lakeside beaches or swim in the dazzling blue, lifeguard-protected waters. You'll find snack bars, swimming and picnic sites at **Ste.-Croix du Verdon**, near the southern end of the lake.

Open *Always.* **Adm** *Free.* **Amenities** 🏞 🅿 🪧

Historic Buildings & Monuments

Citadelle de Sisteron

Sisteron, ☎ 04 92 61 27 57, www.sisteron.com

Perched above the Durance and the red-tiled roofs of Sisteron, this formidable castle has guarded the river crossing since the 13th century—and it's still not finished. It last saw action during World War II, when it was garrisoned by the Germans and shelled by the Allies, but its turrets and bastions are still in pretty good nick, as is the 15th-century stained glass in its chapel. It also houses a small museum dedicated to **Napoleon**, who passed through here after escaping exile on Elba, on the way to reclaiming the imperial throne in 1815. Most children will perhaps find the collection of horse-drawn carriages more fun.

*Open Daily Apr, May and Oct 9am–6:30pm; June and Sept 9am–7pm; July–Aug 9am–7:30pm. **Adm** 7€, children 5–14 4€. **Credit** Cash only.*

Citadelle de Sisteron

Fort de Savoie

Colmars, ☎ 04 92 83 46 88, www.colmars-les-alpes.fr

This solid 17th-century fortress squatting above Colmars was designed by the great French military architect Sébastien de Vauban (1633–1707). From its ramparts, look out over the valley and imagine what it was like to be a French musketeer defending France's border from enemies across the Alps.

*Open Daily 10am–6pm; guided tours hourly July and Aug. **Adm** 10€, children 5–14 5€. **Credit** MC, V.*

Top Museums

Musée de Préhistoire des Gorges du Verdon ★★★

Route de Montméjor, Quinson, 30km east of Greoulx-les-Bains, ☎ 04 92 74 09 59, www.museeprehistoire.com

This is the don't-miss museum in Haute-Provence, and you'll need at least a half-day to make the most of it (although we've spent a whole day here). Designed in the 1990s by British architect **Norman Foster**, it's exciting to look at from the outside, while inside, its exhibits span almost half a million years of human history.

Even better is a themed trail from the museum to the **Baume Bonne grotto**, where many of those exhibits were found. The trail isn't ideal for younger children: allow about 2½ hours to walk to the cave and back, and hold little ones by the hand while on the raised walkways (the trail is buggy-friendly). The grotto was discovered in 1946—a viewing platform lets you see its walls and floor, where archaeologists are still at work, and you can go by boat deeper into the flooded parts of the cave (young children may find this scary).

Further along the trail is an archaeological village where children can try their hand at life Stone-Age style, grinding grain by hand, chipping flints, and trying to light a fire by rubbing sticks together. Keep an eye on any reckless ones along the way—although the trail to the cave is well surfaced and has adequate guardrails, there are some nasty drops.

Open *Wed–Mon 10am–7pm Apr–June and Sept; daily 10am–8pm July and Aug; Wed–Mon 10am–6pm Feb, Mar and Oct–mid-Dec.* **Adm** *7€, children 6–18 5€, family ticket (two adults, two children) 20€; guided visit supplement 1.50€ per person.* **Credit** *MC, V.* **Amenities** 🅿 🎒 💧

Musée Scout Baden Powell
⭐ AGE 12 & UP

6 rue Mission, Sisteron, 📞 *04 92 61 03 16*

It's not entirely clear why Sisteron is so keen on scouting, but the Baden Powell Scout Museum is a good way for families to make new friends in the area. Members of the local Scout group set up the museum in 2007 to mark the centenary of the Scout movement. They say they want it to be a bridge between generations, and you can't fault their idealism. It may all be too earnest for some children, but if yours are already Scouts, Cubs or Guides they will enter into the spirit of the thing. And it's always good to learn the French for 'woggle'.

Open *Wed 3–6pm mid-Mar–mid-Aug; by appointment otherwise.* **Adm** *Free.*

Musée Terre et Temps ★★
AGE 10 & UP

Chapelle des Visitandines, Réserve Naturel Géologique de Haute-Provence, Sisteron, 📞 *04 92 61 61 30, www.sisteron.com; see also www.resgeol04.org*

The **Earth and Time Museum** is a great one for young *Dr Who* fans, who will like the robots, sundials, water clocks and other weird and wonderful devices on display here, including the ever-swinging Foucault's pendulum. There are fossils, petrified trees and meteorites, too.

Open *Daily 9am–midday and 2–6pm July–Sept. Guided visits and activities for children Tues, hourly from 11am.* **Adm** *6€, children under 12 4.50€.* **Credit** *MC, V.* **Amenities** 🅿 🎒 💧

Child-friendly Tours

Le Train des Pignes à Vapeur
Station, Digne-les-Bains, 📞 *04 92 31 01 58, http://gecp.asso.fr/*

This rattling narrow-gauge line makes a fun contrast to the sleek TGVs and Eurostars that whizz you from London or Paris to the Midi. If you're flying into Nice and staying near Digne-les-Bains, the children will find it a novel way of travelling to Haute-Provence (taking 3¼ hours), through spectacular scenery, and a welcome change from sitting in the back of a car.

For an authentic taste of what rail travel was like a century ago, take them on one of the original **'Fir Cone' steam trains** that are operated in summer by the Group d'Etude pour les Chemins de Fer de Provence. They chuff back and forth daily between Puget-Théniers and Annot.

Departures *Daily all year departing Digne 7:29am, 10:55am, 2:25pm and 5:30pm.* **Adm** *Adults 20€; children 16€.* **Credit** *MC, V.* **Amenities** 🅿 🎒 💧

Heating the Trains

Our word 'chauffeur', which we use to mean 'driver', comes from the French verb *chauffer* ('to heat'). Steam-train drivers had to light the wood or coal fire that heated the train's boiler before they could move off. It takes 5 hours to turn the 6 tonnes of water in **Train des Pignes** locomotive into steam—so the driver has to wake up at 5am for a 10am start.

Rando Pitchoun – Les Petits Bricoleurs / Les Aventuriers de la Pigne Magique ★★★
AGE 5 & UP

Departs from Forcalquier tourist office,
📞 *04 92 75 10 02,* **www.forcalquier. com**; *La Compagnie des Grands Espaces,* 📞 *06 80 38 13 23*

These guided walks for children (accompanied by parents) are hands-on adventures in every sense. **Les Petits Bricoleurs** last for 3 hours, but only 45 minutes of that is walking time: the rest is spent pottering around and learning basic countryside skills such as how to mend a fence, move a hive of bees to new pastures or repair a dry-stone wall. The organisers say: 'Bring your hands for odd jobs, your nose for smells, your eyes to admire nature and your feet for walking.' It's definitely a revelation for any urban families who think the simple life is simple— it's really *very* hard work.

Les Aventuriers, also lasting about 3 hours, is for energetic, slightly older children, also accompanied by Mum or Dad. This is where you get to find out who *really* knows how to read a map, as your guides show you basic orienteering and hill-walking skills on the pine-forested slopes of the Montagne de Lure above Forcalquier.

Grands Espaces can arrange car-sharing if you don't want to drive from the village to the beginning of either walk, which can be a great way for your children to make new friends and try out their French.

Open *Les Petits Bricoleurs 5pm Tues; Les Aventuriers 5pm Fri 10–24 July and 7–21 Aug.* ***Adm*** *10€ everyone 5 years and up. Booking obligatory.*

For Active Families

Aboard Rafting ★★★
AGE 8 & UP

Aboard Rafting, 8 place de l'Église, Castellane, 📞 *04 92 83 76 11,* **www. aboard-rafting.com**

Rafting down the Verdon river is the not-to-be-missed Haute-Provence experience for those with older children. Lots of companies in and around Castellane run a huge variety of trips, some of which are frankly terrifying and only for adrenaline-crazed teens and grown-ups. Our favourite trip, run by Aboard Rafting for ages 8 and up, lasts 90 minutes and ends up at the company's private riverside beach at **La Pinede**, an excellent picnic spot where the rafting contingent can rendezvous with younger siblings. Basic training, fully qualified guides and safety equipment are provided including lifejacket, helmet and wetsuit.

Open *Daily Apr–Oct (departures 9:30am, 11:30am and 1:30pm).* **Adm** *33€–75€ (all ages depending on the activity).* **Credit** *MC, V.* **Amenities**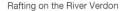

France Montgolfières Balloon Flights ★ ★ ★ AGE 11 & UP

24 rue Nationale, Montrichaud, Forcalquier, ℓ *02 54 32 20 48, **www.france-balloons.com***

Hot-air ballooning is big in France (they invented it, after all); it's also one of the best ways to see Haute-Provence. Lavender fields and olive groves spread out below you as you drift over the Durance valley, with the high country of the Verdon and Valensole stretching off into the distance. You get to watch the balloon being inflated, then scramble into the basket and float effortlessly into the air. Siblings (and parents) who bottle out can join the 'chase convoy' that follows the balloon cross-country and stay in touch by mobile phone. The trip lasts around 3 hours, with just over an hour in the air. If it's your first-ever flight, there's a traditional ceremony on landing involving fizzy drinks and having a lock of your hair scorched off to prove you're a real aeronaut. Minimum age is 6 years old, but younger children may be scared by literally coming down to earth with a bump at the end of the flight, so realistically we think this is one for the over-10s. Note that most flights take off at sunrise.

Flights *Daily June–Aug, sunrise and sunset.* **Rates** *185€–205€, children 6–12 155€.* **Credit** *AE, MC, V.*

Parc Arbres et Aventures ★ ★ AGE 4 & UP

Route de Colmars, Beauvezer, near Colmars, ℓ *06 78 11 89 26, **www.colmars-les-alpes.fr***

You can swing and clamber from tree to tree in this forest adventure park with its 'monkey bridges', tightrope-walkways and 'flying foxes'. Energetic older children with a good head for heights love it—over-10s must

Rafting on the River Verdon

be at least 1.5m tall and accompanied by an adult on the full-on ropeways and swings. For 4- to 10-year-olds there are less demanding, lower-level, un-scary swings and climbing nets too.

Open Daily 10am–5pm June–Sept. **Adm** 19€, children 4–10 12€. **Credit** MC, V. **Amenities** ⓟ ▓ ♀

Shopping

Côté Béa Inspirations

28 boulevard Gassendi, Digne-les-Bains, ☎ 04 92 31 09 76

Every time we pass its window, this posh home decorating and accessories shop has desirable things for younger visitors too, including an extended family of boy and girl bears in hand-made gingham outfits (dresses for girls, dungarees for boys)—the smallest are pocket-sized, cost just 10€ and beg to be taken home. There are also lots of lavender-based gifts—bath oils, bath crystals, creams and oils—that make good presents.

Open Mon–Fri 9am–noon and 2–6pm, Sat 9am–noon. **Credit** MC, V.

Demeter

32 rue du Mitan, Castellane, ☎ 04 92 83 62 34

Demeter pleases young treasure-seekers with its plethora of pretty things made from semi-precious stones at pocket-money prices: choose from amulets, rings, bangles and polished stone eggs made of onyx, amethyst, turquoise and rose quartz. Children also love the little stone animals and the loose polished pebbles of agate, onyx and jasper.

Open Daily 10am–7:30pm. **Credit** MC, V.

L'Échoppe ★★

36 rue Nationale, Castellane, ☎ 04 96 11 11 97

Castellane (p. 225) brings out the adventurer in all of us, and this shop on its main street is the place to kit the family out for an expedition. As well as river-sports kit such as helmets and lifejackets, it sells everything you could possibly need for a camping holiday. It also offers bike

L'Occitane en Provence

L'Occitane (**www.loccitane.com**), which bottles the spirit of ancient Provence, began humbly in 1976 in the Haute-Provence village of Volx. Although it has expanded worldwide and become a high-street name, its signature fragrances have remained true to Provençal roots, rich with olive, lavender, honey, rose and almond. The travel range is particularly handy: we love the shea butter mother-and-baby balm moisturiser, and the biodegradable mosquito repellent towelettes with insect-repelling essential oils, including local lavender. You can visit the factory on the outskirts of Manosque from Monday to Friday. Book via the tourist office in either Manosque or Gréoux-les-Bains. You'll find stores in most towns including Manosque itself.

Food Market, Sisteron

hire and organises rafting, walking and canoeing trips.

Open *Mon–Sat 9am–noon and 2–7pm.* **Credit** *MC, V.*

Magie du Parfum ★★★

18 avenue de la Libération, Sisteron, 📞 *04 92 34 28 12,* ***www.magiedu parfum.com***

This perfumery and museum sells its own range of perfumes and cosmetics for men and women, including their *parfum de Sisteron*, which is blended from lavender and other local aromatics. Mums and daughters will like the on-site museum's vast collection of pretty perfume flasks, bottles, lipsticks and powder boxes.

Open *Mon–Sat 9am–noon and 2–6pm.* **Adm** *Free.* **Credit** *MC, V.*

FAMILY-FRIENDLY DINING

We don't go to Haute-Provence for its gastronomy, yet this part of France offers plenty of solid French cooking at reasonable prices. Because it's so popular with outdoorsy French families all summer, there are plenty of child-friendly restaurants, cafés and snack bars. That said, few go out of their way to provide additional amenities such as highchairs or baby-changing facilities, although you will find these in most hotels and at campsites.

MODERATE

Auberge du Point Sublime ★★

Corniche Sublime, Gorges du Verdon, 📞 *04 90 83 60 35,* ***www.logis-de-france.fr***

This is the perfect spot for a break on a drive through the Canyon du Verdon—the view is spectacular, the food is good and there's parking nearby. As well as a standard burger-and-chips children's menu, there's a second, better-than-average children's menu offering a smaller version of the adult *menu du terroir* (local cuisine), including scaled-down portions of dishes such as crayfish, brochette of

The Best Local Markets

Food market: Place de l'Horloge, Sisteron, Wed morning.

General market: central Castellane, Mon and Wed mornings.

Organic food market: Place du Bourguet, Rue de Bereluc-Perussis and Place St.-Michel, Forcalquier, Mon morning.

Provençal market: central Digne-les-Bains, Wed and Sat mornings.

Provence lamb, fresh vegetable *anchoiade* (anchovy paste), cheeses, fresh fruit and nougat or *crème brûlée* for dessert. The short but steep flight of steps up from the parking to the terrace makes buggy access difficult, and tots will need a hand.

Open *Daily 10am–9pm.* **Main courses** *Menu du terroir 30€; à la carte from 15€; children's menu du terroir 15€; standard children's menu 10€.* **Amenities** 🅿 🎵

La Forge ★

Place de l'Église, Castellane, 📞 *04 92 83 62 51*

This restaurant, set a little apart from the parade of restaurants and cafés on Castellane's main square, has outside tables on a quiet square so you and the children can watch the world go by. The children's menu is basic—*steak haché* and chips followed by ice cream—but satisfying, while for grown-ups and older children the local trout is an excellent bet at 11€, or there are tasty seasonal salads at similar prices. The steps up to the terrace may be difficult for families with buggies.

Open *Daily noon–3pm and 7–10:30pm.* **Main courses** *From 13€, set menu 25€, children's menu 6€.* **Amenities** 🎵

La Taverne ★★

2 place Marcel Sauvaire, Castellane, 📞 *04 92 83 60 23*

This is our favourite spot on a scorching summer day in Castellane: its cooling system intermittently sprays a fine mist over diners on the streetside terrace, provoking squeals of amusement from younger family members. The menu is cheap and cheerful (and translated into English): grills, steaks and pizzas, and a children's menu with a choice of spaghetti bolognaise, burger, ham or cheese pizza, and ice cream or a crepe. The terrace is easily accessible, and the main town car park is just across the street. La Taverne also serves breakfast all morning.

Open *Daily 9am–10pm.* **Main courses** *10€–11.50€. Children's menu 7€.*

Les Affa'mées ★

1 place de la République, Les Mées, 📞 *04 92 34 51 97*

We've long known this cheerful local spot in the middle of Les Mées as a great snack bar for an informal family lunch. It still is, but in addition to its former array of cold drinks, ice creams,

TIP

Picnic with a View

Just outside Les Mées, on the way to Digne, the Aire Touristique at Les Pénitents des Mées lies, literally, in the shadow of the weird grey rock formations for which the village is famous. This grassy picnic spot has plenty of room for children to let off steam, plus benches and tables for family picnics. You can pick up supplies at Mées market on Tuesday or Friday mornings; if it's not market day there's an Intermarché supermarket nearby.

sandwiches and salads to eat at the terrace tables or take on a picnic, it is now a full-on pizzeria with more than 50 choices on the menu.

Open 9am–7pm daily. **Pizzas** from 8.50€. **Credit** MC, V.

FAMILY-FRIENDLY ACCOMMODATION

Haute-Provence isn't over-endowed with good accommodation for families; most hotels and guesthouses in towns and villages are simply too poky. On the other hand, there are heaps of good *gîtes*, many with pools—check them out on **www.gites-de-france.com**. If you want facilities such as a big swimming pool and a play area, think about staying on a campsite—they're mostly great value and far from spartan, and you won't even need to pack a tent because most offer cosy chalets and mobile homes. We've picked two of our favourite sites below.

EXPENSIVE

La Bastide de Moustiers ★★

Moustiers-Ste-Marie, ☏ 04 92 70 47 47, www.bastide-moustiers.com

This bastion of luxury inns and restaurants near to the Verdon gorges (p. 228) is the perfect overnight option for the well-heeled, especially foodies—it's owned by world-renowned chef Alain Ducasse and has a signature fine-dining restaurant. Young children aren't overlooked, though, with children's menus provided on request, plus excellent picnic baskets for alfresco lunches. As well as the heated pool (with Jacuzzi), little ones can enjoy the horses, chickens and Bambi-like deer, and older children can explore the surrounding parkland on mountain bikes.

Rooms 12. **Rates** Packages 190–400€ per night. **Amenities** 🌣 ⋀ 🖼 ⓵ 🛍 **In room** A/C ⊘

MODERATE

Hôtel au Naturel Moulin du Château ★★

St.-Laurent du Verdon, ☏ 04 92 74 02 47, www.moulin-du-chateau.com

For families who want to get away from it all, this is the business. Surrounded by olive groves, the former olive-oil mill is the only hotel within the Parc Naturel Régional du Verdon (Verdon Regional Natural Park, p. 229),

The Best Ice Cream Stop

Wicker chairs and tables surround a splashing fountain on Castellane's pedestrian shopping street, which is lined with shops purveying colourful tat made in Bali. At 22 rue du Mitan you'll find **Le Glacier Chez Jo**—a cool and relaxed spot for ice creams, lollies and cold drinks.

and at almost 500m up, it's pleasantly cool when the rest of Provence is sweltering. Birds and butterflies throng in the sunny garden, so city-dwellers unused to the dawn chorus may find themselves waking early. There's no pool, but you can swim in a small lake 1½km away. Outdoors-loving older children can also take advantage of tennis and riding facilities less than 2km away, while guided walks in the regional park start at the front door.

Rooms 10. **Rates** Doubles from 105€. Rates include breakfast. Extra bed 20€ (15€ under-12s); cot 15€. **Credit** MC, V. **Amenities** 🅿 ☀ 🖼 ♨ ⁇⁇ **In room** ⌐

Camping Les Collines de Castellane ★★★

Castellane, ☎ *04 92 83 68 96,* **www. rcn-campings.fr**

This reasonably priced campsite near Castellane, on the doorstep of the Verdon region with all its adventures, is one of our favou-rites—as well as plenty of activi-ties and a huge swimming pool, it hosts children's entertainment from face-painting to treasure hunts. You don't have to stay in a tent—there are chalets and mobile homes with adequate kitchens for four to six people; you need to bring your own bed

linen. Check the website for spe-cial offers.

Tent pitches 160. **Chalets and mobile homes** 30. **Rates** Tent pitches from 49.50€ (maximum six people), chalets with verandas and mobile homes 108€–800€ week. **Credit** MC, V. **Amenities** 🖢 🖼 🖼 ⁇⁇ 🔒 ⁇ **In room** ⌧

Camping L'International
★★★

Route Palud, Castellane, ☎ *04 92 83 66 67,* www.camping-international.fr

This big campsite with its mobile homes and chalets for four to six people lives up to its name—we always have fun here with fami-lies from all over Europe, com-municating in a weird mixture of English, French, Italian, German and Dutch. As well as a huge pool, children's playground and no-frills barbecue restaurant, there's plenty going on for chil-dren, from table tennis to water polo. Surrounded by woods and fields, this campsite is the perfect base for an adventurous family holiday around the Verdon can-yon country, and is only a short drive from Castellane (p. 225), with its shops, restaurants and activities.

Chalets and mobile homes 60. **Rates** 210€–775€ per week. **Credit** MC, V. **Amenities** 🅿 🖢 🖼 ⁇⁇ 🔒 ⁇ **In room** ⌧

Index

A

Abbaye de Lérins (Île Saint-Honorat), 68
Abbaye de St.-André (Villeneuve lez
    Avignon), 204
Aboard Rafting (Castellane), 232–233
Accommodations, 13–14, 40–46
    Alpes de Haute-Provence, 237, 238
    Avignon and Vaucluse, 217–220
    Grasse and Arrière-Pays, 110–114
    Marseille and Aix-Provence area, 146,
        163–166
    Monaco and French Riviera, 84–88
    Nîmes and Camargue, 190–192
    western Côte and inland Var, 135,
        137–140
Active families, activities for, 76–77
    Alpse de Haute-Provence, 232–234
    Avignon and Vaucluse, 209–212
    Grasse and Arrière-Pays, 104, 105
    Marseille and Aix-Provence area,
        157–159
    Monaco and French Riviera, 76–77
    Nîmes and Camargue, 183–184
    western Côte and inland Var, 130–131
Adventure Golf (Antibes), 76
Aigues-Mortes, 170, 172, 173
Aïoli, 161
Aire Touristique, 237
Air travel, 29–31
Aix-en-Provence, 5, 146
    accommodations, 146, 165–166
    dining, 162–163
    events and entertainment, 145, 146
    historic buildings and monuments, 153
    natural attractions and views, 150–152
    shopping, 159, 160
    top attractions, 144–145
    tours, 156–157
    visitor information, 143–144
Alpes de Haute-Provence, 222–238
    accommodations, 237, 238
    animal attractions and aquariums,
        228–229
    dining, 235–237
    events and entertainment, 225
    historic buildings and monuments,
        229–230
    museums, 230–231
    natural attractions and views, 228, 229
    shopping, 234, 235
    top attractions, 224
    tours, 231, 232
    towns and villages, 225–228
    visitor information, 223–225
Animal attractions and aquariums, 7, 8
    Alpes de Haute-Provence, 228–229
    Avignon and Vaucluse, 203–204
    Grasse and Arrière-Pays, 96–98

    Marseille and Aix-Provence area,
        151–152
    Monaco and French Riviera, 70
    Nîmes and Camargue, 176–178
    western Côte and inland Var, 124, 125
Annonciade Museum (St.-Tropez), 8
Antibes, 5, 62–63
Antibes Bowling, 72
Antibes Land theme park, 76
Antique-car museum (Mougins), 95
ANT Tourisme, 104
Apartments, 43–44
Apt, 198, 199
Aquacity (Plan de Campagne), 155
Aqualand, 121, 123, 129
Aquariums. See Animal attractions and
    aquariums
Aquasplash (Antibes), 76
Aquatropic (Nîmes), 184
Arc de Triomphe (Orange), 201, 207
Archaeological Museum (Nice), 72–73
Arles, 5, 170, 173, 183, 188, 190–191
Arrière-Pays, 90–114
    accomodations, 110–114
    for active families, 104–105
    animal attractions and aquariums,
        96–98
    arts and crafts, 101–103
    events and entertainment, 93, 94
    family-friendly dining, 107–110
    historic buildings and monuments, 99
    museums, 99–100
    natural attractions and views, 96–99,
        101
    shopping, 105–107
    top attractions, 92, 93
    tours, 103, 104
    towns and villages, 94–96
    visitor information, 91–92
Art galleries and museums, 8, 75
Arts and crafts
    Avignon and Vaucluse, 208
    Grasse and Arrière-Pays, 101–103
    Marseille and Aix-Provence area, 156
    Nîmes and Camargue, 182
    western Côte and inland Var, 130
Atelier Paul Cézanne (Aix-en-Provence),
    144, 153
Atelier Terre (St.-Quentin la Poterie), 182
ATMs, 21, 22, 49
Auron ski area, 104
Avignon, 5, 199, 200
    accommodations, 217–218
    for active families, 209, 211
    dining, 213–215
    events and entertainment, 198
    historic buildings and monuments,
        205–206
    museums, 208

Avignon *(cont.)*
  natural attractions and views, 204
  top attractions, 197
  visitor information, 194–196
Azur Express Tourist Train (Monaco), 77
Azur Parc (St.-Tropez), 121, 129

B

Babies, travelling with, 49
Babyland theme park (Le Grau-du-Roi), 178
Badaboum Théâtre (Marseille), 145, 148
Balade en Kayak (Avignon), 209
Banking, 49
Barbajuans, 83
Base Nature, 123, 126
Basse Corniche, 66
Bâteaux Verts (Ste.-Maxime), 121
Baume Bonne grotto (Quinson), 230
B&Bs, 14, 111–114
Beaches
  best, 6, 27
  Camargue, 176
  Marseille and Aix-Provence area, 151
  Monaco and French Riviera, 62, 68, 69
  western Côte, 118, 120, 121, 125
Beaucaire, 170
Beaugensiers Farm (Toulon), 4
Beaulieu-sur-Mer, 65, 66
Beaux Arts Museum (Nice), 65
Benedictine charterhouse (Avignon), 199
Bicycling, 3, 27–28, 40
Biot, 95
Boating, 3
  Alpes de Haute-Provence, 232–233
  Arrière-Pays, 101
  Avignon and Vaucluse, 197
  French Riviera, 59, 62, 74–77
  Nîmes and Camargue, 184
  western Côte, 118–121
Bormes-les-Mimosas, 123
Boucherie Lerda (Mougins), 95
Bowling, 4, 72, 150
Bowling de la Valentine (Marseille), 150
Buggies, 211
Buggy Cross (Mougins), 92, 104–105
Buses, 32–33
Business hours, 50, 51

C

Cabris, 6
Cagnes-sur-Mer, 63
Calanques, 2–3, 144, 147
Calissons (Aix), 144
Camargue, 168–192, 178
  accommodations, 191–192
  for active families, 183–184
  animal attractions and aquariums, 176–178
  arts and crafts, 182
  cities, towns and resorts, 172–176
  dining, 188–189
  events and entertainment, 171, 172
  historic buildings and monuments, 179, 180

  museums, 180, 181
  natural attractions and views, 176, 178, 179
  shopping, 184–186
  top attractions, 170–171
  tours, 183
  visitor information, 169–170
Camping, 14, 44–45
Canadairs (sea planes), 102
Cannes, 63, 64, 82, 83, 86–87
Cannes Bowling, 72
Canoe Evasion (Isle-sur-la-Sorgue), 209–210
Canyon Forest, 63, 76
Canyoning, 101
Carague Safari (Stes.-Maries-de-la-Mer), 183
Carpentras, 200–201
Carré d'Art (Nîmes), 173, 180
Car rentals, 36
Cascade de Courmes, 101
Cascades des Demoiselles, 101
Cashpoints, 21, 22
Cassis, 146, 147
Castellane, 225, 226
Castles, 7–8
Cell phones, 47, 48
Cemenelum (Nice), 72–73
Cézanne, Paul, 144, 153, 156–157
Chagall Museum (Cimiez), 60
Chapelle du Rosaire (Vence), 95
Chartreuse du Val de Bénédiction (Villeneuve lez Avignon), 205–206
Château d'If (Marseille), 153–154, 157
Château du Cirque (Piolenc), 197
Château d'Uzès, 7, 175–176, 179, 180
Château La Barben (Salon-de-Provence), 152
Châteauneuf-du-Pâpe, 214, 218
Children's Festival (Hyères), 128
Christmas in Provence, 165
Cicadas, 114
Cigales, 114
Cimiez, 65, 102
Cinéma Cannet Toiles (Le Cannet), 61
Cinéma Casino (Vence), 94
Cinéma César I and II (Apt), 198
Cinéma Espace Centre (Cagnes-sur-Mer), 61
Cinéma Lido (St.-Raphaël), 119
Cinéma Rialto (Nice), 61
Cinemas
  Alpes de Haute-Provence, 226
  Avignon and Vaucluse, 198
  Grasse and Arrière-Pays, 94
  Marseille and Aix-Provence area, 145
  Monaco and French Riviera, 61
  Nîmes and Camargue, 183
  western Côte and inland Var, 119
Cinéma Sporting (Monaco), 61
Cinémathèque de Nice, 61
Cinéma 3 Casino (Gardanne), 145
Cirque Alexis Gruss (Piolenc), 203
Citadelle de Sisteron, 228–230
Cité Episcopale (Fréjus), 127, 128
Cities, towns, and resorts
  Alpes de Haute-Provence, 225–228
  Avignon and Vaucluse, 198–202
  Grasse and Arrière-Pays, 94–96
  Marseille and Aix-Provence area, 146–149

Monaco and French Riviera, 62–66
Nîmes and Camargue, 172–176
western Côte and inland Var, 120–123
City Pass (Marseille), 157
Climate, 22–23
Colline d'Eutrope (Orange), 201
Collobrières, 123
Colmars, 6, 226
Colorado de Rustrel (Apt), 199
Confectioners, 9
Confiserie Florian sweet factory
(Tourrettes-Sur-Loup), 3, 101
Consulates, 52
Cookery classes, 4
Corniches, 66, 67
Corso de la Lavande (Digne-les-Bains),
225
Côte Bleue, 145, 156–158
Côte Bleue Plongée (Sausset-les-Pins),
157, 158
Côte d'Azur
family highlights, 2–14
maps, 16–17
Courgette-blossom Fritters, 111
Cours Saleya (Nice), 59, 65
Crèche de Haute Provence, 224
Credit cards, 21–22, 52–53
Crin Blanc (film), 178
Cristallerie des Papes (Fontaine de
Vaucluse), 3, 208
Currency, 21
Customs, 19–20

D

Découverte du Terroir en Buggy (Bédoin),
211
Dentelles de Montmirail, 202, 217
Devalkart (Beaumont du Ventoux), 211
Digne-les-Bains, 226
Dining, 11–13, 46–47
Alpes de Haute-Provence, 235–237
Avignon and Vaucluse, 213–217
Grasse and Arrière-Pays, 107–110
Marseille and Aix-Provence area,
160–163
Monaco and French Riviera, 79–84
Nîmes and Camargue, 186–189
western Côte and inland Var, 132–137
Disabilities, travellers with, 20
Diving, 157, 158
Doctors, 51
Dolphin watching, 75, 119
Domaine du Rayol, 125–126
Domaine Paul Ricard Méjanes, 178
Donkey rides, 197
Draguigan, 120
Drinking water, 54
Driving, 32, 34–39

E

Eau Vive Evasion, 101
Ecole de Voile, Yacht Club d'Antibes,
76–77
Ecomusée de la Fôret (Gardanne), 152
Eco-Museum (St.-Martin de Crau), 176

Eldorado cinema (Draguignan), 119
Electricity, 52
Embassies, 52
Emergencies, 52
Enfantillages (Valbonne), 93, 94
Espace Fernandel cinema (Carry-le-
Rouet), 145
Étangs de Villepey nature reserve (Fréjus),
123, 126
Euroméditerranée, 148
Events and entertainment, 5, 24
Alpes de Haute-Provence, 225
Avignon and Vaucluse, 197–198
Grasse and Arrière-Pays, 93, 94
Marseille and Aix-Provence area, 145,
146
Monaco and French Riviera, 60–62
Nîmes and Camargue, 171–172
western Côte and inland Var, 119–120

F

Farmer's markets, 3
Farms, 4, 112, 140, 177, 216
Féria de Nîmes, 171
Ferme aux Crocodiles (Avignon), 7, 197,
203–204
Ferries, 30–32
Festival d'Art Pyrotechnique, 62
Festival d'Avignon, 198
Festival de la Sorgue, 197–198
Festival du Cheval, 172
Festival International du Cirque de Monte-
Carlo, 60–61
Fête de la Bravade (St.-Tropez), 119–120
Fête des Enfants (Hyères), 120
Fête de St.-Pierre, 145–147
Fête du Citron (Menton), 62
Fêtes de la Tarasque (Tarascon), 171
Fêtes Florales (Grasse), 93
Film festival (Cannes), 86
Flayosc (Draguigan), 120
Florian factory, 92
Fondation Maeght art museum (St.-Paul
de Vence), 8, 96, 99–100
Fondation Maeght Giacometti courtyard
(St.-Paul de Vence), 92
Font'Arts (Pernes-les Fontaines), 198
Forcalquier, 226–227
Forest Eco-museum (Aix-en-Provence), 7,
144
Forest fires, 102
Fort de Savoie (Colmars), 224, 230
Fort de St.-André (Villeneuve lez Avignon),
199, 204
Forteresse de Mornas Visites Animées
(Mornas), 197
Four-wheel-drive tours, 103
Fragonard perfume factory (Grasse), 100
Fragonard petit train (Grasse), 105
France Montgolfières Balloon fights
(Forcalquier), 233
Free activities, 2–3
Fréjus, 5, 119, 121–123, 132, 133, 137,
138
French Riviera, 56–88
accommodations, 84–87
for active families, 76–77
animal attractions and aquariums, 70

French Riviera *(cont.)*
 beaches, 68, 69
 cities, towns and resorts, 62–66
 dining, 79–83
 events and entertainment, 61, 62
 historic buildings and monuments, 71, 72
 museums, 72–75
 natural attractions and views, 66–69, 71
 shopping, 77–79
 top attractions, 59, 60
 tours, 75, 76
 visitor information, 57–59
Funboard Center (Hyères), 130
Fun Parc Adventure (Richerenches), 211

G

Gardanne, 151
Gardens, 7. *See also* Natural attractions and views
Gardon River, 175
Geins peninsula (Hyères), 3, 120, 126
Gîtes, 20, 44, 140
Glanum (St.-Rémy-de-Provence), 179
Gonfaron, 123
Gordes, 6, 203
Gorges de Daluis, 3, 92, 101
Gorges de Saorge (Breil-sur-Roya), 3, 101
Gorges du Cians, 101
Gorges du Loup (Grasse), 101
Gorges du Verdon (Moustiers-Ste.-Marie), 3, 228, 229
Gourdon, 96
Graine and Ficelle (Saint-Jean-net), 4, 97, 98
Grand Canyon du Verdon, 224
Grande Corniche, 66, 67
Grands Bateaux de Provence, 208, 209
Grasse, 94
 accommodations, 111
 arts and crafts, 102, 103
 dining, 107–109
 events and entertainment, 93
 museums, 100
 natural attractions and views, 101
 shopping, 105–107
 top attractions, 92
 visitor information, 91–92
Grimaud, 123, 132
Grottes de St.-Cézaire, 4, 96–97

H

Haras d'Uzès National Stud (Uzès), 175, 177
Haribo sweet museum (Uzès), 175, 180–181
Haute-Provence. *See* Alpes de Haute-Provence
Health, 26–27
Héli Air Monaco, 75, 76, 104
Hermann tortoise, 125
Hermes birthplace (Fréjus), 128

Hiking, 101
Hilltop Cabris, 96
Hilltop villages, 5–6, 96
Historic buildings and monuments, 7–8
 Alpes de Haute-Provence, 229–230
 Avignon and Vaucluse, 205–207
 Grasse and Arrière-Pays, 99
 Marseille and Aix-Provence area, 153–154
 Monaco and French Riviera, 71, 72
 Nîmes and Camargue, 179, 180
 western Côte and inland Var, 127, 128
Holiday Bikes (Avignon), 211
Holidays, 23, 24
Holiday villages, 43
Horseback riding, 3, 95, 118, 170, 183–184
Hot-air balloon (Haute Provence), 9
Hôtel du Cap Eden-Roc, 62
Hotel-residences, 42
Hotels, 41–42. *See also* Accommodations
Hyères, 120, 136, 139

I

Ice cream shops, 12–13, 85, 110, 136, 162, 189, 215, 238
Île du Levant, 127
Île Saint-Honorat, 67–69
Îles des Lérins, 63, 67–69
Îles d'Or (Hyères), 118, 120, 126, 127
Îles du Frioul, 154, 158
Île St.-Honorat, 6
Île Ste. Marguerite, 6, 60, 67, 68
Indian Forest Sud (Martigues), 8, 158
Indoor activities, 4
Inland Var
 accommodations, 136, 140
 cities, towns and resorts, 120
 dining, 136–137
 historic buildings and monuments, 127, 128
 visitor information, 117
Insurance, 26
International Festival of Fashion and Photography (Hyères), 128
Internet access, 48–49
Isola 2000 ski area, 93, 104

J

Jardin Botanique (Ste.-Maxime), 121
Jardin Botanique des Cordeliers (Digne-les-Bains), 226
Jardin des Papillons (Digne-les-Bains), 7, 224, 228–229
Jardin d'Eté (Arles), 178, 179
Jardin d'Oiseaux Tropicaux, 124
Jardin du Palais Carnolès (Menton), 71
Jasmin Festival (Grasse), 93
Jazz à Juan (Juan-les-Pins), 62–63
Jazz festivals, 59, 62
Jean-Henri Fabre's Jardin des Insectes, 7, 197
Juan-les-Pins, 62–63

K

Kayak Vert Gardon (Collias), 184
Kiddy Parc (Hyères), 129
Koaland (Menton), 76

L

La Basilique Ste.-Marie-Madeleine (Provence), 3, 127, 128
La Bastide St. Antoine (Grasse), 94
La Bouscarasse (Uzès), 184
Labyrinthe de L'Aventure, 63
Lac de Ste.-Croix, 6, 224, 227, 229
La Crau plain, 176
La Ferme de l'Oiselet (Sarrians), 216
La Garrigue scrubland, 177
L'AM Santonnière (Fréjus), 130
La Petite Ferme du Far West (Antibes), 8, 70, 76
Lasergame Evolution (Marseille), 4, 150
La Strada (Mouans-Sartoux), 94
L'Atelier de la Cuisine des Fleurs (Vence), 4, 102
La Tinée (Vence), 95
La Turbie, 96
La Vallée Sauvage (St. Geniez), 225, 229
La Vésubie (Vence), 95
Le Candille (Mougins), 94
Le Capitole cinema (Uzès), 183
Le Cézar cinema (Marseille), 145
Le Cinéma (Lorgues), 119
Le Cinématographe (Château-Arnoux), 226
Le Félibrige cinema (Gréoux-les-Bains), 226
Le Femina cinema (Cavaillon), 198
Legal aid, 52
Le Grand Tour (Marseille), 157
Le Jardin de César et Léonie (Le Muy), 129
Le Jarditrain (St.-Didier), 4, 201
Le Marzarin cinema (Aix), 145
Le Pagnol cinema (Ste.-Maxime), 119
Le Petit Montmartre (Monaco), 88
Le Petit Train de Pignes (Ste.-Maxime), 132
Le Renoir cinema (Aix), 145
Lérins islands, 83
Le Royal cinema (Toulon), 119
Les Arcades (Cannes), 61
Les Arcades cinema (Salon-de-Provence), 145
Les Aventuriers de la Pigne Magique (Forcalquier), 232
Le Sémaphore cinema (Nîmes), 183
Les Eskimos à l'Eau, 101
Les Folklories de Pernes (Pernes-les-Fontaines), 225
Les Pénitents des Mées, 228
Les Petits Bricoleurs (Forcalquier), 232
Les Poneys de Verderet (Ste.-Maxime), 131
Les Rencontres d'Arles festival, 173
Les Rencontres du 9ème art (Aix), 145
L'Estaque, 146
Le Studio (Grasse), 94
Les Visiteurs du Soir (Vallbonne), 94
Le Tholonet, 151

Le Train des Pignes à Vapeur (Digne-les-Bains), 224, 231, 232
Le Vieux Mas (Beaucaire), 177
Literature, 50, 51, 127
Little Tourist Trains, 4, 77
L'Oblia cinema (Hyères), 119
L'Occitane (Manosque), 234
Lost property, 52
Luna Park (Nice), 76, 123
Lurs, 227

M

Magazines, 53
Magic Land (Carry-le-Rouet), 155
Magic World (Hyères), 129
Maison Carrée (Nîmes), 173, 179
Maison Natale de Jean-Henri Fabre (Serignan du Comtat), 204
Maison Ste.-Victoire (St.-Antonin), 151
MAMAC modern art museum (Nice), 65, 75
Man in the Iron Mask, 68, 69
Marché Médievale (Mornas), 197
Marc Heracle's Cooking School (Aix-en-Provence), 4, 156
Marché République (St.-Raphaël), 123
Marina Baie des Anges (Villeneuve-Loubet), 63
Marineland (Antibes), 8, 63, 70, 76
Markets
    Alpes de Haute Provence, 236
    Avignon and Vaucluse, 212
    Grasse and Arrière-Pay, 106
    Marseille and Aix-Provence area, 160
    Monaco and French Riviera, 79
    Nîmes and Camargue, 185
    Uzès, 170
    western Côte and inland Var, 133
Marseille, 5, 148
    accommodations, 163–165
    for active families, 158–159
    arts and crafts, 156
    dining, 160–162
    events and entertainment, 145
    historic buildings and monuments, 153–154
    museums, 154–155
    natural attractions and views, 149–152
    shopping, 159, 160
    top attractions, 144, 145
    tours, 156, 157
    visitor information, 143–144
Mas (farmhouse), 113
Massif de Maures, 123, 125, 131
Mat & Eau, 101
Medical attention, 25–26
Mercantour National Park (Alpes-Maritimes), 6, 92, 103
Mercury cinema (Nice), 61
Mimosa Festival, 119
Mistral winds, 113
Mobile phones, 47, 48
Monaco, 5, 63–64
    accommodations, 87, 88
    dining, 83–84
    events and entertainment, 60–62
    museums, 73–75
    natural attractions and views, 71

Monaco (cont.)
  shopping, 78
  top attractions, 59, 60
  tours, 75, 76
  visitor information, 57–59
Mons, 6, 123
Mont Faron (Toulon), 118, 123, 124
Mont Pelat (Colmars), 226
Mont Ventoux (Vaucluse), 197, 202, 203
Monuments. See Historic buildings and
  monuments
Mornas Castle, 5
Motorhomes, 38, 39
Mougins, 6, 94, 95, 110–111
Mougins riding school, 104
Moulin de Mougins, 94
Moustiers-Ste.-Marie, 227
Moyenne Corniche, 66
Musée Archéologique (Fréjus), 128, 129
Musée Archeologique Theo Desplans
  (Vaison-la-Romaine), 207
Musée Au Bonbon (Uzès), 170
Musée Cantini (Marseille), 8, 146, 154, 155
Musée de la Lavande (Coustellet), 208
Musée de l'Annonciade (St.-Tropez), 121,
  129, 130
Musée de la Poterie Mediterranéenne (St.-
  Quentin la Poterie), 182
Musée de l'Arles et de la Provence
  Antiques, 179
Musée de l'Empéri (Salon-de-Provence),
  149, 155
Musée de Préhistoire des Gorges du
  Verdon (Quinson), 8, 224, 230–231
Musée des Arts et Traditions Populaires
  (Draguignan), 120
Musée des Beaux-Arts (Nice), 75
Musée du Bonbon (Uzès), 180–181
Musée du Savon Marius Fabre (Salon-de-
  Provence), 149, 155–156
Musée du Vieux Nîmes, 170, 181–182
Musée Granet (Aix-en-Provence), 153
Musée International de la Parfumerie
  (Grasse), 100
Musée Lapidaire (Avignon), 208
Musée Matisse (Nice), 72–73
Musée National Message Biblique Marc
  Chagall (Nice), 73
Musée National Picasso (Vallauris), 75
Musée Nostradamus (Salon-de-Provence),
  154
Musée Oceanographique de Monaco, 73,
  74
Musée Picasso (Antibes), 75
Musée Renoir (Cagnes-sur-Mer), 75
Musée Scout Baden Powell (Sisteron), 231
Musée Souleiado (Tarascon), 182
Musée Terre et Temps (Sisteron), 231
Museum of Provence Landings (Mont
  Faron), 124
Museum of the Sea (Île Ste. Marguerite),
  68
Museums, 8
  Alpes de Haute-Provence, 230–231
  Avignon and Vaucluse, 208
  Grasse and Arrière-Pays, 99–100
  Marseille and Aix-Provence area,
    154–156
  Monaco and French Riviera, 72–75
  Nîmes and Camargue, 180–182
  western Côte and inland Var, 128–130

N

Natural attractions and views, 6–7
  Alpes de Haute-Provence, 228, 229
  Avignon and Vaucluse, 202–205
  Grasse and Arrière-Pays, 96–99
  Marseille and Aix-Provence area,
    149–152
  Monaco and French Riviera, 66–69, 71
  Nîmes and Camargue, 176, 178, 179
  western Côte and inland Var, 123–127
Naturoscope (Marseille), 158–159
Newspapers, 53
Ni Box (Monaco), 59, 72
Nice, 5, 64, 65, 67, 79–82, 84–86
Nice Bowling, 72
Nice Carnival, 61
Nice Jazz Festival, 62
Nîmes, 168–192, 173–175
  accommodations, 190
  dining, 186–188
  events and entertainment, 171
  museums, 180–182
  shopping, 185–186
  top attractions, 170
  visitor information, 169–170
Nostradamus, 149, 154
Notre-Dame de la Garde, 157
Notre-Dame des Anges, 123
Notting Hill (film), 102
Nuits de la Citadelle festival (Sisteron), 228

O

Observatoire de Haute-Provence
  (Forcalquier), 226–227
Occitan language, 10, 11
Oceanographic Museum (Monaco), 7, 60,
  64, 77, 88
Ochre clay, 212
Oiselet Farm (Vaucluse), 4
Olympique de Marseille football club, 150
Open Air Cinema (Monaco), 4, 61
Orange, 201, 215, 219
Outdoor activities, 8–9

P

Paintball 06 (Saint-Paul de Vence), 100
Palais des Festivals (Cannes), 63
Palais des Pâpes (Avignon), 8, 200, 206
Parc Arbres et Aventures (Comars), 8, 224,
  233–234
Parc Borély (Marseille), 152, 157
Parc Départemental de la Brague
  (Valbonne), 98
Parc Départemental de la Valmasque, 98
Parc du Château (Nice), 13, 65, 82
Parc du Pharo (Marseille), 13, 163
Parc National du Mercantor, 98
Parc Naturel Régional du Luberon (Apt), 6,
  198, 204, 205
Parc Naturel Régional du Verdon, 6, 225,
  229
Parc Olbius Riquier (Hyères), 128
Parc Ornithologique du Pont de Gau
  (Stes.-Maries-de-la-Mer), 7, 176, 177

Parc Phoenix (Nice), 65
Parc Princesse Antoinette (Monaco), 71
Parc St.-Bernard (Hyères), 120, 128
Parc St.-Mitre (Aix-en-Provence), 152
Parc Ste.-Claire (Hyères), 120, 128
Parc Zoologique de Fréjus, 125
Parfumerie Molinard (Grasse), 4, 100, 102, 103
Parks. See Natural attractions and views
Passerelle des Cîmes (Isle-sur-la-Sorgue), 8–9, 197, 210
Passports, 19–20
Peillon, 96
Perfume making (Molinard), 92
Petits trains touristiques, 77, 157
Petit Train d'Aigues-Mortes, 182
Pets, travelling with, 20
Pharmacies, 53
Philip Fair, 200
Physicians, 51
Picnics, 13, 82, 109
    Alpes de Haute-Provence, 237
    Avignon and Vaucluse, 217
    Marseille, 163
    Mont Faron, 124
    Square de Verdun, 72
    Uzès, 188
    western Côte and inland Var, 137
Pierre de la Fée (Draguignan), 130
Piscines des Cedres (Orange), 217
Pitchoun Forest (Villeneuve-Loubet), 76
Planétarium Peiresc (Aix-en-Provence), 152
Poissonerie Develay (Mougins), 94, 95
Police, 53
Pont de Gau, 171
Pont du Gard Roman aqueduct, 171, 175, 179, 184
Pont St.-Bénezet (Avignon), 197, 200, 206
Porquerolles, 126
Port Cros, 126, 127
Porte d'Horloge (Lurs), 227
Postal service, 52
Pottery making, 65
Préau des Accoules (Marseille), 3, 148, 156
Prescriptions, 26
Promenade des Anglais (Nice), 65
Promenade des Évêques (Lurs), 227
Promenade des Marronniers (Uzès), 188
Promenade Maurice Rouvier (Beaulieu-sur-Mer), 66
Provence
    cost of items in, 39
    family highlights, 2–14
    maps, 16–17

Q

Quad Location (Crillon-le-Brave), 211

R

Ramatuelle, 123
Ranch La Brouzetière (Camargue), 3, 183–184

Randonnée Pedestre Accompagné d'un Ane de Bat (Le Beaucet), 210
Rando Pitchoun tours (Forcalquier), 232
Renoir Museum (Cagnes-sur-Mer), 63
Resorts, 5. See Cities, towns, and resorts
Responsible tourism, 27–28
Restrooms, 54
Rocher des Doms (Avignon), 217
Rock climbing, 9, 101
Roman amphitheatre (Nîmes), 170, 179
Roman Empire, 179
Roman theatres, 197, 201, 217
Roseraie Princesse Grace & Sculpture Park (Monaco), 7, 71
Roussillon, 6, 203
Roya Evasion, 101
Rues en Fête (Sisteron), 225

S

Safety, 27, 53
St.-Antonin, 151
St.-Eutrope (Orange), 13, 217
St.-Laurent d'Aigouze, 172
St.-Raphaël, 119, 121–123, 133, 137
St.-Tropez, 5, 120–121, 134–136, 138, 139
Saint-Cézaire caves, 92
Ste.-Croix du Verdon, 229
Ste.-Maxime, 5, 120–121, 133, 134, 138
Sainte-Agnès, 96
Saint-Jean-Cap-Ferrat, 65
Saint-Paul de Vence, 95, 96
Salon-de-Provence, 148, 149, 154, 163, 166
Santa Azur, 104
Santa Lucia Marina (St.-Raphaël), 123
Saut du Loup, 101
Scénoparc (St.-Martin Vésubie), 6, 98, 104
Seaquarium (Le Grau-du-Roi), 7, 173, 177, 178
Senior travellers, 20
Sentiers des Ochres (Rustrel), 210, 212
Serre de la Madone garden (Menton), 71
Shopping, 9, 10, 24
    Alpes de Haute-Provence, 234, 235
    Avignon and Vaucluse, 212, 213
    Grasse and Arrières-Pay, 105–107
    Marseille and Aix-Provence area, 144, 159, 160
    Monaco and French Riviera, 77–79
    Nîmes and Carmargue, 184–186
    western Côte and inland Var, 131, 132
Single parents, 28
Sisteron, 227–228
Skating, 59, 72
Skiing, 98, 224
Snowboarding, 93
Soap museum (Salon-de-Provence), 145
Socca, 81
Special needs, travellers with, 20–21
Square de Verdun, 72
Stade Vélodrome (Marseille), 150, 157
Station Kid designation (Villeneuve-Loubet), 63
Swimming, 3, 92, 101, 145, 217, 224

T

Taxes, 53
Taxis, 39–40, 53
Teens, activities for, 3–4
Telephones, 53–54
Tennis, 76
Théâtre Antique d'Orange, 206–207
Theme parks, 8, 63, 76, 129, 155
Time zone, 54
Tipping, 54
Toddlers, activities for, 4
Toilets, 54
Tortoise Village (Gonfaron), 118, 123
Toulon, 123, 132, 139, 140
Tourist trains, 132, 157, 182, 209, 231, 232
Tour Philippe le Bel (Avignon), 200
Tours
    Alpes de Haute-Provence, 231, 232
    Avignon and Vaucluse, 208, 209
    Grasse and Arrière-Pays, 103, 104
    Marseille and Aix-Provence area,
      156–157
    Monaco and French Riviera, 75–77
    Nîmes and Camargue, 183
    package, 33–34
Tourtour (Draguigan), 6, 120
Towns. See Cities, towns, and resorts
Train des Merveilles, 6, 98–99
Train Touristique de Nîmes, 182
Tramways (Marseille), 148
Travellers' cheques, 22
Trophée d'Auguste (La Turbie), 99
Trophée des Alpes, 96

U

Utopia la Manutention cinema (Avignon),
  198
Uzès, 175–176

V

Vaison-la-Romaine, 201, 202
Valberg ski area, 104
Valbonne, 95
Vallée des Merveilles (Tende), 7, 92, 98,
  103
Val Rahmeh garden (Menton), 71
Variétés cinema (Marseille), 145
Vaucluse, 194–220
    accommodations, 219–220
    for active families, 209–212
    animal attractions and aquariums,
      203–204
    arts and crafts, 208
    cities and towns, 198–202
    dining, 215–217
    events and entertainment, 197–198
    historic buildings and monuments,
      206–207
    museums, 208
    natural attractions and views, 202–205
    shopping, 212–213
    top attractions, 197
    tours, 208, 209
    visitor information, 194–196
Vence, 95, 96, 109, 110, 112–114

Verdon Gorges, 6
Verrerie de Biot (Fontaine-de-Vaucluse), 3,
  103
Via Ferrata, 9, 101
Views. See Natural attractions and views
Villa Ephrussi de Rothschild (St.-Jean-
  Cap-Ferrat), 8, 65, 74
Village des Automates (St.-Cannat), 155
Village des Bories (Gordes), 8, 197, 207
Village des Tortues (Gonfaron), 4, 125
Villages Perchés (hilltop villages), 96
Villa Grecque Kérylos (Beaulieu-sur-Mer),
  65, 71, 72
Villa Noailles (Hyères), 128
Villas, 43–44
Villecroze (Draguigan), 120
Villefranche-sur-Mer, 60, 65
Villeneuve lez Avignon, 199
Villeneuve-Loubet, 59, 63
Visas, 19–20
Visiobulle (Cap d'Antibes), 74, 75
Visitor information, 18–28
    Alpes de Haute-Provence, 223–225
    Avignon and Vaucluse, 194–196
    Grasse and Arrière-Pays, 91–92
    Marseille and Aix-Provence area,
      143–144
    Monaco and French Riviera, 57–60
    Nîmes and Camargue, 169–170
    western Côte and inland Var, 117, 118

W

Water, drinking, 54
Waterparks, 8, 184
Watersports, 98, 119, 120, 130
Weather, 22–23
Websites, useful, 18–19, 36
Western Côte, 116–140
    accommodations, 137–140
    for active families, 130–131
    animal attractions and aquariums, 124,
      125
    arts and crafts, 130
    beaches, 118, 125
    cities, towns and resorts, 120–123
    dining, 132–136
    events and entertainment, 119–120
    historic buildings and monuments, 127
    museums, 128–130
    natural attractions and views, 123–127
    shopping, 131, 132
    top attractions, 118, 119
    visitor information, 117, 118
Whale watching, 75
Wi-Fi, 48–49

Y

Yacht Club d'Antibes, 59
Youth hostels, 45–46

Z

Zoo La Barben (Salon-de-Provence), 144,
  149, 151–152